The Ordinary Universe

by the same author

CONNOISSEURS OF CHAOS
Ideas of Order in Modern American Poetry

THE

Ordinary Universe

Soundings in Modern Literature

Denis Donoghue

The Macmillan Company

NEW YORK

To Frances

Acknowledgements and References

This list includes, where relevant, corresponding editions published on the opposite side of the Atlantic to those cited in the text.

Saul Bellow, *Dangling Man*, Vanguard Press; *Seize the Day*, *The Adventures of Augie March*, and *Henderson the Rain King*, Viking Press; *The Victim* and *Herzog*, Weidenfeld & Nicolson.

R. P. Blackmur, *The Lion and the Honeycomb*, Harcourt, Brace & World.

Jorge Luis Borges, *Ficciones*, Weidenfeld & Nicolson.

Martin Buber, *Pointing the Way*, Routledge and Kegan Paul.

T. S. Eliot, *Selected Essays* and *Collected Plays*, Harcourt, Brace & World.

E. M. Forster, *Aspects of the Novel*, Harcourt, Brace & World.

Etienne Gilson, *The Christian Philosophy of Thomas Aquinas*, Heffer & Sons.

G. Manley Hopkins, *Journals* and *Letters to Bridges*, Oxford University Press.

Henry James, *The Tragic Muse* and *Notebooks*, Charles Scribner's Sons; *The Scenic Art*, Hill & Wang.

James Joyce, *A Portrait of the Artist as a Young Man*, Viking Press.

Hugh Kenner, *The Poetry of Ezra Pound*, New Directions Publications; *The Invisible Poet*, W. H. Allen.

D. H. Lawrence, *Last Poems*, Viking Press; *Phoenix*, Heinemann.

H. M. Lynd, *On Shame and the Search for Identity*, Routledge and Kegan Paul.

M. McLuhan, *The Gutenberg Galaxy*, University of Toronto Press.

Marianne Moore, *Collected Poems*, Faber and Faber.

Robert Musil, *Young Torless*, Signet.

Eugene O'Neill, *Long Day's Journey into Night*, Yale University Press.

Richard Poirier, *A World Elsewhere*, Chatto & Windus.

John Crowe Ransom, *God Without Thunder*, Harcourt, Brace & World.

I. A. Richards, *Speculative Instruments*, University of Chicago Press.

Alain Robbe-Grillet, *Snapshots* and *Towards a New Novel*, Grove Press.

Wallace Stevens, *The Necessary Angel*, *Collected Poems*, and *Opus Posthumous*, Faber & Faber.

Charles Tomlinson, *Seeing is Believing* and *American Scenes*, Oxford University Press.

Lionel Trilling, *Beyond Culture*, Viking Press.

Paul Valéry, *Selected Writing*, Routledge and Kegan Paul.

Richard Wilbur, *Advice to a Prophet*, Harcourt, Brace & World.

William Carlos Williams, *Paterson*, Peter Owen.

Ludwig Wittgenstein, *Tractatus*, Humanities Press.

Wilhelm Worringer, *Abstraction and Empathy*, International Universities Press.

W. B. Yeats, *Explorations* and *Autobiographies*, Macmillan N.Y.

I fell over backwards in making that novel explicit. I said to myself, 'Now here is going to be a novel, it's going to be a blow on behalf of the ordinary universe, which I think on the whole likely to be the right one, and I'm going to write it so vividly and accurately and with such an exact programme that nobody can possibly mistake exactly what I mean.'

WILLIAM GOLDING of *Pincher Martin*

Contents

Introduction

There are no bullfights in Hemingway, there is no violence in Faulkner; as Kenneth Burke reminded me in an amiable dispute some time ago. The formalist critic has only to persist in such aphorisms to throw his opponent into despair. The only ready answer is: 'True; but still. . . .' The present book is an attempt to make the desperate dots into a sentence, lest the dispute stop. It takes the strength of the formalist position for granted, and tries to argue from a sense of its own weakness. Some years ago John Crowe Ransom asked Richard Blackmur to acknowledge that 'there are substantive as well as formal values in the poem'.[1] I do not recall that Blackmur answered in one spirit or another, but I fancy him saying, with typical goodwill: 'Yes; and what then?' The issue is rarely joined: so I may be allowed to refer to a few classic occasions, 'anecdotes', to prepare the discussion.

There is the celebrated argument between Henry James and H. G. Wells; but that dispute goes so vividly in its double idiom that it can hardly be taken from its context. Its progress is too much a matter of character and temperament to allow a swift translation into common terms. Perhaps it is better to take the argument in an easier occasion, James's letter to Hugh Walpole, in May 1912, when the matter was a dispute of Form and Substance. James refers to Walpole's 'literary emotions'. And he continues: 'These latter indeed—or some of them, as you express them, I don't think I fully share. At least when you ask me if I don't feel Dostoieffsky's "mad jumble, that flings things down in a heap", nearer truth and beauty than the picking and composing that you instance in Stevenson, I reply with emphasis that I feel nothing of the sort, and that the older I grow and the more

[1] John Crowe Ransom, *Poems and Essays* (New York. Knopf, 1955), p. 108.

I *go* the more sacred to me do picking and composing become—
though I naturally don't limit myself to Stevenson's *kind* of the
same. Don't let any one persuade you—there are plenty of
ignorant and fatuous duffers to try to do it—that strenuous selec-
tion and comparison are [not] the very essence of art, and that
Form is not substance to that degree that there is absolutely no
substance without it. Form alone *takes*, and holds and preserves,
substance—saves it from the welter of helpless verbiage that we
swim in as in a sea of tasteless tepid pudding, and that makes one
ashamed of an art capable of such degradation.'[1]

I have quoted so much of this, and would quote what remains,
to represent the difficulty of the dispute between Substance-men
and Form-men; and the risk, always there, of declaring oneself
an ignorant and fatuous duffer. James survives the dispute; indeed, he comes out on top: but it is strange justice which allows
the praise of Stevenson, praiseworthy as he is, at the expense of
Dostoevsky and, in the next sentence, Tolstoy. We are to believe that Stevenson, an artist of some limitation, is nevertheless
right 'in principle'; while Dostoevsky and Tolstoy are artists of
enormous scale, limited only in the defect of that principle. The
reader will form his own opinion as to the weight to be given to
principle in these cases.

James values Form, it is clear, for many reasons, including this
one; that it guarantees the operative presence of Consciousness.
There is an occasion, hardly less splendid than the first, when he
sends Henry Adams a copy of *Notes of a Son and Brother*. Adams's
letter of thanks has not been traced, but we can infer its tone
from a note in his journal, written the next day: 'I've read Henry
James's last bundle of memories,' he says, 'which have reduced
me to a pulp. Why did we live? Was that all? Why was I not
born in Central Africa and died young. Poor Henry James thinks
it all real, I believe, and actually still lives in that dreamy, stuffy
Newport and Cambridge, with papa James and Charles Norton—
and me! Yet, why!'[2] The date is 8th March 1914, a bad time for
reading memoirs. Presumably Adams's letter conveyed his sense
of James's redundancy, the absurdity of the enterprise. James re-

[1] Henry James, *Letters*, edited by Percy Lubbock (London. Macmillan, 1920),
II, 245–6.
[2] Henry Adams, *Letters*, edited by W. C. Ford (Boston. Houghton Mifflin,
1938), p. 622.

plied in one of his most revealing letters. I give the whole text, to represent a sense of the value it clings to, the value of consciousness, and to suggest that the formalist position, to which I have referred, has this as its chief strength. Nothing in the present book, I hope, will presume to undermine this value. Rather, it is urged that consciousness is an instrument in the service of something other than itself. I quarrel only with those who would make consciousness the end; action, things, and people the means. James writes: 'I have your melancholy outpouring of the 7th, and I know not how better to acknowledge it than by the full recognition of its unmitigated blackness. *Of course* we are lone survivors, of course the past that was our lives is at the bottom of an abyss—if the abyss *has* any bottom; of course, too, there's no use talking unless one particularly *wants* to. But the purpose, almost, of my printed divagations was to show you that one *can*, strange to say, still want to—or at least can behave as if one did. Behold me therefore so behaving—and apparently capable of continuing to do so. I still find my consciousness interesting—under *cultivation* of the intellect. Cultivate it *with* me, dear Henry—that's what I hoped to make you do—to cultivate yours for all that it has in common with mine. *Why* mine yields an interest I don't know that I can tell you, but I don't challenge or quarrel with it—I encourage it with a ghastly grin. You see I still, in presence of life (or of what you deny to be such), have reactions—as many as possible—and the book I sent you is a proof of them. It's, I suppose, because I am that queer monster, the artist, an obstinate finality, an inexhaustible sensibility. Hence the reactions—appearances, memories, many things, go on playing upon it with consequences that I note and "enjoy" (grim word!) noting. It all takes doing—and I *do*. I believe I shall do yet again—it is still an act of life. But you perform them still yourself—and I don't know what keeps me from calling your letter a charming one. There we are, and it's a blessing that you understand—I admit indeed alone—your all-faithful Henry James.'[1]

Is it unfair to say, incited by James's letter, that modern literature is written 'as if' there were nothing; nothing, that is, but consciousness; no values in the given, the finite, only in personal ascription? Even so, we would not deny the salience of such a

[1] James, *Letters, supra*, II, 373.

literature, however extreme its intransigence, as we would not propose the destruction of castles in the air; recalling how useful fictions ('as if') have been found in medicine, economics, philosophy, and virtually every human province. But the old liaisons are under attack. Wittgenstein says: 'In the world everything is as it is, and everything happens as it does happen: *in* it no value exists—and if it did it would have no value.'[1] Robbe-Grillet says: 'The world is neither significant nor absurd: it merely *is*. Things are "there" and they are only things.'[2] Meanwhile the dialogue of man with himself, which Arnold saw as the distinguishing mark of the modern spirit, is an act of the dissociated consciousness: the mind, exercised and assuaged by its activity, ascribes value to that activity for that reason. If a man finds his consciousness interesting, he is thus fortunate. If he finds interesting nothing but his consciousness, his good fortune is to be reckoned along with the price he pays for it. I think the price exorbitant in such writers as Joyce, Musil, and Rilke.

In the third Book of *De Oratore* Cicero rebukes Socrates for trying to separate wisdom and eloquence. Men like Themistocles brought their minds into the arena and spoke there with skill, but Socrates turned away, driving a wedge between rhetoric and philosophy. 'Hence arose a distinction between the tongue and the heart, a distinction entirely absurd, useless and reprehensible; as if some would teach us to be wise, and others would make us eloquent.'[3] The argument has often been impugned, and yet a direct relation between the tongue and the heart is dearly to be wished. The spirit of modern criticism is Socratic in this respect; if for 'heart' we read values, attitudes, motives, choice, preference, commitments; and for 'tongue', speech, literature, the artifact, 'the poem itself'. With Pater we separate the moralist from the poet, for ease and perhaps for peace. With Eliot we separate the man who suffers from the writer who creates, and both from the poem, the verbal icon, the well-wrought urn. These separations have eased our professional lives, and we are furtively grateful to those who sponsored them.

[1] Ludwig Wittgenstein, *Tractatus Logico-Philosophicus* (London. Kegan Paul, Trench, Trubner, 1922), p. 182.
[2] Alain Robbe-Grillet, *Snapshots*, and *Towards a New Novel*, translated by Barbara Wright (London. Calder and Boyars, 1965), p. 92.
[3] Cicero, *De Oratore*, edited by A. S. Wilkins (Oxford. Clarendon Press, 1892), III, 32.

But we have some misgivings. When we read the old writers we are often touched and sometimes shocked by the rigour of their insistence. In his *Report of Germany* Roger Ascham praises Albert of Brandenburgh: 'And when he talketh he so frameth his tongue to agree with heart, as speaking and meaning seemeth to be always at one in him.' Again he says: 'A prince of noble courage should have his heart, his look, his tongue, and his hands so always agreeing together, in thinking, pretending, speaking, and doing, as no one of these four should at any time be at jar with another.'[1] In *The Schoolmaster* Ascham gives Cicero's complaint again, against those who 'make a divorce betwixt the tongue and the heart'.[2] Ascham's terms are old-fashioned, and we sometimes feel that we are well rid of them. But perhaps we have not disposed of his simplicity.

Hence our theme: literature and the attitudes that get into it, secreting themselves in the lines. The present book has an interest in resuscitating the relation between the tongue and the heart. It tries at least to assess the cost of separating the poet from the moralist. Along the margin it recurs to certain issues, including these: the writer's commitment (if he is willing to make it) to the human event, to what James called 'the enormous lap of the actual'; the rivalry between the persuasions of the natural world and the structure of one's own imagination, between Ordinary Things and Supreme Fictions; the further rivalry between Reality and Justice (to invoke a commanding phrase from Yeats's *A Vision*). We advert, perhaps more frequently than tact would advise, to the last rivalry between the world and the word, where the word, the poem, assumes such magical privi-lege that its poet is happy to deny the whole world for the poem's sweet sake.

It might also be mentioned that the book developed from a particular situation. The writer observed that most critics of modern literature assume that the poem's attitudes are beyond dispute. It is commonly agreed that these attitudes, once they reach the poem, subject themselves to a certain formal pressure in the medium itself, and are thereafter freed from other pres-sure. They must not be asked to testify against themselves. This argument is impressive, strategically lively, convincing much of

[1] Roger Ascham, *Works* (London. Smith, 1864), III, 32–3.
[2] ibid., III, 211–12.

the way; but the poem's attitudes, however deeply shaped in the stress of form, seem to declare themselves beyond their strict occasion. Doing so, they seem to expose themselves to a scrutiny that cannot be content with formal recognitions.

Richard Wilbur has a poem which bears upon the matter; the *Ballade for the Duke of Orleans*, 'who offered a prize at Blois, *circa* 1457, for the best ballade employing the line, *Je meurs de soif auprès de la fountaine*'. Like Wilbur, we allow ourselves to be pleased by the condition. A great Prince, himself a poet in two languages, offers a prize for the best ballade. As a master in this *genre* he will require a high performance. The standard edition of the Duke's *Poésies* prints several of the competitive poems, including one by Villon. So it is a highly professional occasion. But lest it fail, becoming a mere technical exercise, the Duke insists that the poems include a line of some substance, in its way profound. The line is splendid and therefore the cause of splendid lines to accompany it. The poets must write up to its mark, or their failure will be shameful. So the poems will be tested by a double criterion: they must be accomplished performances in a *genre* of some delicacy, and they will do well to be profound. The Duke has imposed severe conditions; but anything less would be an insult. In fact, the conditions are the permanent requirements of art, then as now. On high occasions we demand that our poems shall be both accomplished and profound; though some readers are content with accomplishment, and others will take note of accomplishment only in gratitude for the profundity. It is tempting to reject the distinction, insisting that the profundity issues in the accomplishment, the style, or it is not there at all. We have seen many attempts to extend the definition of Style until it means Everything; as Mark Schorer argued that style is achieved content. We are constantly admonished that distinctions between style and content are objectionable. This sounds admirable in Cicero's way, but it has often led to strange conclusions. Thus Dr. Leavis came close to impugning the character of Sir Charles Snow by remarking the style of the novelist C. P. Snow. A short answer to that question is that many good men write badly, and a few bad men have written well. But it is vain to deal in general terms. I mention this matter now only to imply that our criticism is bound to be impure, a messy business. A neat aesthetic theory is one thing, but the experience of reading a poem or a novel is another.

The material considered in the present book is modern literature, or rather, those parts of it in which the issues seem particularly relevant and tangible. It is fair to admit at once that the
author has an axe to grind and grinds it, perhaps, all too noisily.
But he wishes to qualify his argument with the *Envoi* to Wilbur's
competitive ballade:

> Duke, keep your coin. All men are born distraught,
> And will not for the world be satisfied.
> Whether we live in fact, or but in thought,
> *We die of thirst, here at the fountain-side.*[1]

As for the title: the book is a defence of the ordinary universe,
after all; and a motto from William Golding has this particular
merit, that it comes from a writer who finds it difficult to deal
with that universe, directly, without the fabulous mediation of
myth. So perhaps we start with the proper reservations.

[1] Richard Wilbur, *Advice to a Prophet, and Other Poems* (London. Faber and
Faber, 1962), p. 46.

I

The Proper Plenitude of Fact

One might imagine a five-Act drama proceeding along these lines: (1) 'I see a mountain.' (2) 'The mountain exists, owing nothing to me.' (3) 'Now that it exists, however, it will register my feeling, receive its intimation.' (4) 'My feeling, when all is said, is more important than an inert mountain: the mountain will not mind diminishing itself to serve me.' (5) 'I shall now write my poem and it will take the place of the mountain; in this way, incidentally, I shall undo the work of Creation and be my own God. My faith in my own consciousness will move that mountain.' So Wallace Stevens wrote 'The Poem that Took the Place of a Mountain':

> There it was, word for word,
> The poem that took the place of a mountain.

The poem has replaced the mountain because the poet has needed 'a place to go to in his own direction', and he persists until the landscape is exactly 'right', answerable to his imperial mind.[1] The rocks and pines are real now only, as an earlier voice said, 'if I make them so'.[2] 'I am my world,' Wittgenstein says in the *Tractatus*, thus providing a formula that can be slanted in either direction; though later he says, 'The world is independent of my will.'

The imaginary five-Act play is designed to suggest, however, one of the dominant assumptions of modern literature, that nothing is real unless we have made it; the phenomena of earth are tokens of nothing but ourselves. The world is our oyster. Re-

[1] Wallace Stevens, *Collected Poems* (London. Faber and Faber, 1955), p. 512.
[2] ibid., p. 313.

jecting metaphysics, we make a metaphysics of our own, sometimes calling it an aesthetic theory, sometimes a Supreme Fiction. Meanwhile, as Lawrence said, 'To be, or not to be, is still
the question.' Indeed, Lawrence's poems were written to resolve
this problem, or at least to rebuke the imperial imagination. The
novels confront the issue at last, in more problematic terms. In
the poems Lawrence elucidates the relation of birds, beasts, and
flowers, and shows a man acting graciously toward them. Hence
the poems are parables, essays in civility, notes toward a proper
mode of life. If Lawrence compares a pike, 'with smart fins/And
grey-striped suit', to 'a lout on an obscure pavement',[1] it is to
show that the comparison is bogus. The fish is itself, different,
'fish-alive' in its own idiom; not you or I. We are to live in the
world, Lawrence implies, remembering this. John Crowe Ransom has described the poetic attitude to the natural object as one
in which 'we regard the endless mysterious fullness of this object, and respect the dignity of its objective existence after all—
in spite of the ambition to mastery that has become more and
more habitual with us'.[2] As James said in the Preface to *The
Spoils of Poynton*, 'Always the splendid Things.'
   One of the most lucid descriptions of such a world, proceeding under these auspices, is the poetry of Charles Tomlinson,
especially the volume *Seeing is Believing*.
   In the fourth part of 'Antecedents', in stern reply to, 'We lack
nothing/But the milieu', Tomlinson says, 'We lack nothing/But
a significant sun.'[3] Lacking this, he goes down to rock bottom,
to the relation between the individual consciousness and the
Other. This is something, a way out of the prison:

> Out of the shut cell of that solitude there is
> One egress, past point of interrogation.
> Sun is, because it is not you; you are
> Since you are self, and self delimited
> Regarding sun.

We must have it formulated with cool precision:

[1] D. H. Lawrence, *Last Poems* (London. Secker, 1933), p. 79.
[2] John Crowe Ransom, *God without Thunder* (London. Howe, 1931), p. 129.
[3] Charles Tomlinson, *Seeing is Believing* (New York. McDowell, Obolensky 1958), p. 54.

                                                                You accept
An evening, washed of its overtones
By strict seclusion, yet are not secluded
Witheld at your proper bounds.

The fine relation is an act of reverence, propriety, a sense of
limits, identity, dialogue; it is pious, poetic, never predatory. In
'Cézanne at Aix' the mountain is a mountain, irreducible, not an
ambiguous reflection of the speaker or his consciousness; an object, independent of any use we may choose to make of it:

            And the mountain: each day
            Immobile like fruit. Unlike, also
            —Because irreducible, because
            Neither a component of the delicious
            And therefore questionable,
            Nor distracted (as the sitter)
            By his own pose and, therefore,
            Doubly to be questioned: it is not
            Posed. It is. Untaught
            Unalterable, a stone bridgehead
            To that which is tangible
            Because unfelt before. There
            In its weathered weight
            Its silence silences, a presence
            Which does not present itself.

The poem enacts, in the poise of its courtesy, a relationship
equal in grace to that of the mountain and its 'scene'. The lines
swing gently between precise notations, committed to the firm,
modest duty of discrimination. The moral rhetoric, with its
decorous emphases, has that unconscious fastidiousness in which,
as Marianne Moore says, there is 'a great amount of poetry'.
This is the tone of Tomlinson's best poems. The fine relation,
the dialogue, acknowledged and pondered with a sense of its
contractual harmonies, issues in genial assent. Tomlinson gives
the supporting theory in a later poem:

                    Distrust that poet
            Who must symbolize your stair
            Into an analogue of what was never there. Fact

Has its proper plenitude that time and tact
Will show, renew.[1]

This is Tomlinson's reverence, acknowledging that we receive more than we give, and that we make up the difference—if we do—by tact, in wonder and local recognition:

That which we were,
Confronted by all that we are not,
Grasps in subservience its replenishment.

So this poet, acknowledging his role in the scene of Being, is devoted to those relationships—seemingly chained to metaphors of aggression—which are open to more gracious formulation. The oxen and their master; the moss and the rock; the sea and the railway-tracks that seem to deny its glamour; the knife-blade and the apple; the bridge straddling vacancy as a girl's hand composes the air around it:

At Luna
There is a city of bridges, where
Even the inhabitants are mindful
Of a shared privilege: a bridge
Does not exist for its own sake.
It commands vacancy.

Stevens might have been thinking of such a poet as Tomlinson when he spoke of poetry as 'an instrument of the will to perceive the innumerable accords, whether of the imagination or of reality, that make life a thing different from what it would be without such insights . . . a means by which to achieve balance and measure in our circumstances'.[2]

We began with a persuasive relation, in Tomlinson's poems, between the individual consciousness and the Other. Outside the poems, this relationship more often than not is denied; or, if conceded, it seems restless, capricious: hence the temptation to be Master, to set up as God. In Tomlinson's poems the unifying motive is to translate these restless occasions into comelier terms of participation and harmony. The poems try to make marriages

---

[1] Charles Tomlinson, *A Peopled Landscape* (London. Oxford University Press, 1963), p. 14.
[2] Wallace Stevens, *Opus Posthumous* (New York. Knopf, 1957), p. 242.

out of divorces. Tomlinson begins where Freud's *Civilization and its Discontents* leaves off, but he does not forget the sources of discontent. This is the determining figure of his poems; to find in experience justification for a pattern, guaranteed by the poise of its disclosure. The poems aspire to a condition of stillness, in which the self and the Other are acknowledged for what they are, separate but not alien. Like the bowl on a table:

> The laric world where the bowl glistens with presence
> Gracing the table on which it unfolds itself.

It is a 'wooing both ways', in Blackmur's phrase.

Or it is this when everything goes well, when a moral harmony is possible. Tomlinson is not content to enforce relationships, by fiat, setting the poem over against our experience of the daily world in which accords are often broken or frustrate. He brings the daily world as close as possible to the 'ideal' harmonies of the poem, by going back over the world's relationships and seeing whether at least some of the tangled ones are not, after all, open to more engaging interpretation. Stevens has argued for this, or something like it, as the essential poetic programme, to be 'in agreement with the radiant and productive world in which (the poet) lives'. Only when this proves impossible is Tomlinson defeated. Often, indeed, it is impossible, or too late. When the object is abused, there is no chance of liaison; we are baffled by guilt, watching defilement. Tomlinson thinks of such occasions as the wanton demolition of a house, or its defacement. In a ruined house the hearth is a focus for nothing:

> Within, wet from the failing roof,
> > Walls greened. Each hearth refitted
> For a suburban whim, each room
> > Denied what it was, diminished thus
> To a barbarous mean. . . .

A potentially vivid relation has been undermined. To speak of it in aesthetic terms is innocent if we bear in mind that for this poet aesthetic terms have weight only in a moral context of feeling.

But the fine relation can be subverted by the abuse or the exorbitance of its other member, the 'I'. The fact of 'otherness' is a beautiful necessity that invites recognition; if the 'I' turns

back upon itself, it commits a breach of tact, falls from the condition of grace. This is the Symbolist impasse. Tomlinson has
several poems that ponder the situation, and one that enacts its
rebuke:

> She looks. And a flawed perfection
>   Disburses her riches. She is watched
> And knows she is watched. The crimson reveals itself
>   Recommending her posture and assured by it
> Both of her charm and her complicity: . . .

She has become a component of the delicious 'and therefore
questionable'; distracted—as the sitter—by her own pose and
therefore 'doubly to be questioned'. Thus one poem glosses
another in Tomlinson's single world.

To describe that world, we should consider its relations and
its definitive terms. The terms of distaste include these: inert,
mean, politician, romantic, prodigal, suburban, diminished,
whim, ugly, waste, barbarous, negligence, empty, sullen,
menial, excess. Some of the terms of praise are: replenishment,
civil, order, ceremony, profuse, natural, consent, lucid, relation,
stable, equable, comity, seasoned, human, stillness, recognition,
temper, deft, haven, accomplished, supple, presence, dependence, grace. It is a Yeatsian vocabulary in the sense that Tomlinson, using such words as 'ceremony', 'civil', and 'accomplished',
takes advantage of the resonance earned for them and their like
in such poems as 'A Prayer for my Daughter' and 'In Memory
of Major Robert Gregory'. This is a dependence, an acknowledged relation, rather than a debt; like the relation to Marianne
Moore's 'Silence' in Tomlinson's 'The Castle'. The world defined by Tomlinson's key-terms is a world of pieties and accords,
a world of rooted men, gestures, pictures, cities, bridges, and
apples. This is why he speaks, in one poem, of the release from
'knowing' to 'acknowledgement'.

I have mentioned situations apparently encased in aggression,
ascribing to them a dominant force in modern literature. In many
writers the only proof of reality, the only sign that can be taken
seriously, is the mark of violence. But by now every trivial
novelist knows how to forge the signs. Can anyone doubt that
hundreds of contemporary novels are trading upon an induced
violence, a mass-produced extremity? Lionel Trilling has re-

cently entered a dispirited protest against the literature that features 'an accredited subversiveness, an established moral radicalism, a respectable violence'.[1] Tomlinson distrusts this literature so deeply that his distrust has the defect of its quality: if his poems reveal a danger-sign, it is their tendency to retreat to a merely passive position in the moral world. Some time ago the poet endorsed Martin Buber's early redaction of certain Chinese emphases in philosophy as a timely critique of our own: in particular, the 'containment of the will' and the 'potentialities of quietude' sponsored in the *Tao*.[2] It is obvious that the West has much to learn from the East in this respect, but the Taoist position itself is no real help. This is less China than chinoiserie: there must be a more Confucian way out. Tomlinson's own poems are not quietist: it is enough that they are quiet.

Perhaps at this point we might resort to the philosophers to rehearse the idiom of participation. Clearly, this idiom depends upon our acknowledgement of Being as the first commitment in an intelligible life. Before Stevens could posit a relation between his jar and Tennessee, he had to assent to the separate being of each, the ABC of being. As in his 'Study of Two Pears', 'The pears are not seen/As the observer wills.' This is provisional in Stevens, though he commits himself to it, as we shall see, in many of his last poems. Etienne Gilson has pointed out that, among the philosophers, Aquinas had a lively sense of the plenitude and continuity of being, but he remarks also that it is difficult to express this sense by the concept of Being. A philosopher who would begin with that, and that alone, undertakes to deduce the concrete from the abstract. To avoid this difficulty he would try to enrich the concept by giving it the vigour of an existential intuition. Subject and object must be connected by an intuition of the 'act'. Otherwise, Gilson says, 'an essence is dead when it is deposited in the understanding as a quiddity, without preserving its contact with the act-of-being'.[3] Let us say that the act of being must be acknowledged by a correspondingly 'active' sense. It is this sense, I would argue, that explains the eventfulness of Wordsworth's poems, the muscular exertion in Hopkins's

[1] Lionel Trilling, *Beyond Culture* (London. Secker and Warburg, 1966), p. 86.
[2] *Poetry*, Vol. 93, No. 6, March 1959, p. 411.
[3] Etienne Gilson, *The Christian Philosophy of St. Thomas Aquineas*, translated by L. K. Shook (New York. Random House, 1956), p. 370.

poems, and the urge in some parts of Stevens and many parts of Tomlinson to render essence by deploying existents in lithe relationships. It is the relationship, the movement of energy between the objects, that certifies their participation in the act-of-being.

Rounding this out a little: we think of Aquinas and his modern pupil as supplying a theory in support of Hopkins's practice, with more cogency than the maverick Scotus normally invoked for this purpose. (But we revert to this later.) For Wordworth's moral ballads we have his own theory. Beside this we might place a passage from Ortega's *Meditations on Quixote*, where he discusses 'Things and their Meaning'. Things have their meaning, he says, in relation to themselves and to other things. 'The "meaning" of a thing is the highest form of its co-existence with other things—it is its depth dimension. No, it is not enough for me to have the material body of a thing; I need, besides, to know its "meaning", that is to say, the mystic shadow which the rest of the universe casts upon it.' Hence what we call Nature is only 'the maximum structure into which all material elements have entered'.[1] For Stevens's poems we have his own theories, fabulous in their resource, with only this disability, that they are neater than the poems themselves in the matter of consistency. The poems flout the essays time and again, as perhaps they should. For Tomlinson's poems there is a certain amount of theory, often in his verse. But perhaps we might supplement it by recourse to two passages from older poets. There is a splendid letter in which Rilke, writing to his Polish translator, puts a case for Nature. Nature, he says, meaning all the objects of our context, is but a frail thing. But as long as we are here we should not abuse it. We should not 'pollute and degrade the Actual', if for no other reason than this, that its transitoriness is held in common with our own. Many of the things which our grandfathers valued are disappearing; in their lives, almost every object with which they lived was 'a vessel in which they found something human or added their morsel of humanity'. These things have gone and cannot be replaced. 'We are perhaps the last to have known such things': we are already replacing them with things that resist our humanity. It is our

[1] Jose Ortega y Gasset, *Meditations on Quixote*, translated by Evelyn Rugg and Diego Marín (New York. Norton, 1961), p. 88.

responsibility not only to remember them but to endorse 'their human or "laric" value'.[1] We may think that, in some of his later poems, Rilke freed himself a little from this admonition; but this is by the way. The second text to put beside Tomlinson's poem is a stanza from the *Song to David*, where Smart shows what laric value means by rendering the mutual relation of things:

> For ADORATION rip'ning canes,
> And cocoa's purest milk detains
>   The western pilgrim's staff;
> Where rain in clasping boughs inclos'd,
> And vines with oranges dispos'd,
>   Embow'r the social laugh.

I give this as an accompaniment to Tomlinson's poems, to emphasize a particular continuity of feeling at a time when dissociations are more often in the news. In the 'Ode to Arnold Schoenberg' Tomlinson speaks of proceeding

>   through discontinuities
>   to the whole in which
>   discontinuities are held
>   like the foam in chalcedony
>   the stone, enriched
>   by the tones' impurity.[2]

This is the direction of his recent poems. He still retains the old liaisons, recognizable in such phrases as 'the mystery of fact', 'the trust of seeing', the marriage of eye and mind. In Machado's Castilian ilexes, Tomlinson finds, 'strength and humility agree'. It is entirely in keeping with these poems that, quoting *The Deserted Village*, he should invoke 'the seasons' sweet succession'.

On the first page of *American Scenes* Tomlinson speaks of 'terror and territory'; at the end of the book we read of 'pause and possibility'. Between these extremes we find him accepting every invitation of language, provided its terms are gracious and rational. It is a good omen, a sign of proper nonchalance. Some

[1] Rainer Maria Rilke, *Selected Letters 1920–1926*, translated by R. F. C. Hull (London. Macmillan, 1946), p. 290. Letter of 13th November 1925, to Witold von Hulewicz.
[2] *A Peopled Landscape*, p. 50.

of Tomlinson's poems in the early years were a little too tight for their own ease. They refused to speak beyond their contract; as if, like Flaubert in Henry James's phrase, they felt of their vocation almost nothing but the difficulty. The recent poems are wrought with the old care, but they move more genially. There is no loss of their qualifying merit.

The collection is divided in four parts. The first, 'Negotiations', is continuous with the idiom of *A Peopled Landscape*. Sometimes the figures are rather monolithic, as if they were hired for the occasion to represent an aesthetic theory: they do not move with their own energy. A girl climbing a hill is a moral emblem, acting in that capacity before she is fully established as a girl climbing a hill. The second part, 'American Scenes', is Tomlinson's response to the landscapes of Arizona and New Mexico. Some of these poems are satirical, a new mode for this poet and still, it seems, difficult for him to gauge. In the weaker satires we hear an outraged English sensibility finding itself in Barstow, California, 'a placeless place' featuring an 'execrable conjunction/of gasoline and desert air'.[1] A sensibility in pain may be allowed the privilege of roaring as loud as it wishes; and yet one thinks of Austin Clarke's satires, poems like 'Martha Blake' and 'The Loss of Strength', where the pain is given in the cadence. In 'American Scenes' the lovely poems are the memorials to people like Homer Vance, Thomas Eakins, Mr. Brodsky, Emily Dickinson. The third and fourth parts contain a group of Mexican poems and a longer Idyll from San Francisco. Some of these pieces are like short stories; incidents, things seen from a bus, a Chinese adolescent in San Francisco reading a book called *Success in Spelling*.

The nonchalance of this poetry is partly Tomlinson's readiness to accept the invitations of language, and partly an equal readiness to accept the casualties of event, whatever the day offers. He still pares his poetic apples with concern, but he is now responsive to the yield of chance. He takes things as they come. This was implicit in his terminology from the beginning, but held back by some scruple. Now it is free. Tomlinson trusts, of course, that things, as they come, will not come too violently: his poems are not yet ready for the big storms, the 'violence without', in Stevens's phrase. When things come, the poet re-

[1] Charles Tomlinson, *American Scenes, and Other Poems* (London, Oxford University Press, 1966), p. 34.

ceives them with the values already declared in the earlier books.
So we hear of 'a loving lease/on sand, sun, rock', and the splendour of 'Castilian grace'. If we need a motto to hold these poems
in mind, we have one: 'the tranquillity of consciousness/for-
gotten in its object'. This may be Tomlinson's answer to those
modern writers who insist upon remembering their consciousness, whatever the fate of the object. So Tomlinson proceeds,
compiling an anthology of minor occasions to endorse a per-
vading tact. His masters in this transaction are Ruskin, Lawrence,
and Williams, so far as one can see: there is still a trace of Marianne
Moore, but hardly a sign of Stevens, an early master. Ruskin is
audible particularly in 'A Given Grace', where two cups on a
mahogany table are seen to 'unclench the mind, filling it with
themselves', a figure elsewhere invoked for the tranquillity of
consciousness. Lawrence seems to underwrite those poems in
which the acknowledgement of separateness is a first step toward larger courtesies. Williams is invoked, mostly in the
American scenes, to guide the younger poet in dealing with
casualty and 'rankest trivia', the things that come into the
poems because they are true, they were there at the time. In
'Chief Standing Water' we read of the *Book of Mormon* for the
same reason that in Marianne Moore's poem we are told of four
quartz crystal clocks, because there were four, neither three nor
five. The casual is not enough, as Stevens says, but the ability to
receive the casual, giving it a flick of feeling, is rare in poets.
Tomlinson's happiest development is in this direction. Seeing is
still believing:

> To love
> is to see,
> to let be
> this disparateness
> and to live within
> the unrestricted boundary between.[1]

We think of Isabel Archer, and of her interest, as James says, in
'the things that are not herself'.[2]

[1] ibid., p. 3.
[2] Henry James, *The Art of the Novel* (New York. Scribner, 1950 reprint), p. 51.

One of Randall Jarrell's favourite poems was 'During Wind and Rain'. Hardy's poem invokes the lost worlds, the songs of *Under the Greenwood Tree*, the English villages, the gallantry of bright things on the lawn. In each stanza there are seven lines, five to bring back the old images, two to concede their loss; but these two have the last word, the 'sick leaves', the 'white storm-birds', the 'rotten rose', and the rain cutting the names on the gravestones. 'Ah, no; the years, the years.' It is a noble poem, keeping up appearances when there is nothing else to be done. The stanzas begin with a lift of feeling: to every dog his day of remembered ease. The loss is held at memory's length, but in the last two lines the years break in upon reverie. It is easy to guess that the poem pleased Jarrell because of its gallantry, the bravery of its tone in defeat. Gallantry: as in *King Lear* when Edgar says

> Men must endure
> Their going hence, even as their coming hither,
> Ripeness is all, come on . . .

And Gloucester answers

> And that's true too.

This is the burden of Jarrell's poems: 'And that's true too.'

The poems begin with loss. The lost world is, to use Eliot's phrase, 'the ground of our beseeching', Act I. An entire book is called *Losses*. In 'When I Was Home Last Christmas . . .' the poet says:

> There is no one left to care
> For all we said, and did, and thought—
> The world we were.

'Never again,' the voice in 'Moving' says, recalling dear dead school-days, 'Never again/Will Augusta be the capital of Maine.' 'Children's Arms' calls to 'this first Rome/of Childhood', and several poems are elegies for the penny world of Pop, Mama, and Dandeen 'in her black silk'. In 'The Lost Children' a mother, observing that her daughter has grown up and that the air of home is thin, reflects:

> She makes few demands; you are grateful for the few.

In 'Woman':

> A girl hesitates a moment in mid-air
> And settles to the ground a wife, a mother.

There is more to be said, and the poet says it in the same poem, but this is Act 1, the cause of all. The figure the feeling makes is given in 'Thinking of the Lost World':

>   Back in Los Angeles, we missed
> Los Angeles.

The terms of loss are the inveterate relationships: father, mother, child, wife, husband. Jarrell's poetry is a sequence of Mutabilitie Cantos, tracing the crucial situations back to the point at which, changing, they withered into a new and darker truth. The tracing is done, mostly, in fear. In 'The Märchen', 'the darkness quakes with blood'. Sometimes the tone tries to hold itself well back from the edge. There is a time for speaking of the woe that is in marriage, but Jarrell tries to postpone that speech; meanwhile, keep the cry muted. In 'Next Day' a woman at the supermarket, her pilgrim's progress confined to a choice between Cheer and Joy, is troubled by what she has become, 'commonplace and solitary'. Life makes few demands upon her and perhaps, like the other mother, she is grateful for those few. The demands she makes upon life are not exorbitant.

>   Now that I'm old, my wish
> Is womanish:
> That the boy putting groceries in my car
> See me. It bewilders me he doesn't see me.

Not 'enrages' or even 'annoys'; just 'bewilders'. In this first act there is bound to be a moment in which the bewilderment is complete and fixed. In Jarrell's poetry it occurs when the voice says something and then, since the something said is disconsolate, says the opposite, hoping that this is the trick, the key; and finds that it makes no difference:

>   The husband answers, 'Life is life,'
> And when his wife calls to him from the kitchen
> He tells her who it was, and what he wanted.
> Beating the whites of seven eggs, the beater
> Asks her own opinion; she says, 'Life

Is Life.' 'See how it sounds to say it isn't,'
The beater tempts her. 'Life is not life,'
She says. It sounds the same. Putting her cake
Into the oven, she is satisfied
Or else dissatisfied: it sounds the same.

I have spoken of this as Act 1, where the dramatist gives the first hints. With the wisdom of hindsight we say, looking at Jarrell's poetry: there, there is where it began. The poems in *Blood for a Stranger* and *Little Friend, Little Friend* are not his choice work. In these the feeling is raw, and Jarrell was not good with raw wounds. He needed, for the good of the poetry, a wound not quite healed and yet as close to healing as it would ever come. He needed to be able to go a little way off, far enough to talk about the experience. He was not a dramatic poet. Reading his poems is not like seeing *King Lear*: it is like the relief of breaking a wounded silence, letting the pain drain away in words, in companionable talk. When we say that his idiom is conversational, we mean that it is like the conversation that helps, in trouble; balm to hurt minds.

Meanwhile there is Act 2, since we cannot live forever in loss even if the loss lives forever in us. As Gloucester says, 'O cruel! O you Gods.' Act 2 is the place for blame, recrimination, fighting back. As Jarrell says, 'Oh, it's not *right*,' the italics the fury in the words of 'The Night before the Night before Christmas', heard again in 'The Face'. Some of Jarrell's most celebrated poems come from this second act: cadences of protest, as in 'The Prince'. 'A man dies like a rabbit, for a use'; followed by: 'What will they pay me, when I die, to die?' The war poems are here, and poems like 'Jews at Haifa' about the war after the War. Some years later we hear the protest, rueful now, *diminuendo*, in the prose of *A Sad Heart at the Supermarket* and many of the poems in *The Woman at the Washington Zoo*. Perhaps it is the residue of the war feeling which, turning sour, sets the cruel moments astir in *Pictures from an Institution*. In 'The Snow-Leopard' Jarrell speaks of 'the brute and geometrical necessity'. In 'Siegfried' this necessity is reported as dull fact:

It happens as it does because it does.
It is unnecessary to understand; if you are still
In this year of our warfare, indispensable

In general, and in particular dispensable
As a cartridge, a life . . .

This is the 'murderous dull will' invoked in '1945': 'The Death
of the Gods', arranging, as in 'The Sick Nought', that the soldier
is 'something there are millions of'. 'The book is finished. I tell
you you're not in it,' the poet says to the men in the Overseas
Replacement Depot. Reading the protest poems again when
another protest is in the air, I find that those which have not sur-
vived intact are dead in their public manner. They sound as if,
for a proper reading, they need a megaphone and Hyde Park, a
public-address system and Madison Square Garden:

Man is born in chains, and everywhere we see him dead.
On your earth they sell nothing but our lives.
You knew that what you died for was our deaths?

There is nothing wrong with these lines, in principle, except
that they come from a poetic world that Jarrell never owned. He
did not lose it, because he never had it. The lines witness a failure
of the feeling to secure its proper voice, its proper form. In an
early poem Jarrell invokes 'that strange speech/In which each
sound sets out to seek each other'. In poems like 'The Emanci-
pators' the sounds set out to seek each other but, not finding,
settle for other sounds, more accessible, merely because they are
there. The sounds have a better chance when they are less por-
tentously directed, left to find their own companions. This is to
say that Jarrell's poems are best when scored for a voice, like
Cordelia's, 'soft, gentle, and low'; even when the words are
large in content:

                    . . . nothing comes from nothing,
The darkness from the darkness. Pain comes from the
     darkness
And we call it wisdom. It is pain.

There is nothing remarkable in these lines except the tone of
their delivery. The crucial moment is in the gap between the last
two sentences: what is said, in the words, is only important because it frames the silence between one apprehension and the
next. Among the modern poets Eliot is the greatest master of
these silences. But Jarrell is more than Eliot's pupil in this re-

source. He is particularly vivid in the relation between silence and speech, the flow of feeling between them. So he does wonderful things with a full stop, a colon, a question mark. In 'A Street off Sunset' the voice speaks of Mama, her face 'half a girl's', wringing a chicken's neck; and the child thinking:

> . . . Could such a thing
> Happen to anything? It could to a rabbit, I'm afraid;
> It could to—
> 'Mama, you won't kill Reddy ever,
> You won't ever, will you?'

This experience, which recurs in several poems, is beautifully registered. Its horror is domestic: this is not to say that the horror is small. Jarrell's special area of feeling is the private loss, held but not resolved in the structure of daily things; where the domestic order conceals—but not really, and not for long—the private anarchy; where speech is bewildered in silence. His sad hearts are most warmly felt at the supermarket, his wounded souls at the Washington Zoo. This is why the conversational idiom is so close to the shape of the poems, the shape of their feeling; why, too, this poet got so much, in this way, from Hardy, Yeats, and Frost. Saying, 'Oh, it's not right,' is momentous when things seem to be right: right, meaning normal, ordinary, daily. There is no point in saying, 'Oh, it's not right,' if you are in Hiroshima. In 'Three Bills' we are to imagine a man, the poet perhaps, in the restaurant at the Plaza, breakfast time, overhearing a conversation between a man, his wife, and another woman, all rich. The man goes off to the lavatory and his wife complains to her friend:

> We can't stay anywhere. We haven't stayed a month
> In one place for the last three years.
> He flirts with the yardboys and we have to leave.

The friend is sorry; and the poet in turn is sorry; sorry that the wife, the blonde, 'the suffused face about to cry/Or not to cry'——

> was a face that under different
> Circumstances would have been beautiful, a woman's.

I.E.: 'Oh, it's not *right*.'

Act 3 : 'An English Garden in Austria' ; a voice asking, 'And how shall we bear it?' The first answer is: by recalling everything else. Jarrell is a little Proust to whom, as someone has said, the only real paradises are lost paradises, spectrally recovered in memory and vision. Memory is compulsive in this poet, as if he feared that by losing anything he would lose everything. This is why so much of Jarrell's experience is seen under glass, and the death of the ball-turret gunner, in a famous poem, is a sinister version of the boyhood image, the magic gone wrong. In 'Children's Arms':

> The glass encloses
> As glass does, a womanish and childish
> And doggish universe. We press our noses
> To the glass and wish . . .

In 'The One Who Was Different' the poet thinks of a dead woman and, rearranging the conditions, thinks of her, instead, lying

> Encased in crystal, continually mortal,
> While the years rolled over you . . .

Hence the mirror's magic, sometimes black, sometimes the whitest white; as in 'Woman', where the morning sun, 'greyer for its mirroring', is 'perfected' in the wife's shining eyes. Hence also the dream poems, sometimes nightmare, sometimes what we see when we press our noses to the glass and wish. In 'A Sick Child' the child longs so hard for things to be different that they must be different, mustn't they?

Jarrell has a wonderful feeling for dreams and for the children who attend them, for those countries to which a child creeps 'out of his own life'. He wrote many poems to chart those countries, planting them with their proper vines. In the nightmare poems the proof of desolation is the thought that the dream things are just the same as daily things. In 'The Truth', when the bombs on London drive a child away from father and mother and the father is lost in one way and the mother in another, the child knows that the mother is no longer the same:

> Sometimes she was the same, but that was when I dreamed it.
> I could tell I was dreaming, she was just the same.

The wounded soldier in 'A Field Hospital' comes out of his dream: 'the old mistake'. Dream is a way of bearing it. So is fiction, anything to make it new. Jarrell wrote several poems about children seen in a lending library. He speaks of 'one cure for Everychild's diseases/Beginning: Once upon a time there was. . . .' We live, the same poem has it, by 'trading another's sorrows for our own'; trading 'another's impossibilities, still unbelieved in, for our own'. Stevens said of the Supreme Fiction: 'It Must Change.' To Jarrell, that kind of change is the fiction itself, 'dear to all things not to themselves endeared'. So in 'Children's Arms' the island sings to the child: 'Believe! Believe!' We bear it, if we can, by make-believe, dreams, figments, fictions. The verbal equivalent, in the detail, is wit, where the poet, almost a child, creeps out of his own life, fighting the good poetic fight, slaying the prosaic dragon. Mostly the dragon comes as authority, the way of the world, Army Regulations, public cliché. The poet bears these things by gulling them, tripping them on their own banana skins. In 'A War':

> There set out, slowly, for a Different World,
> At four, on winter mornings, different legs . . .
> You can't break eggs without making an omelette
> —That's what they tell the eggs.

When the poet asks, 'And how shall we bear it?' his answer is: 'Lightly, lightly.' This is his way into Act 4, the place where, traditionally, the dramatist releases 'the pity of it all'. Jarrell is lavish in pity. Indeed, he is never afraid of his feelings, or ashamed of them, or even proud of them. He is always pleased to appreciate the natural thing, liking the way a baby bat holds on tight to its mother's tail and the different way an owl tests the corners of the night. The poet's special feeling in Act 4 is care; its particular cadence, 'And yet, and yet.' He does not parade his care. Simply, he cares. It is typical of his sensibility that in an art gallery he notices the guard before he looks at the pictures; that when a girl talks of 'the dailiness of life' he saves the day with an image of water:

> Water, cold, so cold! you cup your hands
> And gulp from them the dailiness of life.

After the cruelty of the gods we have to care for what remains, such as it is. If the rules of the game are unjust, so much the worthier those men of chance who play it well. Character is a game splendidly played: therefore good like the other good things, 'to go on being', life itself with all its cruelty, ordinary things like sunshine, rain, childhood, the life of Nollekens. Or literature, one of the best ordinary things. In criticism, in teaching, praise was the highest form of Jarrell's care. Robert Lowell has written that eulogy was Jarrell's glory as a critic, praise that moved mountains of inertia and condescension. Who has ever spoken so well for Whitman's lists merely by saying of them: yes, but what lists! Jarrell's own lists make an impeccable anthology, the classic unexpected poems from Hardy, Ransom, Rilke, Frost, Williams, Shakespeare, Marianne Moore. When he was wrong, as I think he was wrong in that early essay on Stevens, he found an occasion to try again and this time got it right. Indeed, his reading of favourite poets was so devoted that he seemed to think his response a paltry effort until he had almost made himself over in their image. So I think of 'A Soul' as a Ransom poem, 'To the New World' an Auden poem, 'The Märchen' a Tate poem. And if someone loved Hardy so much that he wanted to write a Hardy poem, could he do better than Jarrell in 'The Blind Sheep'? I am surprised that Jarrell did not write a Yeats poem, but there are Frost poems, like 'Money' and 'Field and Forest'. These poems are thank-you notes mailed to the poets who showed Jarrell what might still be done.

I am not sure about Act 5. We are accustomed to muted endings, as in *King Lear* when Edgar says simply, 'The weight of this sad time we must obey.' In Jarrell's Act 5 the crucial poem is 'Thinking of the Lost World'. A man goes back, in reverie, to California, finding smog in Los Angeles where a child knew sunshine. 'The orange groves are all cut down.' So he tries to bear it, lightly:

> I say to my old self: 'I believe. Help thou
> Mine unbelief.'

The images of boyhood, the strangled chicken and the woman with the lion, are now parts of science fiction: this is not to say that they have been replaced, in belief, by anything else. There

is a moment in *Timon of Athens* when Timon, who has been
composing his epitaph, says to Flavius:

> My long sickness
> Of health, and living, now begins to mend,
> And nothing brings me all things.

It is a moment entirely in keeping with that all-or-nothing play.
'Thinking of the Lost World' is also written, imaginatively, at
the end of the line. So it goes back to the old images and gestures: one thing copying its opposite, a shadow miming a
shadow, trading one emptiness for another. The poem ends, the
last poem in Jarrell's last book:

> Where's my own hand? My smooth
> White bitten-fingernailed one? I seem to see
> A shape in tennis shoes and khaki riding-pants
> Standing there empty-handed; I reach out to it
> Empty-handed, my hand comes back empty,
> And yet my emptiness is traded for its emptiness,
> I have found that Lost World in the Lost and Found
> Columns whose grey illegible advertisements
> My soul has memorized world after world:
> LOST—NOTHING. STRAYED FROM NOWHERE. NO REWARD.
> I hold in my own hands, in happiness,
> Nothing: the nothing for which there's no reward.

Gloucester speaks to Edmund of 'the quality of nothing'.
Stevens speaks, in 'The Snow Man', a poem dear to Jarrell, of
the 'mind of winter', the superbly qualified mind of one who
willingly sees wintry things:

> the listener, who listens in the snow,
> And, nothing himself, beholds
> Nothing that is not there and the nothing that is.

This second nothing is the one that brings all things, Timon's
nothing in Act 5. In 'Prologues to What Is Possible' Stevens
writes of

> The way the earliest single light in the evening sky, in
>   spring,
> Creates a fresh universe out of nothingness by adding
>   itself . . .

This is what the mind of winter comes to, after the long sickness. Where there is nothing, Stevens implies, there is man, there is his imagination. Stevens thinks of it as a wonderful resilience of perception. It is what Jarrell comes to at the end: winter, and then, in happiness, the mind of winter. In his case I think of it as a resilience, equally wonderful, of love. Call it gallantry. As Yeats sang:

> Man is in love and loves what vanishes,
> What more is there to say?

I have implied that Charles Tomlinson is an accomplished rhetorician. His poems imply an aesthetic, a morality, an ethic. They do not pale in the presence of ideas. Tomlinson hopes to endorse the validity of human life by showing the resources of its attendant idiom, the language of fact and being. He knows that in these days the weight of poetic evidence is against him. Robert Martin Adams has studied the opposition in terms of Void, the engrossment of modern writers in modalities of Nothing.[1] The chief quality of Nothing, as he discloses, is that it releases man from his bondage to things, from the immediacy of experience, from the terror of fact, time, and history. Void is 'an ultimate without responsibilities'. The motto is given in 'Les Fenêtres', where Mallarmé says: 'Mais, hélas! Ici-bas est maître', pondering ways of escape even at the risk of falling through eternity. So in the literature of Void the status of the natural object is greatly diminished, things are reduced to shadows. The whole middle range of experience, ici-bas, is waved aside. In Mallarmé's poems, as Mr. Adams shows, the unexpectedly literal and physical images represent the tissue of material things 'imposing a lattice on a texture of woven abstractions, behind which lies the deeper darkness of void itself'. To Samuel Beckett the Wordsworthian assumption of a relation between man and Nature is 'the farce of giving and receiving'. The only recourse, in Beckett's terms, is parody, the poetry of negation. To read Mallarmé's poems and then to read Cézanne's letters to Émile Bernard and Charles Camoin is one way of meeting the

[1] Robert Martin Adams, *Nil: Episodes in the Literary Conquest of Void during the 19th Century* (New York. Oxford University Press, 1967).

fundamental crisis of modern imagination; the status of the given world and our available ways of apprehending it.

Santayana is helpful in this setting. In *Interpretations of Poetry and Religion* he considers the meaning of three terms, Understanding, Imagination, and Mysticism. Understanding, he says, is 'an applicable fiction, a kind of wit with a practical use'.[1] 'Those conceptions which, after they have spontaneously arisen, prove serviceable in practice, and capable of verification in sense, we call ideas of the understanding.' The imagination is a higher power because it expresses 'the universal self' and goes far beyond the serviceable. But it can be abused. 'If the imagination merely alienates us from reality, without giving us either a model for its correction or a glimpse into its structure, it becomes the refuge of poetical selfishness. Such selfishness is barren, and the fancy, feeding only on itself, grows leaner every day.' Mysticism is the final mode of abstention: 'instead of building a better world, it would undermine the foundations even of the world we have built already'. The mystic cannot be satisfied with 'anything short of Absolute Nothing'. Meanwhile there is the natural world. We cannot do better, Santayana implies, than to live in it, guided by understanding and the constructive imagination. 'When we compare the temple which we call Nature, built of sights and sounds by memory and understanding, with all the wonderful worlds evocable by the magician's wand, may we not prefer the humbler and more lasting edifice, not only as a dwelling, but even as a house of prayer?' Charles Tomlinson is one of those poets who would, as far as possible, make us at home in the world.

Marianne Moore is another. Indeed, it may be useful to look at Miss Moore's poems in this context, to see another relation between poetry and fact.

Miss Moore's first book was called, simply, *Poems*. Her second was *Observations*. The titles are interchangeable. 'I like to describe things,' she remarks in 'Subject, Predicate, Object', an aesthetic given in three modest pages of *Tell Me, Tell Me*. Her favourite mood is the indicative, pointing to things. Optatives are rare; imperatives are normally addressed to herself. The pleasure of writing a poem, she has said, is 'consolation, rapture,

[1] George Santayana, *Interpretations of Poetry and Religion* (New York. Harper and Row edition, 1957), p. 15.

to be achieving a likeness of the thing visualized'. Poetry is a way of looking, various because vision is irregular, reasonable because, irregular, it is not indiscriminate. Yeats distinguished between the glance and the gaze, and William Empson took care to discover what a man sees through the corner of the eye. The distinction between appearance and reality is not to Miss Moore a cause of persistent distress. To think appearance significant is not a mark of folly; it is a mode of appreciation, or predilection. Things may be deceptive, but a relation between one thing and another is something achieved. So it is good to look at things, observing.

Mostly, the observations in Miss Moore are her own; of plants, animals, birds, the giraffe, the pangolin, clocks, baseball, jewels. But this poet, gorgeous in observation, is the first to acknowledge that someone else has been observant. 'Blue Bug' started from a photograph by Thomas McAvoy in *Sports Illustrated*; of eight polo ponies, one of them like a dancer or the acrobat Li Siau Than. 'The Arctic Ox' was set astir by an essay in the *Atlantic Monthly*, the essayist John J. Teal, who rears musk oxen on his farm in Vermont. A recent poem praises Leonardo da Vinci, impassioned calligrapher of flower, acorns, and rocks. The hero of 'Granite and Steel' is John Roebling, praised for inventing Roebling cable. Throughout her poems Miss Moore is on hand to defend the rights of 'small ingenuities', keeping open the 'eye of the mind'. Gracious, she delights in grace, skill, gusto, charity, the rescue of Carnegie Hall, the 'enfranchising cable' of Brooklyn Bridge.

So Miss Moore's poems are poetic as natural science is poetic; botany, meteorology. Some years ago she defended the comparison of poet and scientist. 'Both are willing to waste effort. To be hard on himself is one of the main strengths of each. Each is attentive to clues, each must narrow the choice, must strive for precision.' In 'The Staff of Aesculapius' she writes in praise of cancer research, virology, knowledge 'gained for another attack' upon suffering. There are several poems in defence of experimental waste. Anything is poetic, Miss Moore implies, conducted in the proper spirit of disinterestedness and charity. A poet writes a poem, perhaps, to revive a root meaning long buried. The reader consults a large dictionary, finds the old meaning, and recognizes it, revived, in its new setting. These are

poetic acts, honourably wasteful. One of Miss Moore's favourite
writers is Christopher Smart, author of *Jubilate Agno*. Another is
Landor, praised in a recent poem, who could throw a man
through a window and yet say, 'Good God, the violets!' Miss
Moore loves dapple, dappled things, the evidence of spirited
acts. She does not like a big splash. She likes circumstance, released from pomp. She thinks Caesar a great writer and Defoe
observant to the degree of genius.

'Accessibility to experience' is Henry James's phrase, invoked
for admiration in Miss Moore's poem 'New York' and elsewhere recalled in prose. It is reasonable to say that this is Miss
Moore's way of being an American, like James in this respect a
characteristic American. When she quotes a sentence from
James's study of Hawthorne, its light returns upon herself. Hawthorne was dear to James because he 'proved to what a use
American matter could be put by an American hand'. An
American 'could be an artist, one of the finest, without "going
outside"; quite, in fact, as if Hawthorne had become one just by
being American enough'. We think of Williams in Rutherford,
Stevens in Hartford, Miss Moore in Manhattan. 'The Gods of
China are always Chinese,' Stevens said. Miss Moore likes to
quote from James the advice to Christopher Newman: 'Don't
try to be anyone else'; and if triumph comes, 'let it then be all
you.' But she does not endorse a predatory grasp of reality. Instead, she is the first to concede to a thing its own independent
right; an acknowledgement rather than a concession. In her
colony of the spirit there are no chain gangs. It does not gratify
her to brings things to heel, seeing them cower. She is a poet of
finite things; she does not lust for the absolute. She is always
patient in the presence of limitation. A recent poem, 'Charity
overcoming Envy', says: 'The Gordian knot need not be cut.'

Of eternal things in this poetry there is little to be said. Miss
Moore has her own sense of them, but it is private. She praises
Landor for a corresponding reticence; who, considering infinity
and eternity, would only say: 'I'll talk about them when I understand them.' Miss Moore does not claim to understand everything; not even everything she sees. She speaks when, observant,
she has something to report. She is no mystic. This is the measure
of her care for things, relationship, words; a care habitually engaged in accuracy. Quoting Martin Buber: 'The free man be-

lieves in destiny and that it has need of him'; she adds, 'Destiny, not fate.' A sentence culled from James's *Notes of a Son and Brother* is to her 'an instance of reverent, and almost reverend, feeling that would defend him against the charge of casualness in anything, if ever one were inclined to make it'. Miss Moore's poems are full of quotations because she has come upon many things which have only to be exhibited to be appreciated, and appreciation is poetic. One thing, placed beside another, if both are judiciously chosen, sets a new relation in train. The main duty is to get the words right. This is why Miss Moore is stern in revising her poems.

So the revisions are always instructive. Usually they are the result, she says, of 'impatience with unkempt diction and lapses in logic, together with an awareness that for most defects, to delete is the instantaneous cure'. Sometimes the change is designed to strengthen the syntax, where the burden is excessive. In *Tell Me, Tell Me* the poem 'Sun' is revised. An earlier version included the lines:

> O Sun, you shall stay
> with us. Holiday
> and day of wrath shall be one,
> wound in a device
> of Moorish gorgeousness,
> round glasses spun
> to flame hemispheres of one
> great hour-glass dwindling to a stem.[1]

The internal rhymes are gay, but perhaps they are too much, gaudy. The repetition of 'one', if not unkempt, is loose. But the author of 'The Pangolin' would not wish to delete the invocation to the sun, 'that comes into and steadies my soul', so she tidies the diction by eliminating the repetition, letting the rest stand:

> O Sun, you shall stay
> with us; holiday,
> consuming wrath, be wound in a device
> of Moorish gorgeousness, round glasses spun
> to flame as hemispheres of one
> great hour-glass dwindling to a stem.[2]

[1] *A Marianne Moore Reader* (New York. Viking Press, 1961), p. 88.
[2] Marianne Moore, *Tell Me, Tell Me* (New York. Viking Press, 1967), p. 49.

The relation between the holiday and the wrath is changed, but the new relation is more in keeping with the urgency of the prayer. Miss Moore cares for these things, her small ingenuities. She likes to recite the fable of La Fontaine about the song that preserved the life of the swan mistaken by the cook for a goose; the moral of the story being, 'Sweet speech does no harm—none at all.' Admiring 'an elegance of which the source is not bravado', she writes as if every poem were a swansong, sweet but not lugubrious. There are things a swan may not do, even to save her life. Many of the poems are the result of stitching and unstitching, but they sound like 'a moment's thought' (Yeats's test in 'Adam's Curse'). Some of them, speech after long silence, have that fatality of cadence which is Miss Moore's trademark:

> You understand terror, know how
>   to deal
> with pent-up emotion, a ballad,
>   witchcraft.
> I don't. O Zeus and O Destiny!

But these cadences are not, as we say, 'merely verbal', they are a form of good manners, 'values in use'. Miss Moore's poems have the kind of grace, civility, and candour which we find in English verse epistles of the sixteenth and seventeenth centuries. When her lines are unforgettable, it is not because 'in the accepted sense' they do things 'in a big way'; it is because they are true, genuine, and because they have that 'tame excitement' on which she thrives. The objective is 'fertile procedure'. In a recent poem Envy is delineated:

> Envy, on a dog, is worn down by
>   obsession,
> his greed (since of things owned by
>   others
> he can only take *some*).

Things well done are 'inventions with wing'.

So the relation between Miss Moore and the language she uses is remarkably intimate. She can do more with abstractions than any modern poet, Eliot excepted: reticence, propriety, mobility, probity, deference, magnanimity. Her favourite word, I guess from internal evidence, is ardour, in French and English: '*Sentir avec ardeur*: with fire; yes, with passion.' Her favourite image, by the same guess, is the kite. 'With no resistance, a kite staggers and falls; whereas if it catches the right current of air it can rise, darting and soaring as it pulls and fights the wind.' Hence 'the mind is an enchanting thing', and poetry is 'the Mogul's dream: to be intensively toiling at what is a pleasure'.

So, thinking of Miss Moore's poems in general before looking at one of them in particular, we think of activities at once work and play; or things like ice-skating which are hard play. The function of a poem, when Miss Moore writes it, is to provide for distinctive energy of mind a sufficient occasion; a direction. The mind moves from its presumed rest; ranges abroad through materials congenial to its nature; comes to rest again. This is the figure the poems makes; a sequence, a curve, the trajectory of a mind well aimed. If we ask why one curve is chosen in preference to another, there is no ready answer: it is so. The assumption is that energy of mind is good, and its release in action is good. The note is experimental, exploratory. This is one of the differences between Miss Moore and Mr. Tomlinson. In Tomlinson's poems the poetic materials seem to be subdued before the poem begins. Too often the poem has an air of illustration, almost of allegory. This poet cares for certainty and lucidity so much that he waits for them to come before he writes the poem to prove them. Miss Moore seems to achieve her lucidities in the process of sending her mind abroad. So the relation between the moral and the story, in Tomlinson's poems, is often a diplomatic relation; in Miss Moore's poems it is a more daring relation, along lines of feeling now laid down for the first time.

'The Pangolin' is a celebration of difference, of the benign force which makes a thing what it is and keeps it in that state. The first stanzas disengage the pangolin from any human use, invasion of its privacy: observation guarantees this. Gertrude Stein said that 'description is evaluation', an admonition congenial to Miss Moore, who is content to have the evaluation reside silently in descriptions almost scientific. Once the pangolin is safe in its own nature, the poet can afford to let the mind roam a little:

> Pangolins are not aggressive animals; between
> dusk and day they have the measured

> tread of the machine—
>   the slow frictionless creep of a thing
>   made graceful by adversities, con-
>
> versities. To explain grace requires
>   a curious hand. If that which is at all were not forever,
> why would those who graced the spires
>   with animals and gathered there to rest, on cold luxurious
>   low stone seats—a monk and monk and monk—between
>   the thus
>   ingenious roof-supports, have slaved to confuse
>   grace with a kindly manner, time in which to
>   pay a debt
>   the cure for sins, a graceful use
>   of what are yet
>   approved stone mullions branching out
>   across
>   the perpendiculars? A sailboat
>
> was the first machine.[1]

I have quoted the final version, somewhat tidied in diction be-tween 1951 and 1961. We assume that Miss Moore came upon the first 'graceful' in the ordinary way, since it is a word near at hand and natural. The first event of distinctive imagination is the jump from 'adversities' to 'conversities'. 'Adversities' is moral in its first meaning, since the Latin is dead there, until it is restored to figurative life by the recognition of the Latin in 'conversities'. The poet does not spurn an extensive meaning even if it comes by linguistic chance. The effect is to light up both words; and then to throw this double light back upon 'graceful'. So the next passage is derived from this happy chance. 'To explain grace re-quires a curious hand.' Already the word is moving buoyantly between a spiritual and a secular meaning. 'Curious', meaning now 'careful', because Latin is in the air. 'Hand', because the true explanation is to do it: no explanation but in action. 'If that which is at all were not forever'; a variant of Yeats's 'All lives that has lived'; just as one word, 'grace', serves two or several

---

[1] *A Marianne Moore Reader, supra*, p. 38. The text of this passage differs some-what from that in *Collected Poems* (New York. Macmillan, 1952), p. 120.

masters, natural and supernatural, so anything that exists is, in a sense, eternally existent. The next lines are a lively illustration of the fact that, as Miss Moore says in 'The Sycamore', 'there's more than just one kind of grace'. To set an animal upon a spire is to bring the several worlds together, honouring all. The monks are the appropriate adepts, graceful in two worlds. Miss Moore's monks live at once in both worlds, not painfully divided and distinguished but genial. Hence they have slaved to confuse grace (supernatural) with its several human forms, social, legal, ecclesiastical, architectural. These are various enough to stand for all the other forms, unspecified. The basic pattern of the verse, then, is the observation, followed by an elucidation sufficient to make the observation shine; text and gloss. The nature of grace is enlivened by sentences involving 'graceful', 'graced', and so on. I. A. Richards once set the opening lines of Donne's *First Anniversary* beside Dryden's *Ode to Mrs. Anne Killigrew*; the point being that in Donne's verse 'there is a prodigious activity between the words as we read them'.[1] Following, exploring, understanding Donne's words is not a preparation for reading the poem: 'it is itself the poem'. In Dryden, on the other hand, 'the words are in routine conventional relations like peaceful diplomatic communications between nations'. Dryden's words 'do not induce revolutions in one another and are not thereby attempting to form a new order'. Can we not say, allowing for the differences, that in 'The Pangolin' the activity between the words as we read them is great, if not prodigious? The words, as we cope with them, are forming new relations in our minds; or, what is often the same thing, breaking up dead relations already entombed there. The verse is purifying 'the dialect of the tribe' by sending an imaginative force to range through tribal words. Think, to illustrate again, what 'luxurious' does to 'cold low stone seats', otherwise conventional enough: it sets the common phrase stirring from within.

So the question to ask about a poem by Marianne Moore is not: what are all these details doing here?; but rather, what, given these details, is the principle of their relation? The ethic of Miss Moore's verse implies that if we treat objects as objects, rather than as functions of ourselves, and if we send the mind to

[1] Reprinted in Irving Howe (editor), *Modern Literary Criticism* (New York. Grove Press, 1958), pp. 85 foll.

explore them in their own terms, the encounter of subject and object is likely to be rewarding. If the spaces of life are occupied by generous perception, there is less room for nasty things; belligerence, bravado, cruelty, condescension. No other poet writes like Miss Moore: not even William Carlos Williams, who learned from her how lightly a poet may travel. The reason is partly the choice of objects; and about this there is nothing useful to be said, except that the choice is personal and intimate. 'The Pangolin', for instance, begins *de facto* and ends *de jure*. Her preoccupation: the personal and moral possibilities of *ici-bas*, despite everything.

2

Plot, Fact, and Value

'Theories of values have all but lost contact not
only with morals and preferences but even with
ethics and aesthetics, and our judgment of what
is good or beautiful has little bearing on our
analysis of action or taste.'
R. P. MCKEON, *Thought, Action and Passion*

I

It is either too early or too late to attempt a definition of plot.[1]
In the Preface to *The Portrait of a Lady* Henry James speaks of the
germ of his idea as consisting 'not at all in any conceit of a "plot",
nefarious name, in any flash, upon the fancy, of a set of relations,
or in any one of those situations that, by a logic of their own,
immediately fall, for the fabulist, into movement, into a march
or a rush, a patter of quick steps; but altogether in the sense of a
single character, the character and aspect of a particular engaging
young woman, to which all the usual elements of a "subject",
certainly of a setting, were to need to be superadded'. What
James resents is the notion of a commanding plot, a moving pattern of events to which the characters must conform, so that the
pattern will be protected, the movement free. In the naturalistic
novel the characters conform, and the plot leads the way because it is the finger of Fate, Determinism, or whatever monster
is the villain of the piece. The characters are dragged along.
James resented this, because he would not have his characters
abused: they must be free to go at their own pace in their own
direction. But the going will be so often a matter of consciousness and sensibility that the movements are likely to be too fine
for public record. The plot often seems to stand still while the

[1] See R. S. Crane, *Critics and Criticism, Ancient and Modern* (Chicago. University
of Chicago Press, 1957 edition), p. 66.

characters are buzzing with internal event. Later in the Preface
he reverts to the question: 'I might envy, though I couldn't emulate, the imaginative writer so constituted as to see his fable first
and to make out its agents afterwards: I could think so little of any
fable that didn't need its agents positively to launch it; I could
think so little of any situation that didn't depend for its interest
on the nature of the persons situated, and thereby on their way
of taking it.' This sounds like E. M. Forster's condescension to
plot in *Aspects of the Novel*, but the position is sensible; the
answer is clearly a matter of proportion. Even in Forster, the dis-
proportion of the theory is corrected by the measure of his practice, notably in *Howard's End* and *A Passage to India*, which have
quite enough in the way of story to engross the nature of the
persons situated. But there are novels like *To the Lighthouse* in
which the buzz of sensibility without an adequate commitment
to story and event is deadly, and a problem we considered unreal rears itself again to imply that at least a certain minimum of
plot is necessary.

There are two points to be remarked at this stage. James will
lean toward 'character' rather than 'plot' if we insist upon taking
a vote, but he uses a strikingly 'plotty' word, 'agents', in preference to the normal word, 'characters'; in the Preface to the
Portrait he thinks of his fictional persons not at all as pictures but
as agents in a world of action; clearly a dramatic image. He sees
Isabel Archer not as a static figure but 'in motion and, so to
speak, in transit . . . as bent upon its fate—some fate or other'.
The motion, the transit, and the fate largely constitute what we
call plot. We have a particular case in mind, the great Chapter
XLII, which James rightly considered the best thing in the book,
Isabel's 'meditative vigil' far into the night by a dying fire.
James says: 'Reduced to its essence, it is but the vigil of searching
criticism; but it throws the action further forward than twenty
"incidents" might have done. . . . It is a representation simply of
her motionlessly *seeing*, and an attempt withal to make the mere
still lucidity of her act as "interesting" as the surprise of a cara-
van or the identification of a pirate.' James is leaning rather
heavily here, implying that the best a fabulist can manage is to
think up large, rough 'incidents', as if the only choice were between *The Waves* and *Ben-Hur*. But if plot is a sequence of
incidents the greater part of its meaning consists in its being a se-

quence of incidents; the incidents are the experience of which the sequence is the meaning. The merit of James's great chapter, however, is entirely consistent with placing a high valuation upon plot. Isabel's meditative vigil depends upon a defining context; it could not exist without forty-one chapters of fairly stout events. Given those chapters, the vigil becomes momentous, an act of recognition, an earned epiphany. The act itself is not a buzz of sensibility; it has separate stages, in each of which Isabel ponders a relationship, holds it up to an inner light that becomes more intense as the firelight wanes. The vigil has a plot of its own. Isabel begins by thinking of the hovering but manageable relationship between herself and Warburton; then of Gilbert and Madame Merle; of herself and Gilbert; of herself and Ralph; finally returning to the recognition scene, the remembered vision, 'that of her husband and Madame Merle unconsciously and familiarly associated'. Action, perception, and passion are inseparable.

There is no quarrel, then, with James's theory, or with his practice on this occasion. The great middle novels commit themselves to time, place, event, to the finite, the realm of action as the scene of disclosed value; this is what the 'solidity of specification' comes to, a belief in the value of being, a commitment to action and vision in a human world acknowledged as real. It is part of James's history that these commitments wavered in some of his later fiction, notably in *The Golden Bowl* which one tends to praise as 'poetic' before reflecting that its poetry is induced as in *The Blue Bird* rather than inseparable from the represented transit and conflict of feeling, as in *Hedda Gabler*.

A survey of the history of plot in modern fiction is unnecessary for our purposes. In any event the general outline is fairly well known. I propose to discuss only one or two novelists and to comment a little upon the embarrassment of their dealing in plot. Later, we return to the *Portrait of a Lady*.

II

Conrad is clearly a major novelist, and his works are clearly *fiction* in the sense that it is as fiction we should read them rather than as poetic dramas or tone poems. The fiction seems to divide itself readily into two kinds; the novels and tales which disclose

most of their meaning through the events as exhibited, notably
Under Western Eyes, *Nostromo*, 'The Secret Sharer', 'The End of
the Tether', 'The Shadow Line', and *The Nigger of the 'Narcissus'*; and those novels and tales in which the meaning is largely a
matter of quasi-philosophic assertion, comment and critique, the
narrator's essays, sheer verbal 'business', as in the Conradese of
'Youth', the smoky symbolism of 'Heart of Darkness', the portentous Marlow of *Chance*, the narrative insistence of 'The
Lagoon'. I should argue that the best of Conrad is in his plots;
the worst arises when his faith in the actual breaks down and he
conceals the rupture with a coating of scarlet prose.

Chance, for instance, is grossly overwritten. James was fascinated by its exhibiting 'the way to do a thing that shall make it
undergo most doing', but the truth is that the book groans under
the weight of its 'art', its elaborate multiplication of producers
and reporters, its 'circumferential tones', Marlow's 'prolonged
hovering flight of the subjective over the outstretched ground of
the case exposed', the nervous tic that sends the narrator into
verbiage about night and evil because Marlow needs time to get
another cigar. The residual strength of the novel consists in the
moral implications of its plot, the story of Flora de Barral, the
Fynes, the financier, and Captain Anthony; this is what the
reader trusts, and his confidence is greater than Conrad's, for the
reader does not acknowledge the necessity or the propriety of
the 'doing' which for the most part consists in building up a
Holmesian *persona* for Marlow with the aid of garrulous remarks about fate, chance, responsibility, the sea, women, greed,
stupidity, and the Inscrutable. Here is a case in point, Marlow's
account of the Fynes and their reaction to the disappearance of
Flora de Barral:

'I supposed they would wish to communicate, if only as to the
disposal of the luggage, with the young lady's relatives. . . .

'Fyne, he looked rather downcast by then, thanked me and
declined.

' "There is really no one," he said, very grave.

' "No one," I exclaimed.

' "Practically," said curt Mrs. Fyne.

And my curiosity was aroused again.

' "Ah! I see. An orphan."

Mrs. Fyne looked away weary and sombre, and Fyne said,

"Yes," impulsively and then qualified the affirmative by the quaint statement: "To a certain extent."

'I became conscious of a languid, exhausted embarrassment, bowed to Mrs. Fyne, and went out of the cottage to be confronted outside its door by the bespangled, cruel revelation of the Immensity of the Universe. The night was not sufficiently advanced for the stars to have paled; and the earth seemed to me more profoundly asleep—perhaps because I was alone now. . . .'[1]

This is curious. Conrad is often credited with the power of a symbolist, the power to make a strict notation take on a special tone, a visionary resonance, a halo; Lord Jim's jump from the boat, Flora de Barral's dog, the statue of Rousseau, the stained front of the Mint. But just as often he tries to enlarge the significance of the event by surrounding it with breathless prose and ominous suggestion for which no reasonable preparation has been made. D. H. Lawrence's Paul records a few moments of lofty intimation on the last page of *Sons and Lovers*, but they are securely grounded in the tumult of his mother's death and the lesser tumult of his own failure in 'dialogue'. The Immensity of the Universe has nothing to do with Flora de Barral or the Fynes; it is commandeered to lend interest to Marlow, a piece of shadow-boxing set up because Conrad thought the facts were not enough. In this case the facts would have been quite enough. Mr. Fyne's quaint remark is a brilliant invention: it is perfectly appropriate that the remark should strike Marlow as quaint and that he should go off to wonder about it; but the sudden jump to the capitalized Immensity is a provincial touch. Conrad's genius was restless, problematic, insecure; he could not trust it; he could not sit still in its possession. In *Chance* he committed himself to fact and event only when they were spectacularly intense; Flora's, 'But I don't want to be let off,' de Barral's drinking his own poison, Captain Anthony's implacable magnanimity, 'I own myself beaten.'

The Secret Agent seems quite different. There are no detachable lumps of philosophy, no halos of lurid significance. The great scenes achieve representative force without in any way invalidating their strict function as events within the plot. The remarkable Chapter XI, for instance, the great scene in which Verloc tries to explain things to Winnie, depends for its power not

[1] Joseph Conrad, *Chance* (London. Gresham, 1925), pp. 60–1.

at all upon verbal insistence but upon the disclosed gap between the endorsed formulae of communication and the actual transaction between husband and wife. The network of events is made up of Verloc's pathetically benign thoughts, his fatalistic explanations, Winnie hiding her face in her hands, Verloc eating bread and meat—a marvellous invention—Winnie staring at the blank whitewashed wall as she ponders Belgravian memories. These events are given as a human situation, deployed by a narrative voice which is sufficiently identified to be 'there' but not to intrude. Elsewhere, the voice proclaims itself that of a compulsive cynic, and the effect is demoralizing. The splendid things in *The Secret Agent* are the scenes so strong in themselves and already so naturally and properly ironic that an additional irony inserted by the narrator would obviously have been crude. But in several chapters, while most of the meaning is entrusted to the actual—to act and event—it is given to these only as qualified by the 'knowing' and corrosive narrator. The reservations that Conrad imposed upon the actual as the locus of value and meaning in *Chance* are squeezed, in *The Secret Agent*, into the gap between each event and its corrosive gloss. Hardly a single character is allowed to stand undisgraced: Verloc, Vladimir, the anarchists, the police. Winnie's love for Stevie is retroactively degraded by her transaction with Ossipon; Winnie's mother plays the beggar too competently. And Stevie, Myshkin's shadow, embodies something in human feeling but nothing that one could take seriously as Value. Even poor Michaelis is a harmlessly anarchist butterfly broken upon the narrator's wheel:

'The perspiration of the literary labour dropped from his brow. A delightful enthusiasm urged him on. It was the liberation of his inner life, the letting out of his soul into the wide world. And the zeal of his guileless vanity (first awakened by the offer of five hundred pounds from a publisher) seemed something predestined and holy.'[1]

The spirit at work is ungenerous. To divert attention from the facts—in which he does not believe—Conrad stations the narrator at the side of the stage, jeering at the fat revolutionary. Indeed, the narrator's interventions in *The Secret Agent* reveal Conrad's self-indulgence just as clearly as the high talk of *Chance*. Conrad, by nature one of the finest of storytellers,

---

[1] Joseph Conrad, *The Secret Agent* (London. Gresham, 1925), p. 120.

could never quite manage, even in *Nostromo*, to commit himself and his fortunes to the case exposed; he had not enough faith left over after the demands of an exorbitant Self. In *The Secret Agent* the only force, the only value, allowed to persist without question is the narrative voice itself, and the voice is full of contempt.

Perhaps we can say that facts are, in one sense, roots, incarnations; and Conrad, having cut his Polish roots, was never again to be fully at ease with facts. He would never again commit himself to facts, and he was distressed by the vague perception that disembodied values—values-without-fact—are pathetic; that—as C. I. Lewis has argued—'values are attributes which do not wander outside some substance; they can be realized or contemplated only as characters of something in particular, or of some specific *kind* of thing'.[1] Conrad could not tolerate this: hence he tended to divert the perceived values, assigning them to the 'self' of his narrative voice. Even in *Under Western Eyes*: having set up a moral jungle in the great opening scenes of the novel, Conrad fled from its implications, sending in his English narrator to cut off the revolutionary claws before any Western citizens could get hurt; and, at the end, inserting Natalie Haldin's gesture as at once a moral statement and a repudiation of the 'substance' of political action. This statement is itself circumscribed by the neutralizing narrator: in the last pages he offers the critique that 'there was no longer any Natalia Haldin, because she had completely ceased to think of herself. It was a great victory, a characteristically Russian exploit in self-suppression'. Conrad is putting his thumb on the scale. This is a failure of narrative tact, but it reveals why Natalia's new commitment serves only to allow Conrad to evade the hazards of his novel; because he does not understand the act and cannot perceive the meaning, the value, it should possess. Natalia's portentous silence merely dissolves the world of political Fact and locates Value in private service to the weak and the bereaved. On the selected ground, the world of political action, nothing is fulfilled.

Conrad's greatness consists, almost despite himself, in the moral resonance of his fables, the source of which lies in sequences of acts and events, in plots; the rest—and notably the high scepti-

[1] Clarence Irving Lewis, *An Analysis of Knowledge and Valuation* (La Salle, Illinois. Open Court Press, 1946), p. 369.

cal talk—is dispensable. Reality offered itself to him in acts and sufferences, human events; like a divine gift, like faith. It came upon him prostrate before the idols of the Self. The conversion, the assent, was incomplete. Hence the impression of his successes as precariously achieved; hence the embarrassment of his lapses, and the impatience one visits upon his failures. It is not surprising that he is at his best in his plots. Indeed, while the art of fiction is various and inventive in its procedures, the centre of its circle of reference is still the story, the human events. True, the novel has shown itself hospitable to many kinds of action and discourse; it has found a place for essays, lyrics, catalogues, blank pages, documentation; but these in the nature of the form itself are marginal to the central commitment, to event, act, and time. In 'Emotion of Multitude' Yeats argued that 'there can not be great art without the little limited life of the fable, which is always the better the simpler it is, and the rich, far-wandering, many imaged life of the half-seen world beyond it.'[1]

III

'The great discovery of the French symbolists was the irrelevance, and hence the possibility of abolition, of paraphrasable plot.' This report was made by Hugh Kenner, writing of Ezra Pound.[2] Mr. Kenner's approval was elicited by 'the fact that juxtaposed objects render one another intelligible without conceptual interpositions': again, 'as things are set in relation in metaphor, according to an acute intuition of their similarity and dissimilarity, so actions, passions, places, times, blocks of experiences are set in relation in a more extended poem. This is as true of the *hokku* as of the epic, of *King Lear* as of the *Cantos*.' In these observations Mr. Kenner showed no concern for the fate of plot, concept, copula, syntax, or transitive verbs, or for the modes of mind and feeling which they serve. Recently he has argued that in a universe where intelligibility does not need to be imposed by the mind, syntax is optional: the poetic microcosm is not the statement but the Aristotelian action, 'the process by which the poem gets from its own first word to its own last word, some-

---

[1] W. B. Yeats, *Essays and Introductions* (London. Macmillan, 1961), p. 216.
[2] Hugh Kenner, *The Poetry of Ezra Pound* (London. Faber and Faber, 1951), p. 91.

times a syntactic process, sometimes not'. This action, it appears, can be called *mimesis* 'because it parallels the similar movements of apprehension performed by a mind moving among intelligible things and situations, knitting webs of intelligibles'.[1]

A critic who endorses Aristotelian *praxis* and *mimesis* while dispensing with *mythos* is a strange adept of discriminations. The gesture is not convincing. It is still necessary to ask what is implied in a rejected copula, in the elimination of plot, in dispensing with the concept, in economizing on syntax and transitive verbs. I am ready to agree that 'juxtaposition without copula' is one of the feasible methods of expression—we will return to it in thinking of Joyce—but its functions are far more restricted than Mr. Kenner allows. It is appropriate mainly for ironic comparisons and contrasts, as in *Ulysses* and *Madame Bovary*, and even there its special temptation is to be arch, pseudo-profound, glib, evasive. It claims vast resources of implication and hovers on the brink of commitment. It would and it would not. Being arbitrary, it protects itself from the risk of interrogation; since a relation of some kind can be established between practically any juxtaposed objects. Mr. Kenner claims that it parallels the movements of apprehension performed by a mind moving among intelligible things and situations; but such a mind does far more than this, it seeks formulations, explicit relations, and—urgently —an answer to the question, 'how should one live?' A mind thus engaged will find its full resources barely adequate to the task in hand, and it will not be tempted to give up its conceptual powers because Laforgue walked some steps without their aid; nor will it be greatly intrigued by the possibility of eliminating transitive verbs without falling into lunacy. The irony of sophisticated juxtaposition is sometimes necessary, but it forms an inadequate 'way of life': it tends to be self-righteous, arrogant, Olympian. Commitment is often silly, but irony is often repulsive.

We should push the question a little further. When a writer undermines plot or subverts the prosaic piety of the copula he is really revolting against Time, refusing to accept the limitation of successiveness, that one event in some sense happens after another. For him, as for Shakespeare's Ulysses, Time is the great calumniator, the monster of ingratitudes. Ulysses had his own suggestion for evading the monster, and the 'angelic' writer who

[1] Hugh Kenner, *Gnomon* (New York. McDowell, Obolensky, 1958), pp. 187–8.

fights this battle devises several stratagems. He blurs 'before' and 'after' by setting up spatial rather than temporal analogues, offering in support a devious interpretation of 'organic form'. He cultivates all possible impressions of simultaneity, in an effort to make his poem appear simultaneously 'there', not a discourse in which words are spoken in a certain order of time, but a field upon which suggestive 'things' are so placed that they are all simultaneously apprehensible. Driven into a corner he often insinuates the grace of cyclicism, the myth of the Eternal Return, as a refuge from time and history. To avoid committing himself to the metalled ways of time he sets up spatial relationships in which the resultant meanings are indefinite, multiple, and portentous: much of the poem's business is found to be subterranean, far below the journeyman commitments of intention and verification. And yet, I should argue, the poet does well to assent to Time as one of the incorrigible but valuable conditions of his art. If his assent is full and simple, all the better; in a novel, as Forster remarked, there is always a clock.[1]

It seems clear that the rejection of plot and the revolt against Time are deeply involved in philosophical Idealism as well as Symbolism; the connexion between these procedures is close. The theory of Symbolism implies that a man makes his own reality, that reality is not there to be discovered and disclosed, that the grammatical relation of subject, verb, and object has nothing to do with the mind's way of knowing and is therefore an arbitrary imposition. These are also the assumption of Idealism, which undermines the validity of a subject-object relation by transferring the 'object' to the dissolving attentions of the 'subject'.

On the other hand, the writer who commits himself to plot and time assumes that the real is to be disclosed rather than invented, that man is not God, that the human mind devising concepts is fallible but not feeble. The corresponding epistemology holds that the real exists 'independent of how we think it',[2] that 'empirical reality does not need to be assumed nor to be proved, but only to be acknowledged'.[3] With these commitments a

[1] E. M. Forster, *Aspects of the Novel* (London. Edward Arnold, 1947), p. 46.
[2] Philip P. Wiener (editor), *Values in a Universe of Chance: Selected Writings of C. S. Pierce* (Stanford. Stanford University Press, 1958), p. 80.
[3] Lewis, *supra*, p. 361.

genial relation between Fact and Value becomes feasible without the insinuation of a predatory Self.

I. A. Richards has described the question of Fact and Value as 'this truly central problem of all philosophy'.[1] When Troilus asks, 'What is aught but as 'tis valued?' he summarizes a problem which is still a vexation to philosophers and critics. Indeed, it is not surprising that we hear a great deal, these days, of giving up the problem altogether and treating criticism as a 'purely' descriptive act. I would argue that existence, being, and fact are valuable because they are sponsored by something properly if loosely called an intention, and by an intention properly if loosely called divine; what Buber calls 'the speech of God articulated in things and events'. In this sense fact is the locus of value, for without fact value cannot reside in the human condition at all. The human mind, man in society, the given world, the little limited life of the fable; these are, it seems to me, feasible terms, if we are to live and if our living is to be serious. Pater acknowledged that a writer must have a 'sense of fact'. Pater would emphasize the sense, the naturalists would point up the fact. We need the tension of the two, a sense of fact.

IV

There is an essay in *Beyond Culture* which bears upon these questions. Mr. Trilling's official text is Hawthorne, but he surrounds that text with two more, James and Kafka. James is the name he gives to a writer who works on the understanding that 'the world is *there*: the unquestionable, inescapable world; the world so beautifully and so disastrously solid, physical, material, "natural"'. Such a writer relishes the density of the world, the pleasure of life, Paris, women, the vivid things. To Hawthorne, the world is there, 'in a very stubborn and uncompromising way', but he makes it his business to show the moral life 'as a mystery, as being hidden, dark, and dangerous, and as having some part of its existence in a world which is not that of our ordinary knowledge'. Hawthorne's theme is 'the interpenetration of the two worlds'; in his last years, when he lost all belief in the second world, the world of mystery and spirit, he lost his

[1] I. A. Richards, *Speculative Instruments* (London. Routledge and Kegan Paul, 1955), p. 202.

governing theme, and found no other. Those readers who are 'of the modern dispensation' find Hawthorne unsatisfactory, largely, Trilling suggests, because his imagination was not sufficiently intransigent: 'he always consented to the power of his imagination being controlled by the power of the world'. The name given to the intransigent imagination is Kafka; who 'gives very little recognition, if any at all, to the world in its ordinary actuality'. Kafka's imagination is autonomous: to read him is to have ourselves imposed upon; and for this, apparently, Kafka is our hero. He gives us authority to think our own spirit autonomous, and this is our deepest desire: for this we are ready to regard 'the actual' as 'the creation of some inferior imagination'.[1]

Trilling's co-ordinates have been examined with some severity in England and America. It is unnecessary to prolong the dispute; as, for instance, by questioning the names given to his three writers. The motives ascribed to Kafka seem to me accurately described; but Tolstoy would be a better name than James for the sense of life described under that rubric; and the second position should perhaps be filled by Dostoevsky than by Hawthorne. But the names matter little. What is more disturbing is that 'we' are identified with 'the modern dispensation' and thereafter with a sense of life which seems to me arrogant and sentimental. There are many readers who are not intimidated by the autonomous imagination; who are not exhilarated by the rift between matter and spirit; who ask of literature that it shall help them, in its own ways, to live their lives in the given historical world. I do not understand the 'modern dispensation' which excludes them, or the critical intelligence that does not heed them.

But this is quarrelsome. Indeed, Trilling's descriptions are so perceptive that I wish he would extend them far enough to say that often in modern literature one can see the three 'positions' in a single writer. It is a common pattern; a 'James' phase, then a 'Hawthorne' phase, and finally a 'Kafka' phase. It may be useful to look at Joyce in this connexion.

Dubliners is Jamesian in Trilling's sense, if in no other. The world is there, vivid in its penury, beyond doubt: Joyce commits himself to its actuality, the sounds and shapes and colours of its life. In 'Clay', for instance, the story is given as Maria's wandering apprehensions: these are defined by the warm, damp

[1] Lionel Trilling, *Beyond Culture* (London. Secker and Warburg, 1966), p. 205.

clichés of lower-middle-class respectability. Jobs are *positions*, kitchens are *spick and span*. Reality to Maria is a trail of modest hopes, some of them genially fulfilled. There are disappointments: Protestants in Dublin adorn their walls with tracts; Joe and Alphy are cross. But there is Hallow E'en and there is plumcake and most people, like Ginger Moore, mean well. Maria is a vulnerable character. But Joyce is content that she should inhabit the earth. He does not feel required to protect her as he protects Stephen in the *Portrait*; self-preservation is not involved. He is utterly willing that she should 'be', and her being does not require the demolition of others. He does not formulate her on a pin, like the lady in Eliot's cruel *Portrait*. At the party he gives her the Prayer Book rather than the ring, and she forgets the stanzas of 'I Dreamt I Dwelt' which tell of love and marriage: the irony is clear, but it is gentle, and the faded song gives Maria the modest enchantment of accomplishments and dreams. We are not invited to sneer. Nor is there any suggestion that these facts are cut adrift from value. They are not bogus; not chimerical.

Ulysses is a 'Hawthorne' book, in Trilling's sense, however peculiar the description sounds. On the face of it, it seems rich, dense, earthy, a Dublin book; memorable scenes, places, characters. But its irony is problematic, none the less. Joyce has begun to ask, as he did not ask in *Dubliners*, where is reality, what constitutes the real? Increasingly, as the book proceeds, the answer has more to do with the autonomous imagination and less with the density of the world. In this it differs, of course, from Hawthorne's bias. Hawthorne leans, when he has to lean, the other way. But we can see in the Holles Street chapter and again in the interrogations of Bloom and Stephen in Eccles Street that Joyce's interests are not primarily represented by such words as character, life, relation, and so forth. It may be said that the last chapter contradicts this; it does not. That chapter is a *tour de force*, and some of its paragraphs are splendid in the old rich way; but it is like a rhyming couplet at the end of a sonnet, masterfully added to a book that had already ended in 7 Eccles Street with 'the cold of interstellar space'. Writing the book, Joyce discovered something much more exciting than characters and relationships; he saw that language has resources far beyond the call of duty; 'purely linguistic' resources that have only as much to do with character and action as they are prepared to allow. Joyce tended to finish off his later books with a 'human' passage, often beautiful like the great curve of Anna's feeling in the last pages of *Finnegans Wake*, but for hundreds of pages before the end he gave himself up to his own demands, and these are linguistic. Wittgenstein said that to imagine a language means to imagine a form of life. The form of life to which the Holles Street chapter corresponds is solitaire; not in the sense that the writing is hard to penetrate. Some of it is hard, some not. This is not a quarrel about communication. I am arguing that some of the possibilities which Joyce discovered while writing *Ulysses* were linguistic, 'internal' possibilities; as a rhyme is an internal possibility which, often, has nothing to do with the communicative or expressive aim. I am also arguing that Joyce became more and more interested in these possibilities, less and less in the human reference. *Finnegans Wake* is the most exciting anthology ever compiled, but it is organized on the principle that the only reality is the imagination, that the imagination when it knows itself is autonomous. In that sense it is a 'Kafka' book, however different its tone. Hannah Arendt says in *The Human Condition*: 'One of the most persistent trends in modern philosophy since Descartes and perhaps its most original contribution to philosophy has been an exclusive concern with the self, as distinguished from the soul or person or man in general, an attempt to reduce all experiences, with the world as well as with other human beings, to experiences between man and himself.'[1] In *Finnegans Wake*, as Hugh Kenner has remarked, the mind is detached from its responsibility to things. This is the purpose of its dream-structure, to reduce all experiences to experiences between one man and himself. This is what we mean when, thinking of Joyce's last years, we mark the loneliness, the pain, the blindness. In the dream he is free; and there is always the new, golden toy, the wonderfully self-delighting words, the sweet language, detached now from all the old, killing tasks. This is where Joyce, like Kafka, becomes a modern here: turning away in distaste now from the phenomenal world, they represent the Nietzschean imagination, virtually identified with the will. No one would deny to Joyce the consolation of sweet sounds and dreams; but this is not to say that his strategy is

[1] Hannah Arendt, *The Human Condition* (New York. Doubleday, 1959), p. 230.

'available' to us, or that we would be the wiser for sharing it. Iris Murdoch remarked some time ago that Kant 'was especially impressed by the dangers of blind obedience to a person or an institution'. But, she continues, 'there are (as the history of existentialism shows) just as many dangers attaching to the ambiguous idea of finding the ideal in one's own bosom. The argument for looking outward at Christ and not inward at Reason is that self is such a dazzling object that if one looks *there* one may see nothing else'.[1]

V

There is a famous scene in Joyce's *Portrait* in which Stephen converses with the Dean of Studies in the Physics Theatre of the University. Walking towards the Theatre, Stephen has felt the corridor alien and watchful, 'as if the Ireland of Tone and of Parnell had receded in space'. In the chilly grey light he sees the Dean lighting the fire; after a brief exchange he takes revenge in a skirmish about Aquinas and Beauty. When he wins, his prize is a vision of 'the silent soul of a jesuit' looking out at him 'from the pale loveless eyes'. The Dean returns to the aesthetic question with some goodwill, Stephen with a show of patience: then the Dean tries a little parable in the light of Epictetus's lamp:

' "To return to the lamp," he said, "the feeding of it is also a nice problem. You must choose the pure oil and you must be careful when you pour it in not to overflow it, not to pour in more than the funnel can hold."

' "What funnel?" asked Stephen.

' "The funnel through which you pour the oil into your lamp."

' "That?" said Stephen. "Is that called a funnel? Is it not a tundish?"

' "What is a tundish?"

' "That. The . . . the funnel."

' "Is that called a tundish in Ireland?" asked the Dean. "I never heard the word in my life."

' "It is called a tundish in Lower Drumcondra," said Stephen, laughing, "where they speak the best English." '[2]

[1] Iris Murdoch, 'The Idea of Perfection': *Yale Review*, Spring, 1964, p. 368.

[2] James Joyce, *A Portrait of the Artist as a Young Man* (London. Cape, 1954 reprint), pp. 210 f.

This scene brings together many of the factors that conspire to defeat communication. The Jesuit's world is alien to Stephen; alien also the priest's language, his bourgeois prudence, his 'excelsior' clichés, his dry concessions. Stephen, connoisseur of epiphanies, sees in the Dean only a faded soutane, an old body without beauty, a limp, and pale loveless eyes: he does not see an individual soul, only the soul of a Jesuit; he does not see a person. One does not need to be Martin Buber to recognize that Stephen's denial of the person makes communication impossible: his denial culminates in the malice with which he wields the tundish. This incident is the formula of communication, but not the form; words, words, words. The priest teaches, but does not delight or persuade; a grim pedagogy is the best he can disclose from his resources of vocation and personality. Stephen, obsessed with the hazards of an engrossing self, can encounter others only in a spirit of corrosion and aggression. He is Amateur Shadow-Boxing Champion of the Western World. His gestures are not the free play of the intelligence; his favourite game is cat-and-mouse. His attitudes are those of the technologist, the bureaucrat, not the artist. Philip Wheelwright has noted that the great evil encouraged by a technological and bureaucratic way of life is 'to forget that the individual exists and to treat him as a mere instance of a generality'.[1] Precisely: to Stephen the Dean of Studies is not a person but the Order of Jesus for which he supplies a gothic scenario. The haze with which Stephen surrounds this man is the smoke of a dialectically induced battle between Stephen and 'Authority'; it is not Stephen's acknowledgement of the privacy, the mystery, of the self, the uniqueness of the person. Stephen the artist has the mind of a statistician: he lives only for himself: he loves only himself. Joyce connived with Stephen by protecting him with a circle of inflamed prose. He failed to 'detect' him. I take this word from one of T. S. Eliot's observations on Henry James, and the particular passage is relevant. Eliot has been discriminating between the James of *Roderick Hudson* and of *Daisy Miller*, *The European*, and *The American*. He remarks that in the later edition James toned down the absurdities of Roderick's sculpture a little, 'the pathetic thirst and the gigantic Adam', but he 'too much identifies himself with Row-

---

[1] Philip Wheelwright, *The Burning Fountain* (Bloomington. Indiana University Press, 1954), p. 78.

land, does not see through the solemnity he has created in that character, and commits the cardinal sin of failing to "detect" one of his own characters'.[1] For similar reasons, perhaps, Joyce failed to detect Stephen—at least until *Ulysses*, where his main interests moved toward Leopold Bloom and Stephen's concerns were no longer formidable.

There is an equally famous moment in *The Great Gatsby*, when Gatsby's party for Daisy has lurched to a fatigued conclusion:

' "I wouldn't ask too much of her," I ventured.

' "You can't repeat the past."

' "Can't repeat the past?" he cried incredulously. "Why of course you can!"

'He looked around him wildly, as if the past were lurking here in the shadow of his house, just out of reach of his hand.

' "I'm going to fix everything just the way it was before," he said, nodding determinedly. "She'll see." He talked a lot about the past, and I gathered that he wanted to recover something, some idea of himself perhaps, that had gone into loving Daisy. His life had been confused and disordered since then, but if he could once return to a certain starting place and go over it all slowly, he could find out what that thing was.'[2]

Why does Gatsby exist, here and throughout the book, to a far greater degree than Joyce's Stephen? We know from *Tender is the Night* and 'The Diamond as Big as the Ritz' that Fitzgerald entertained his fantasies to a degree dangerous in anyone and peculiarly so in a writer; his daydreams of the beauty and style of wealth are not unlike Stephen's proud exertions. But in *Gatsby* and again in *The Last Tycoon* the dream is rendered in all its beauty and 'placed'—not discarded. A distinguished intelligence that yielded to the dream in *Tender is the Night* now insisted upon its rights. But the real explanation is that for Fitzgerald the person existed; *The Last Tycoon* is all person. The person was not a bank balance, or a Packard, or the Order of Jesus, or a box of beautiful shirts. The person was unique, mysterious; if you assigned him a place on a map, it could only be the point toward which your feelings conspired—your feelings of reverence and piety—on the crucial occasion; and you did not aspire

[1] Reprinted in Edmund Wilson (editor), *The Shock of Recognition* (New York. Doubleday, 1943).

[2] *The Bodley Head Scott Fitzgerald* (London, Bodley Head, 1958), I, 211.

to make him a mere function of yourself or to tear away his strict privacy. Each of the characters in *The Great Gatsby* has a *being* far in excess of the qualities and apprehensions specifically ascribed to him, a bright halo of ambiguity not to be confused with vagueness in transcription. The halo indicates Fitzgerald's assent to their being, without claiming to touch it, measure it, or take its pulse. By strange contrast, most of the characters in *Stephen Hero* and the *Portrait* seem less than the sum of qualities specifically ascribed to them; even Simon Dedalus remains cutely 'picturesque', like the citizens in the fiction of Somerville and Ross. Fitzgerald's narrator, Nick, takes the poetic attitude to Gatsby: he says 'yes' to him, acknowledges his being, his individuality, his strangeness, his otherness; he allows for the sad-and-yet-saving gaps between moments of direct communication; he doesn't try to deprive Gatsby of his silence or his bewilderment.

I have described Nick's attitude as poetic, not only because it rejects the statistical simplifications of experience, but because it assents to the moral complexity of persons, the vibrant silences, the unpredictable notations, the leaps of apprehension; like the moment in which Gatsby remarks of Daisy's love for Tom, 'In any case it was just personal.' Nick knows that Gatsby's dream is part of his 'heightened sensitivity to the promises of life', but he also apprehends the 'foul dust' that floats in the wake of the dream: the poetic attitude allows for this. It also makes possible the remarkable poise that Nick exhibits: 'The truth was that Jay Gatsby of West Egg, Long Island, sprang from his Platonic conception of himself. He was a son of God—a phrase which, if it means anything, means just that—and he must be about his Father's business, the service of a vast, vulgar, and meretricious beauty.' The inclusive and generous critique; the transcription of feeling, with nothing lost and everything gained in the transcription; the genial irony which offers saving impurities to the otherwise pure poetry of Gatsby's dream: these depend upon the poetic attitude, upon assent and piety, upon dialogue.

We are again discussing two attitudes, two ways of confronting experience. One is full of power, but a little rude, a little short of wisdom, formidably efficient in its limited purposes, rarely in error and never in despair. The other is more vulnerable, its truth is always in a future that can never be called as a supporting witness; it seeks genial, humane, wise notations at the risk of being fatally inconclusive. We think of James's Nick Dormer as an 'answer' to Stephen Dedalus.

Indeed, *The Tragic Muse* is less a novel about the artistic life than about these two attitudes in their bearing upon human relationships. Peter Sherringham wants to take possession of Miriam Rooth; Nick Dormer, in the mildness of his strength, celebrates her. Nick is the only real artist, real poet, in the world of this novel. James gives us a motto for these considerations in the passage in which he describes the 'quality' of Julia Dallow's love for Nick: 'If the affection that isolates and simplifies its object may be distinguished from the affection that seeks communications and contacts for it, Julia Dallow's belonged wholly to the former.'[1] Julia, as much as Peter, wants possession: at this stage Nick is a desired object to be manipulated; 'and, indeed, the cause of her interest in him was partly the vision of his helping her to the particular emotion that she did desire—the emotion of great affairs and of public action'. The dramatic action of the novel is the movement of feeling by which Julia gives up the 'simplifying' kind of affection for Nick and assents to the other kind; her assent is given in the request to have Nick do her portrait. At that moment the sight of Gabriel Nash's portrait fills Nick with 'an unreasoning resentment': we can guess that Nash's arrogant claim to *being* as a condition far superior to the mere *action* of others is now revealed as chic but faintly absurd.

VI

A writer who assents to the Person does so not as a casual acknowledgement but as part of that larger, more inclusive assent which is a reverence for life. It is usual to give ourselves the protection of inverted commas when we use such terms, but this is an impertinence. Reverence for life involves saying 'yes' to the human situation, limited and finite as it is; it disposes us to respect persons, to value them, to find the human predicament full of hazard and therefore full of significance; to find that moral choice is important and that life is possibility if not promise. (This is not a case in which we shout 'Lawrence' when someone else says 'Eliot'.) As Buber has argued, the Person must

[1] Henry James, *The Tragic Muse* (London. Rupert Hart-Davis, 1948 reprint of the 1890 edition), p. 119.

be acknowledged as 'the ground which cannot be relinquished, from which alone the entry of the finite into conversation with the infinite became possible and is possible'.[1]

The Portrait of a Lady—to return to it at last—is clearly a great novel, and clearly the product of a certain view of life. These facts are closely related; the quality of the book depends upon the magnanimity of the view of life that informs it.

The idea of the novel, as James gives it in his *Notebooks*, is 'that the poor girl, who has dreamed of freedom and nobleness, who has done, as she believes, a generous, natural, clear-sighted thing, finds herself in reality ground in the very mill of the conventional'.[2] Isabel Archer, we are told in Chapter IV, 'carried within herself a great fund of life, and her deepest enjoyment was to feel the continuity between the movement of her own soul and the agitations of the world'. Her affections, then, are not of the 'simplifying' kind. And in Chapter VI: 'It had been her fortune to possess a finer mind than most of the persons among whom her lot was cast; to have a larger perception of surrounding facts and to care for knowledge that was tinged with the unfamiliar.' For James, as for Isabel Archer, 'Life' is a matter of consciousness and vibration, but these move in time and place, prompted by people, by facts, by a sense of human continuity. Not 'mere' consciousness. As he said in the Preface to *Roderick Hudson*, 'the continuity of things' is 'the whole matter of tragedy and comedy'. Isabel's consciousness is not deployed upon argument or the shrill clash of ideas—she is almost Yeatsian in her sensibility; she does not discuss Lord Warburton's 'advanced' views, nor is she perturbed by them, since they are evidently and engagingly summarized in that gentleman's 'excellent manner with women'. Liking Gilbert Osmond's company, she 'had what always gave her a very private thrill, the consciousness of a new relation'. This is her 'yes' to life, and clearly it is James's, too. It is defined again in her relation to Caspar Goodwood, 'a straight young man from Boston'. There are many attractive features in this man, but he will not 'answer'. 'His jaw was too square and set and his figure too straight and stiff; these things suggested a want of easy consonance with the

---

[1] Martin Buber, *Between Man and Man* (London. Collins, 1961), p. 108.
[2] F. O. Matthiessen and Kenneth B. Murdock (editors), *The Notebooks of Henry James* (New York. Oxford University Press, 1947), p. 15.

deeper rhythms of life.' They also suggested 'that he was naturally plated and steeled, armed essentially for aggression'. He is unfit for the dialogue that constitutes a fine marriage.

Isabel's error—to describe it mildly—is that she does not perceive in Gilbert Osmond a sinister version of Caspar Goodwood's aggressiveness. She recognizes aggression only when it is visibly armed. In Chapter XXVIII we are reminded that Gilbert 'was fond of originals, of rarities, of the superior and the exquisite' and, now that Isabel has rejected Lord Warburton, Gilbert 'perceived a new attraction in the idea of taking to himself a young lady who had qualified herself to figure in his collection of choice objects by declining so noble a hand'. The hint is clear enough. This has nothing to do with relation or mutuality. The gentle Ralph sees that Gilbert's collection is a 'cage' in which poor Isabel has now been 'caught': 'one ought to feel one's relation to things—to others. I don't think Mr. Osmond does that.' Gilbert's egotism, which 'lay hidden like a serpent in a bank of flowers', expresses itself in 'a sovereign contempt for every one but some three or four very exalted people whom he envied'. Isabel's real offence in this emotional police-state is 'her having a mind of her own'. Eventually and too late she recognizes 'the staring fact that she had been an applied handled hung-up tool, as senseless and convenient as mere shaped wood and iron'. Her vision of a 'multiplied life' reveals itself now as that of 'a dark, narrow alley with a dead wall at the end'. But she must bear some of the blame. She connived a little with Gilbert, speaking his language. She did not know enough: she was immersed in exquisite appearances; her aesthetic—itself a little thin —served as ethic most of the way and persuaded her to think that it was enough. She was somewhat tainted with the exquisite, and abstract, and she enforced her human rejections a little righteously. Furthermore, she had tried to diminish herself for Osmond's pleasure, tried to deny her own truth: 'she had made herself small, pretending there was less of her than there really was'. She yielded too much, and at the wrong time, and she should not have yielded at all. 'But she was, after all, herself— she couldn't help that': this, in Chapter XLII, Isabel's silent refusal to deny herself any longer, is the core of the fiction. Ralph made Isabel rich so that she could meet the requirements of her large imagination; the highest requirement would be to *live*, to choose, to 'go before the breeze', to enter into the richest dialogue with persons, with things, with places, to be beautifully herself—which meant being graciously in relation to herself and to other existents. But she tried to enter into a dialogue with Gilbert Osmond, and though the attempt was natural and proper it was doomed because Gilbert, as we have seen, lived only in a world of possessed objects, objects possessed not for their own value but for his power. The only genuine dialogue in Isabel's entire history, too late, is the great relation to the dying Ralph.

James's sense of the person is the animating value of his fiction: it accounts for the scope, the radiance of *The Portrait of a Lady*. The sense of identity, the relation of fact and value, the risk of moral freedom, Isabel's 'haunting sense of the continuity of the human lot', the will to live with freedom and space, the clash of choice and chance, Ralph's 'Dear Isabel, life is better; for in life there's love. Death is good—but there's no love': these are the apprehensions that give the novel its depth and reverberation. It could not 'sound' without them.

It comes back to the embodied relation between imagination and reality. Reality is the certifying pressure of things, their weight and density; if it is 'the whole envelope of circumstances', it is also Rome, London, Gardencourt, Florence, the people who live and suffer. The novel begins in Gardencourt, and the place, the house, is a measure of the disclosed feeling in the sense that the feeling has to live up to the record of the house, its history and fortune. 'I like places in which things have happened,' Isabel says; and later she hands over her sorrow to the more capacious sorrow of Rome, 'the large Roman record'. Imagination is Ralph's 'boundless liberty of appreciation'; it is Isabel's love of knowledge, her 'immense curiosity about life'; it is visible in Isabel's eyes, which have 'an enchanting range of concession'. Above all, it discloses itself in the relation of a person to the multiplicity of his experience, 'the accretions of human contact'. It is, to be brief, a mode of appreciation. The engagement of reality and imagination is the energy of the novel; a dynamic balance nowhere more beautifully achieved than at the end of the book, when Isabel, sure now, turns back to her fate. This is an act of imagination; as in *The Ambassadors* Lambert Strether sets aside the gift of Maria Gostrey lest he should gain anything for himself from the general wreck, so Isabel turns back to Osmond. Imagination is her sense of moral propriety; duty ('One must accept one's deeds'), her promise to Pansy, 'the sense that life would be her business for a long time to come'. This is a new kind of renunciation. To Osmond, renunciation was a mode of aggression: he has always been like his house in Florence, where the windows 'seemed less to offer communication with the world than to defy the world to look in'. The windows are Osmond's eyes. Isabel's renunciation is her vision of responsibility, to herself and to others.

Much earlier, in Chapter XXIV, when Gilbert charms Isabel with a dry recital of his life, Isabel does not believe him, the record is too small to be believed; so she fills it out on his behalf. 'Her imagination supplied the human element which she was sure had not been wanting.' It had, of course, been wanting, but she was not to know this or to feel it. This is how imagination lives, by adding to the given record 'the human element', if that is what the record wants. It is not the mark of her imagination to yearn beyond the world. The world is enough, if only the human element is enough. This is what her appreciation comes to. When Ralph dies and poor Mrs. Touchett is left with nothing but her limitations, Isabel's 'old pity' comes back to her, 'for the poor woman's inexpressiveness, her want of regret, of disappointment':

'Unmistakeably she would have found it a blessing today to be able to feel a defeat, a mistake, even a shame or two. She wondered if she were not even missing those enrichments of consciousness and privately trying—reaching out for some aftertaste of life, dregs of the banquet; the testimony of pain or the cold recreation of remorse. On the other hand perhaps she was afraid; if she should begin to know remorse at all it might take her too far. Isabel could perceive, however, how it had come over her dimly that she had failed of something, that she saw herself in the future as an old woman without memories.'

This is to add to Mrs. Touchett a measure of the human element which she has done little to deserve. But Isabel's imagination is lavish in such additions. *Etiam peccata*; *etiam* sorrow, defeat, shame, anything, so long as it is 'life'. To Isabel life is a matter of feeling, being able to feel; she is not rigorous in measurement. Her imagination often leads her astray because it leads her too far; she is never fanciful, but her estimates are too generous. Her imagination is like the light which falls on the pictures in Gardencourt; in Chapter V, when Ralph is showing Isabel the pictures in the gallery. 'The lamps were on brackets', we are told, 'at intervals, and if the light was imperfect it was genial.' It is a Coleridgean word, meaning responsive, open, exposed, willing to go too far rather than to fail, not going far enough. These are the intimations of the word in this scene and elsewhere in the novel. Isabel 'goes too far'; Mrs. Touchett cannot move at all: Osmond calculates to a nicety how far he should appear to go.

At the end, Isabel feels again, talking to Ralph, 'the good of the world'. To reconcile the demands of the imagination with the impositions of the world is a delicate exercise; especially if the natural idiom of the imagination is a language of freedom, mobility, and range, and the idiom of the world is, for the most part, deception and abuse. In the great conversation with Madame Merle, early in the book, Isabel said that she could not consider herself expressed by anything. 'Nothing that belongs to me is any measure of me; everything's on the contrary a limit, a barrier, and a perfectly arbitrary one.' But she does not insist upon a Platonic poetry. Indeed, the momentum of James's fiction works against that recourse. To be an old woman without memories is dreadful, but the worst escape is in transcendence, where the good of the world, such as it is, cannot be felt. James was sure of little, but he was sure of this. It is the informing principle of his fiction.

I would recommend this view with a certain emphasis because it has recently been impugned, notably by Richard Poirier in an exceptionally vivid book, *A World Elsewhere*.[1] Mr. Poirier is to show that the American tradition in literature is characterized by resistance, within its pages, to the forces of environment that otherwise dominate the world. American writers, he argues, tend to substitute themselves and their imaginations for the world and its thrones and powers, so that their books become rival worlds in which their characters can live. Language provides the conditions denied in time and place. Style is therefore a mode of freedom, achieved in American literature under in-

[1] Richard Poirier, *A World Elsewhere* (New York. Oxford University Press, 1966).

ordinate pressure of need. It is the writer's way of changing the
rules so that he and his characters can breathe. The function of
the Book (as in Mallarmé: 'L'Oeuvre, le Grand Oeuvre, comme
disaient les alchimistes, nos ancêtres') is to offer the beleaguered
consciousness a home fit to live in, a new 'environment of
nakedness' to replace a deadly 'environment of costume'. Costume is Society, institutions, manhood, Emerson's 'buzz and
din'. Nakedness is Nature, childhood, wilderness, Emerson's
'dream of the self'. Call nakedness, for the pun, a tropical freedom. Mr. Poirier knows that this freedom is necessarily limited;
as Valéry knew that the words of a poem cannot, alas, be
separated from their daily habits; as James knew and said in his
study of Hawthorne that 'it takes a great deal of history to produce a little literature'. Indeed, Mr. Poirier concedes that James,
Thoreau, and Faulkner 'honor something outside of style'. He
does not push his thesis, even if he shows its unmistakable bearing on such writers as Cooper, Emerson, Hawthorne, Mark
Twain, James, Dreiser, Edith Wharton, and Scott Fitzgerald. In
a rough paraphrase Mr. Poirier's argument sounds like the
standard account which says that for various social reasons
English fiction is the novel and American fiction is the romance.
True, he endorses this in some respects while disavowing it as a
standard thesis. He allows that George Eliot could rely upon a
society in which 'grave and endearing traditions' were still
operative; while Edith Wharton could only improvise, extem-
porize, lacking public forms of the feelings engaged. But Mr.
Poirier goes far beyond the standard account in describing the
'world elsewhere'. In some parts of the book I feel that his ideas
are engaging in such vigorous alliance that they threaten to put
the literature itself under constraint. I cannot share his impression, for instance, that in James the 'world elsewhere' has quite
the exorbitant status the critic gives it. The Ambassadors, he says,
'offers remarkably beautiful instances of the hero's effort to
transform the things he sees into visions, to detach them from
time and from the demands of nature, and to give them the
composition of objets d'art'. There is a sense in which this is true.
James does not commit himself, as Whitman does, to the idiom
of Contact. There is always a distance. James knew this, and
ponders it in his Autobiography. The distance is the price his
temper pays for the privileges of vision and consciousness, since

these require a gap between the perceiver and the thing perceived. The gap is not, however, a guarantee of protection, because in James vision and consciousness are moral risks. This is where James's position differs from, say, Robbe-Grillet's. In his essay on Tragedy Robbe-Grillet provides a scenario for man's relation to the world:

'The time comes when this man's eye falls on certain things, positively and emphatically. He sees them, but he refuses to take possession of them, he refuses to entertain any questionable understanding or complicity with them. He asks nothing of them, he feels neither in harmony nor in disagreement with them. He may perhaps use them to reinforce his emotions, or as something to focus his eyes on. But his eyes are content just to measure them, and his emotion, too, alights on their surface, with no wish to penetrate them, since there is nothing inside them. It makes no pretence of appealing to them, for there would be no answer.'[1]

That this is a possible way of living in the world, one does not dispute. But it is not James's way. It is not the way of his heroines. These characters are always entering into complicity with things; even though entry is effected by the eye rather than the hand. To be in harmony with the natural appearance is to James's characters a profoundly important experience. To have their feelings tested by the quality of the natural appearance is an experience of equal moment. It is not self-indulgence which brings Isabel Archer to visit again the Roman ruins:

'She had long before this taken old Rome into her confidence, for in a world of ruins the ruin of her happiness seemed a less unnatural catastrophe. She rested her weariness upon things that had crumbled for centuries and yet still were upright; she dropped her secret sadness into the silence of lonely places, where its very modern quality detached itself and grew objective, so that as she sat in a sun-warmed angle on a winter's day, or stood in a mouldy church to which no one came, she could almost smile at it and think of its smallness.'

Here an imputed relation between one sadness and another has the effect of imposing upon the personal feeling a testing perspective; as a human event is judged but not denied or obli-

[1] Alain Robbe-Grillet, *Snapshots and Towards a New Novel*. Translated by Barbara Wright (London. Calder and Boyars, 1965), pp. 77–8.

terated by the larger record of history. This is one test. Very
often James calls upon Art to supply the critical test of life. But
he is always concerned that the poor thing will pass the test. In
The Ambassadors, to return to Mr. Poirier's occasion, Lambert
Strether is not concerned to 'transform the things he sees into
visions': he is tested to acknowledge the spirit in the matter he
sees, to respond to it, to the people, the French landscape, the
scene, the composition. Art (the Lambinet landscape painting,
for instance) imposes the standard by which his life is to be
judged, but only because that standard is available and high. Indeed, I would argue that what distinguishes James's central fiction is a remarkably dynamic relation between the admitted
claims of the two worlds, this world and the world elsewhere; it
is 'the ache of the actual', as James called it, an ache of acknowledgement as well as an ache of dream.

3

Hopkins, 'The World's Body'

On 24th September 1870, Hopkins wrote in his Journal: 'First saw the Northern Lights. My eye was caught by beams of light and dark very like the crown of horny rays the sun makes behind a cloud. At first I thought of silvery cloud until I saw that these were more luminous and did not dim the clearness of the stars in the Bear. They rose slightly radiating thrown out from the earthline. Then I saw soft pulses of light one after another rise and pass upwards arched in shape but waveringly and with the arch broken. They seemed to float, not following the warp of the sphere as falling stars look to do but free though concentrical with it. This busy working of nature wholly independent of the earth and seeming to go on in a strain of time not reckoned by our reckoning of days and years but simpler and as if correcting the preoccupation of the world by being preoccupied with and appealing to and dated to the day of judgment was like a new witness to God and filled me with delightful fear.'[1]

It is an informal occasion. But the pressure applied to the event issues in a pattern of meditation which we find in most of Hopkins's poems. There is the event itself, all the better if it is fortuitous, freely given and received. Hopkins describes it, attending to the detail with such precision that we think of the spirit of the attention as scientific, until we reflect that it is, more deeply, poetic. He is trying to register the mysterious density of the event, so that he will be equal to it and his response will not shame the occasion. When he has done what he can in this way, he withdraws, and moralizes the event a little. The 'busy working of nature wholly independent of the earth' is a good omen:

[1] *Journals and Papers of Gerard Manley Hopkins*, edited by Humphry House and Graham Storey (London. Oxford University Press, 1959), p. 200.

it enforces upon us a touch of modesty, a sense of proportion. The pressure of meditation brings Hopkins in a long sentence from our days and years to the day of judgement, from us to God. At this point he is filled 'with delightful fear'. This phrase has a technical ring, we hear it a good deal in the history of literature; it refers to that category of high, intense experience which we call the Sublime. So Hopkins has brought himself a long way from the common event, the Northern Lights. But the common event is not forgotten or slighted. It would be wrong to imply that the common things were useful to Hopkins because they gave him something to transcend. One might say this of Emerson or of Leopardi with more justice, though the justice would be incomplete. The natural occasions were never mere grist to Hopkins's mill. Indeed, one of the most admirable things in him is the care he brought to those occasions; and he wanted to leave them as they were, finite and historical, and not to smear them with his own mystery. The Northern Lights are not dimmed by the meditations they inspire. A poet's piety is the quality of his attention to what he has received, and we think harshly of him if he does not respect its integrity or if he converts it too ruthlessly to his own purpose. We think him lacking in tact. There are many ways of knowing the world, and each has professional defenders. But it is possible to have a knowledge of the world which is too imperious, too much a function of its own demanding insight. The cost of its success is that we are often ashamed of the amateur ways of knowing the world, we think them provincial. The poet is an amateur. He has one skill, the use of language, but this does not give him a special insight or a technical qualification. Besides, the range and depth of the language warn the poet that he must not be content with a technical knowledge of the world. He must remain an amateur. He must not use violence in taking from the world what he thinks he needs. All the better for his poems if he leaves the world as he finds it, merely adding his own appropriate feeling. John Crowe Ransom, rehearsing this theme some years ago, asked: 'Where is the body and solid substance of the world?' And he answered: 'It seems to have retired into the fulness of memory, but out of this we construct the fulness of poetry, which is counterpart to the world's fulness.'[1] So we add that the poet seems to have a

[1] John Crowe Ransom, *The World's Body* (New York. Scribner, 1938), p. x.

special disposition to respect the world's body, to leave it as he finds it, a world of 'whole and indefeasible objects', each one itself. Or if he lacks this disposition we think him barbarous and disabled.

It is appropriate that Hopkins gives us a motto for this disposition, because he was an amateur of great endowment. In one of his poems he asks, 'To what serves mortal beauty?' and immediately answers, 'See: it does this: keeps warm/Men's wits to the things that are.' It is a definitive statement of the function of poetry; but it would not do at all without that word 'warm', which makes the figure homely and tactful, an amateur figure. The poetic attitude to life is warm and attentive; it comes to know the objects of the world by acknowledging them in their fullness and integrity. If there is any danger of mutilation, it leaves off. 'Man's spirit will be flesh-bound when found at best,' Hopkins says, not because he has a theory to sponsor this unity, but because he has the poetic disposition.

We often say, in moments of simplicity, that poetry helps us to see the world. But there are poets for whom sight is not enough. We have been told, notably by Alain Robbe-Grillet, that the function of sight is to keep things at a safe distance, so that we will not be drawn into complicity with them. But there are poets who are willing to risk this complicity: they do not resent the intimacy of contact. They want to know the world's body by touching it. Hopkins is such a poet. So is Whitman. William Carlos Williams is a third. This accounts for the kinship between Hopkins and Whitman; between Whitman and Williams, in *Paterson*. When Hopkins wrote 'The Leaden Echo and the Golden Echo' Bridges suggested that he was imitating Whitman. At that time Hopkins had read only a few fragments of Whitman's poetry, culled mainly from Saintsbury's review in the *Academy*. But he remembered them, and would not refute Bridges's suggestion: 'But first I may as well say what I should not otherwise have said, that I always knew in my heart Walt Whitman's mind to be more like my own than any other man's living.' And he added: 'As he is a very great scoundrel this is not a pleasant confession.'[1] The kinship is easy to explain. Both Hopkins and Whitman sought a knowledge of the world by attend-

---

[1] *Letters of Gerard Manley Hopkins to Robert Bridges*, edited by C. C. Abbott (London. Oxford University Press, 1955), p. 155.

ing to it in its fullness and individuality. They were, in that special sense, naturalists; poets for the same reason that we think of botany as a poetic vocation. They do not want the safe distance of sight. We meet something of this feeling again when Thoreau attends to the natural forms and configurations, and the record of this attention is *Walden*, a botanic and poetic book. There are differences. Whitman's knowledge of the world's body is achieved by bringing thousands of its common forms into contact, into intimacy. In *Leaves of Grass* these forms are often strung out in long lines and we forget the care that holds them together. It is a poetic care, never aggressive. Thoreau and Hopkins have the same care, but it is lavished upon the particular case, the sample. They assume that by attending to one natural form they are attending to all, as a poem that invokes one bird invokes all birds. This is their way of accepting the ordinary human limitations of time and place; if the quality of their feeling is warm enough, one object will stand for everything. This is how Thoreau lived at Walden Pond. Robert Frost used to say that all a poet needs is samples; touching the hem of the garment. Most of Hopkins's poems begin with the particular occasion, a sample of the natural life, and the attention he gives to it is the measure of his assent. The poems show that he thought of this attention in dynamic terms, as if the experience had muscles and ligaments. His response to the world's body is itself bodily, animated by bodily metaphors and gestures. In a letter to Bridges he mentions 'The Leaden Echo'. The word 'Back', in the second line, he says, 'is not pretty, but it gives that feeling of physical constraint which I want'.[1] So, admiring Milton and Keats, he admired Dryden perhaps more than these. 'He is the most masculine of our poets,' he tells Bridges; 'his style and his rhythms lay the strongest stress of all our literature on the naked thew and sinew of the English language.' In Hopkins's own poems the idiom is a matter of thew and sinew. Even when the natural event is placid, Hopkins is so urgent in his attention that the event, when he has apprehended it, seems all storm and stress. We have to go to an early poem like 'Heaven-Haven' or an unfinished poem like 'Moonrise' or 'On a Piece of Music' to find one mode of calmness answered by another. Normally, Hopkins cannot believe in an experience unless it is guaranteed by

[1] ibid., p. 162.

bodily metaphors. The first lines of 'Spelt from Sibyl's Leaves' describe the passing of evening into night. We think of this as an occasion charming in its ease, an image of all those occasions on which the grace is natural and easy. But Hopkins thinks of it as a time of ethical strain; or he reads the parable in that sense. So, even in the description, the twilight is forced to share the ethical problem, to register the strain of distinguishing right from wrong:

> Earnest, earthless, equal, attuneable, vaulty, voluminous . . .
>   stupendous
> Evening strains to be time's vast, womb-of-all, home-of-all,
>   hearse-of-all night.

It is possible to say that this is a predatory description and to resent the denial of a calm evening. Hopkins seems to demand an exorbitant share in the proceeding. But I would not press the charge. Hopkins's involvement in the event is so much the measure of his care that it is easily entertained. He is always afraid that his response to the natural event will be unworthy of it, too weak in its feeling. We are always afraid that his attention, so forceful, will end by destroying the valued object. Hopkins's fear is like Coleridge's in the 'Dejection' Ode, that he is sullen in his reception of nature, and therefore unworthy. Both poets know that in these matters 'we receive but what we give'. Hopkins felt this with peculiar force because he committed himself so deeply to the single occasion. Sullen on Monday, he could never persuade himself that there would be another day.

There was another consideration. It was part of Hopkins's Christianity to believe that the world was 'charged with the grandeur of God'. This had nothing to do with Baudelaire's world as a forest of symbols. If you failed in care and attention to the world, you were sullen to God's creation and therefore churlish to God. It was an ethical matter and a matter of belief. This is the difference between Hopkins and Ruskin, both poets who were lavish in their attendance upon the natural forms. Ruskin cared for the detail of the world because it was natural for him to do so, but he did not bring God into the question. In *Praeterita* he makes the secular nature of his care quite specific. He has been describing his first sight of the Swiss Alps, and now he says:

'St. Bernard of La Fontaine, looking out to Mont Blanc with his child's eyes, sees above Mont Blanc the Madonna; St. Bernard of Talloires, not the Lake of Annecy, but the dead between Martigny and Aosta. But for me, the Alps and their people were alike beautiful in their snow, and their humanity; and I wanted, neither for them nor myself, sight of any thrones in heaven but the rocks, or of any spirits in heaven but the clouds.'[1]

Later, Ruskin speaks of 'the bond between the human mind and all visible things', but he offers no account of that bond, its source, the auspices under which it persists. He assumes a natural affinity between snow and humanity: that is enough. Hopkins was never content with this. When he thought of the world, he saw it as a flow of energy between three terms, God, Nature, and Man. Snow and man seemed to need a third term, the ground of their being and beseeching. This allowed him to think of the natural world as a great body mediating between himself and God. He would not try to address God directly, except in the privacy of prayer. Rather, he would devote himself to the natural forms in all their miraculous detail, on the conviction that they were 'signatures' of God.[2] There is an early reference in his Journal, 6th November 1865: 'On this day by God's grace I resolved to give up all beauty until I had His leave for it.' When this was written, his role as communicant and his role as poet seemed to fall apart; but with God's leave, as he calls it, the roles would merge into one. Attending to Nature, he devoted himself to God; poetry became prayer. In this spirit he wrote a poem comparing the Blessed Virgin to the air we breathe. In poems like 'Harry Ploughman' and 'Felix Randal' God remains as the apex of the triangle, the self remains as the communicant, and the third term is man himself, now linked with Christ in the imagery of Incarnation. The danger comes when Hopkins, in the descriptive poems, presses his analogies so hard that a relation is forced to become an identity; as in 'Hurrahing in Harvest' the hills are God's shoulder, because Hopkins insists. Sometimes his engagement with the natural forms is so intense that it comes close to breaking the barrier between subject and object. This matters little to Hopkins: he was pleased to find that in Par-

[1] *Praeterita* (London. Hart-Davis, 1949), p. 103.
[2] Kenneth Burke, *A Rhetoric of Motives* (New York. Braziller, 1955), p. 314.

menides 'the distinction between men or subjects and the things without them is unimportant'.

When everything was going well, then, there would be an endless flow of feeling between God, Nature, and Man. Hopkins could become what Yeats said Blake was, a 'literalist of the imagination', convinced that the forms of Nature were the 'letters' of God. This distinguishes Hopkins from such poets as Tennyson and Leopardi, to whom the given world, more often than not, was merely an obstacle or, at best, an instrument; from Leopardi especially, to whom the world was, in itself, unworthy of a sigh, even the sighs he gave it, 'nè di sospiri è degna/La terra'. Hopkins needed the world as his mediating term, and valued it for this among a hundred reasons, that it answered his need. He was terrified that the circuit of feeling might be broken; then he would be lost. The most reliable side of the triangle was the line between God and Nature: he seems never to lose faith in that. But the other lines depended upon the weather of his feeling. There are several poems in which the circuit is broken and we hear a cry of despair. In some of these the break comes between himself and Nature; as in the poem 'In the Valley of the Elwy' where the intimations of Nature are vivid but, as Hopkins says, 'Only the inmate does not correspond.' And when the line between himself and God is broken, we have the 'terrible sonnets' of his despair. In 'I Wake and Feel the Fell of Dark, not Day' the spirit turns back upon itself, 'My taste was me'; a desolate image, testifying to the failure of all the more congenial forms of sustenance. The image is developed in 'Selfyeast of spirit a dull dough sours', which points the absurdity of the self as its own declared source.

This is to speak of those moments in which Hopkins's world caves in. Normally, the structure was strong enough to hold his world together, his sense of the world's body was so vigorous. A. O. Lovejoy argued many years ago that what distinguishes the Romantic writer is a constantly renewed delight in the plenitude of the world. Variety, difference, and plenitude were the qualities in which the value of the world was most evident. A classic occasion is Blake's marginal commentary on Reynolds's *Discourses*. Reynolds thought that the Good was embodied in an objective standard, called Nature, to which the good man 'conformed': its mode was universal, categorical. Blake despised this view of things. To him the miracle of the world was its variety as the miracle of man was his imagination, his vision. To Blake, one man is distinguished from another in the degree of his imagination; the power released is energy, intensity. Among ten chestnut-trees Reynolds was concerned with the qualities common to all. Blake was concerned with the minute differences making each tree itself, distinct. So we call Blake's vision Romantic if we allow his devotion to 'minute particulars' rather than to general truths; his commitment to the imagination which permits us to see things in their intimate variety. To Blake, as to Berkeley, matter was an incitement to perception: granted the primacy of the imagination, the relation between imagination and matter could be vivid, intimate, nuptial. Like Yeats, Blake rejected any doctrine that 'drives mind into the quicksilver'; hence his scorn for Newton and Locke. The Romantic principle is given in *The Marriage of Heaven and Hell*: 'Exuberance is Beauty'.

There is no reason to bring Hopkins and Blake too violently together. The differences are great. But if we now emphasize Hopkins's continuity with the English Romantic tradition, after many years in which it was customary to think of him as an eccentric poet lost in his time, the reason is clear: the spirit of his poems, the energy and *brio* of the work, are best understood in Blake's terms. To read 'Glory be to God for dappled things' after reading the Pickering Manuscript of Blake is to feel, all the differences registered, a remarkable continuity of feeling. If Blake is prepared to see a world in a grain of sand and a heaven in a wild flower, Hopkins is quick to report that the changelessness of God is manifested in a world of dazzling change. What is common to the changing things is the unchanging spirit behind them. All things, to Hopkins, are 'counter, original, spare, strange'. This is in Blake's idiom. There is an entry in Hopkins's Journal: 'All the world is full of inscape, and chance left free to act falls into an order as well as purpose: looking out of my window I caught it in the random clods and broken heaps of snow made by the cast of a broom.' We are accustomed to say that Hopkins was indebted to Duns Scotus for this kind of idiom, and there is a poem in which the debt is handsomely paid. But it seems likely that we have made too much of this obligation. Hopkins read Scotus with unusual care, but mainly because he admired the

finesse with which the philosopher treated the problem of Freedom and Necessity. But he did not need Scotus to sponsor a delight in being and individuality which he felt, richly, from the
beginning. Whether he attended to these things as a Romantic
poet or as a Christian endowed with a sacramental sense of
reality, makes little difference. He had merely to acknowledge
the minute particulars, the dapple of life and, as he urges in 'The
Golden Echo', give it back to God, 'beauty's self and beauty's
giver'. Then, 'See; not a hair is, not an eyelash, not the least lash
lost.' This was his way of certifying his imagination, giving it a
crucial part in the worship of God.

This word, imagination, is one of three or four inescapable
terms which we use in describing our engagement with literature. We are never quite sure what it means. A modern poet tells
us that it is a power like light, in the sense that it adds nothing to
its objects, except itself; but he implies that the addition makes
all the difference. There is some dispute about the last clause, the
difference it makes. There are moments in which we think we
are touching a reality that has no need of a remoter charm, by
thought supplied; the best way is to touch it, nonchalantly, without any thought. At the other extreme, there are moments in
which the world's body seems peculiarly inert and we think that,
unless the imagination brings it from the grave, it will die for the
last time. These are extreme conditions: we exert a choice, or we
do not. But the dependence of *esse* upon *percipi* is not merely an
academic dispute. The same modern poet, Stevens, tells us that
the happiest occasion is when imagination and reality seem to be
equal and inseparable, and he thinks that, in drama, the conditions are fulfilled when Horatio says, 'Now cracks a noble heart.
Good night, sweet prince,/ And flights of angels sing thee to thy
rest!' I would offer another occasion, when Hopkins in 'The
Windhover' says:

> I caught this morning morning's minion, kingdom of
>   daylight's dauphin, dapple-dawn-drawn Falcon, in
>   his riding
> Of the rolling level underneath him steady air, and striding
> High there. . . .

There is still a lively dispute about this poem, or at least about a
few of its details. But I do not recall any of the disputants re-

marking what a splendid figure the bird offers to represent the poet's own vocation. It would be difficult to find a figure more lucid in suggesting the relation between the imagination and reality, when that relation is a mutual excellence. The bird flies of its own volition and yet it needs the sustenance and the opposition of the air, a happy meeting of necessity and freedom coming from a poet who was interested in such things. The continuity of the energy from line to line, from 'striding' to 'High', suggests the imagination going about its proper business. The poet's imagination is, like the bird, daring and self-contained but it needs the opposition of reality; and the air, like reality, is dense even when it is transparent. In the poem 'To an Old Philosopher in Rome' Stevens, a great master of the relation between reality and imagination, invokes two Romes:

> The threshold, Rome, and that more merciful Rome
> Beyond . . .

as if to imply that reality, graced by the imagination in one way, aspires to a second grace, supernatural in kind as in degree. The two Romes, Stevens goes on to say, are 'alike in the make of the mind'; where all the dreams cross. Hopkins's bird is a kind of Rome and it is a form of imagination. If we take it as representing not only poets in general but Hopkins in particular, we emphasize the degree of its daring. Hazlitt remarked of Cowper that he always wrote with an air of precaution; and, if it is true, we think it a serious restriction. R. P. Blackmur said of a modern writer that he always insists on using a mind never entirely his own; cultivating 'always deliberately to some extent what he understands to be the mind of society'.[1] The modern writer is prepared to cut back his own insights, unless they are somehow acknowledged beforehand, in principle, by the society he addresses. Blackmur had a mild rebuke in mind, I suppose, because he valued private intelligence too much to allow it to be constrained by the public intelligence. He liked his own thoughts to be a little wild, full of risk. We recall these occasions to quicken our sense of Hopkins's independence, the risks he was prepared to run. Indeed, it would be neat to say that he always insisted on using a mind entirely his own, and to point to the poems for proof and the letters for corroboration. The letters to

[1] R. P. Blackmur, *The Lion and the Honeycomb* (London. Methuen, 1956), p. 23

Bridges and to Canon Dixon especially record the poet's intransigence, the daring to say that he was right. He was often right; not always. But, neat or not, the assertion cannot hold. No one ever uses a mind entirely his own; no one, that is, who writes and, using language, uses thousands of minds not his own. Hopkins was perhaps more isolated in his thoughts than most poets of his day; though if we think of Dostoevsky, Kafka, Musil, Svevo, he seems by comparison almost domestic. The point to make is that he did not isolate himself from the composite mind which includes the single minds of Shakespeare, Milton, Dryden, Wordsworth, Keats, Whitman, and many other writers. There was also, richly available, the classical mind which he touched in his reading and teaching. And there was the reality, not all mind, which he knew as a Christian. His relation with this body of experience was always a matter of risk and strain: he did not possess it with the familiar air, second nature, which we find in a poet like Herbert. But we can hardly regret the strain or the risk, the animation of his most resplendent poems.

The special problem of Hopkins's poetry can be marked quite simply: what happens when the dapple is at an end? When a poet invokes Nature as the mediating term between Self and God, he faces an incipient ambiguity: is God naturalized, or is Nature deified? Many of Hopkins's ostensible descriptions are acceptable only on the understanding that Nature is deified. But if Nature is deified, what happens when the world's body is distant or invisible? Surely these occasions must at least hint, by their imagery, the disappearance of God. It is necessary to posit something along these lines if we are to take the strain of Hopkins's gestures. There is an interesting version of this in Spinoza, as a paraphrase will show. 'The more reality or being a thing has, the greater the number of its attributes.' Next: 'God possesses infinite attributes.' Finally: 'The human mind is capable of perceiving a great number of things, and is so in proportion as its body is capable of receiving a great number of impressions.' But the religious sense must be defeated if the supply of impressions is cut off; as it is cut off when darkness falls. This may suggest why Spinoza tried the experiment of discussing evil, sin, pain, joy, and all the other human factors as if he were dealing with geometrical lines, planes, and surfaces. In 'Spelt from Sibyl's

Leaves', to revert to that poem for a moment, what emerges when the dapple is at an end is fear. A poet who holds to Hopkins's aesthetic is bound to be afraid of the dark. If we compare this poem with Fulke Greville's 'In night, when colours all to black are cast', which is based upon the same figure, we see at once the difference. Grammatically, Greville's poem is an easy movement of indicatives; the analogy runs until its breath is used, but there is no impression of ethical strain. The security of Greville's world does not depend upon dapple or the continuity of sensory impressions. He writes of fear, but he is not afraid. Hopkins's poem begins with indicatives, but already they have registered the strain. In 'As Kingfishers catch Fire' and other poems the verbs are the points of contact between reality and imagination. Hopkins glories in them for that reason. But in 'Spelt from Sibyl's Leaves' the syntax is a prayer for security and the verbs rush to the imperative, 'part, pen, pack/Now her all in two flocks', and so on. Hopkins is as deeply afraid of the night as Pope in *The Dunciad*; though the fears of one are ethical, and the other social and moral. Ralph Barton Perry remarked, paraphrasing William James, that all views of the universe as a whole are based on the analogy of one of its parts. In Hopkins the chosen part is the body, the human body, then as the first circle of analogy 'the world's body', the earth, the natural forms. Finally, when all was well, the Body of Christ. It is an aesthetic of daylight, dapple, colour, form, time, and symbol.

4

From Tennyson to Eliot

In the fourth poem of *In Memoriam* Tennyson composes a little ritual to strengthen his will against the assault of life. He pictures himself asleep, his mind suffused with images of distress; and in the morning his will awakes and cries, 'Thou shalt not be the fool of loss.' Later in the poem we read: 'His night of loss is always there.' Tennyson's poetry may be approached in this image; the man who feels himself the fool of loss in an unending night, sometimes acquiescing, sometimes girding his will to resist. It is a commonplace that his poems are heavy with an air of numbed sadness: he wrote as if he had suffered a dreadful shock. Many of his poems are written as if to soothe a nameless wound, and sometimes to crawl back into a safe place. I would try to show a close relation between Tennyson the fool of loss and Tennyson the sweet singer of moody songs.

It is customary to say that the wound in Tennyson was religious, a loss of faith caused by the new sciences, the verdict of Biblical scholarship, the evidence of Nietzsche's murdered God. We know that he voted for Christianity when it was a question of voting, but we judge that his Christian belief was thin and fretful; it was not enough to sustain a thoughtful life. But we have to go a little further. There is a chapter in John Crowe Ransom's *God without Thunder* which offers a hint. Ransom's theme is not so much the gradual loss of belief in God, but rather the loss of belief in the God of the Old Testament, as distinct from the Christ of the New. And he explains it somewhat as follows. He points out that Christ did not identify himself with His Father, the God who sent Him to redeem the world by sacrifice. But over the centuries the world has given up its belief in that God: it has enforced an identity which Christ was the first to deny. Refusing to believe in God, the world—or part of it—has compromised by believing in Christ, and identifying this Man-God with God.[1] But in this compromise God becomes man, a fine man by common agreement but still man; so that God is merely a finer edition of oneself, not different in kind, but in degree. Christians have perverted the image of God by assimilating God to man. We have denied to God His thunder. Joseph Campbell says in *The Hero with a Thousand Faces* that man is now the object of his own wonder. 'The descent of the Occidental sciences from the heavens to the earth (from seventeenth-century astronomy to nineteenth-century biology), and their concentration today, at last, on man himself (in twentieth-century anthropology and psychology) mark the path of a prodigious transfer of the focal point of human wonder. Not the animal world, not the plant world, not the miracle of the spheres, but man himself is now the crucial mystery. Man is that alien presence with whom the forces of egoism must come to terms, through whom the ego is to be crucified and resurrected, and in whose image society is to be reformed.'[2] Man is now ready to worship himself: or rather, his imagination refuses to acknowledge a mode of being higher than his own. Tennyson asks:

> What find I in the highest place,
> But mine own phantom chanting hymns?
> And on the depths of death there swims
> The reflex of a human face.

Clearly, man's worship of man may be gay or rueful. In Stevens's 'Sunday Morning' the woman regrets that even Paradise is likely to be smeared with our own lineaments, vivid only in our own vividness:

> Why set the pear upon those river-banks
> Or spice the shores with odors of the plum?
> Alas, that they should wear our colors there,
> The silken weavings of our afternoons,
> And pick the strings of our insipid lutes!

[1] John Crowe Ransom, *God without Thunder* (London. Howe, 1931), Ch. VII.
[2] Joseph Campbell, *The Hero with a Thousand Faces* (New York. World, 1956), p. 391.

We live, Stevens says, in 'an old chaos of the sun'. In *In Memoriam*
God is merely a function of man, living on man's goodwill.
Tennyson asks:

> The wish, that of the living whole
> No life may fail beyond the grave,
> Derives it not from what we have
> The likest God within the soul?

This is why he finds it a consolation to identify Hallam with
Christ; as Hallam becomes 'the man I held as half-divine', and
'dear heavenly friend that canst not die'. As the poem proceeds,
Tennyson pictures Hallam encompassing God and Nature, as
the greatest term subsumes all lesser terms. He does this because
Tennyson's need requires him to do so.

There is another aspect. Christ said, 'Thou shalt love the Lord
thy God . . . and thy neighbour as thyself,' but the world has
suppressed the first clause and remembered only the second: so
that as belief waned, and the God of Thunder was rejected,
Christians tried (and are still trying) to pass off as Christianity
what is merely a vague neighbourliness. Religious truths are
softened in translation to social gestures; Christ becomes a kind
of David Riesman, in high standing with the profession. Instead
of a belief in God, we have a rhetoric of good works. Ransom
says at one point: 'The classical, Oriental, and early modern
literatures dealt, when they were serious, chiefly with the issue:
Man versus Nature, or Man versus God. They defined for individual or generic man his private economy, letting him take
the best course he might with a nature over which he had better
not think his rights were supreme. They showed him the error
of pride and *hubris*. They bade him remember God. But modern
Western literature, most of our literature since Milton, has presented in the main only one single issue: Man versus Man, or
Man versus Society. . . . This literature is marked by the absence
of metaphysical interest. It has no God. Discussing only the
social problems, it seems perfectly confident that society has
justified its aggressive scientific programme, and that the only
problem remaining to be decided is that of the reciprocal relations of persons within that society.' These sentences were
written in 1930, when scientific confidence was higher than it
is now, but they may be allowed to stand. They remind us,

reading Tennyson, that in 1850 to be a reasonably contented
man without a deep religious conviction, you had to be assured
that the relevant questions were personal and social, and you had
to be free from metaphysical nostalgia. If you genuinely believed that man lives by bread alone, and if you had no hanker-
ing for the old God, you were happily placed. But even a stubborn secularist like Stevens concedes that 'to speak of the origin
and end of gods is not a light matter'. It was not a light matter
to Tennyson.

Nostalgia for the old God is audible on every page. Even
when he speaks of merging in form and gloss 'the picturesque of
man and man', the merging is never complete. And while he
attended to his social concerns, he was never assured that the
real depths were there. In fact, there was only one way out, and
Tennyson was not ready to take it. One of Christ's strangest
sentences is: 'The Kingdom of God is within you.' In the new
ethic it was easy to rob this of its content by taking it to mean
that the truth of things resides within the human psyche. In
modern literature from Blake to Stevens it has been understood
to mean that 'God and the imagination are one'. If Tennyson
had been ready to believe this and to act upon it with Blake's
vigour or Stevens's nonchalance, it would have carried him
through a lifetime. Stevens says that God and the human
imagination are one and the same, because he equates God with
that creative power which the artist feels within him. For the
same reason Braque says, 'The senses deform, the mind forms.'
And according to Stevens, God could do no more than that.
Stevens was pleased by this conclusion; there were some
moments in which he was in doubt, and many in which he was
bored, but there was a point beyond which it seemed unnecessary to care. Tennyson could not solve the problem in this way.
To him, God and the human imagination did not seem one and
the same; two, rather, and God immeasurably more inscrutable
than the other term. Stevens made a religion of the aesthetic;
often replacing the structures of belief by those of his own
Supreme Fiction. But Tennyson could not do this, though there
is some evidence that he tried in his way. To him, fiction was
fiction because it was not fact, and a need of fact was not satisfied
by a profusion of fictive possibilities. He knew that his sensibility
could not unify the world. Hallam speaks of the rift between

community and idiosyncrasy; we think of the rift between the present and the past; the past a womb from which the poet has been wrenched.

This is where the imaginative propriety of *In Memoriam* is felt. By a kind of synecdoche the loss of one person, Arthur Hallam, becomes the loss of all; a loss, of which Tennyson is the fool. The effect of one death is to make a universe of death; as the loss of Desdemona made Othello's world into loss. For Tennyson, there were no 'healing' resources, Wordsworth's way was shut. Wordsworth's major poetry assumes a liaison between Man and Nature, a spousal relation, as he called it in the Preface to *The Excursion*. Blake objected to this from one point of view; Tennyson, like Tuckerman, distrusted it from another. Indeed, Tennyson is much closer to Hardy than to Wordsworth, whatever his official commitment. His idiom is rarely as stark as Hardy's; there is nothing in Tennyson to put beside Tess's image of the blighted planet; but there are moments in which a similar implication comes through the moodiness of the verse. As in this part of *In Memoriam*:

> O Sorrow, cruel fellowship,
>   O Priestess in the vaults of Death,
>   O sweet and bitter in a breath,
> What whispers from thy lying lip?
>
> 'The stars,' she whispers, 'blindly run;
>   A web is wov'n across the sky;
>   From out waste places comes a cry,
> And murmurs from the dying sun:
>
> And all the phantom, Nature, stands—
>   With all the music in her tone,—
>   A hollow echo of my own,—
> A hollow form with empty hands.'
>
> And shall I take a thing so blind,
>   Embrace her as my natural good;
>   Or crush her, like a vice of blood,
> Upon the threshold of the mind?

This is a hesitant assertion and, as Wittgenstein warned, we are not to confuse a hesitant assertion with an assertion of hesitancy.

It is also a whistle in the dark. Tennyson was not ruthless enough to crush things upon the threshold of his mind. Besides, he must find somewhere the intimations of womb and nursery; if not in the natural forms and appearances, then where? In a later poem he laments the failure of natural liaisons. 'How changed,' he says, 'from where it ran/Thro' lands where not a leaf was dumb;/ But all the lavish hills would hum/The murmur of a happy Pan.' He had not enough to live by, unless he was prepared to live in one idiom, almost on one note. He often disappoints us by doing so.

To come to the technical meaning, the difference it made in the poems: the first sign is a loss of narrative power. Tennyson envied those poets, like Crabbe, who were at home in the terminology of action, but he could not emulate them. He was hesitant in that sense of life which gives it as dramatic, dynamic; this feeling was blocked off. It is tempting to associate this with a failure of will, because this is how it often appeared to Tennyson himself, as a certain inner lassitude. Irritation and ennui are the notes of his age. Every now and again Tennyson tries to stir his will, making it confront the 'folly of loss'. Near the end of *In Memoriam* he makes another effort:

> O living will that shalt endure
> When all that seems shall suffer shock,
> Rise in the spiritual rock,
> Flow thro' our deeds and make them pure. . . .

It is not his best poetry, but he had to make the gesture, to keep things going. When he knew himself better, he committed himself to a terminology of feeling as a rueful alternative to action. He made a virtue of that necessity.

In Tennyson's case the language of feeling was 'the picturesque', a technique by which the opulence of static perception makes up for the loss of other terminologies. Baudelaire gives the key when he speaks of transforming sensation into consciousness. Poulet argues that this is the real revolution in the history of Romanticism; the shift from sensation to a consciousness of the means by which sensation is transformed into art. In the earlier Romantic writers the nature of the sensation was matter enough. But the later writers value sensation only as grist for the mill of consciousness: the problem was to keep the mill going. Conceptual thought was not enough; any journalist could manage that. The poets were not engaged by the task of 'saying things'. They were concerned with states of mind, and these seemed far more interesting, because far more complex, than anything likely to issue in a concept. The problem of language was to find a verbal equivalent of those states of mind; especially those which were locked in themselves, with no release in action. This was the problem that engaged such poets as Tennyson, Arnold, and Clough. Failure in this effort is the cause of the fretful note which dominates the poetry of the middle years of the century.

Marshall McLuhan has argued that, in Tennyson's case, the necessary hint is: Landscape. Or rather, landscape in itself and the landscape painting. Landscape in itself was fine, except that until the Impressionists the artist was intimidated by the presence of what was there in front of his eyes, and the absence of what was not. But as landscape painting developed, the intimidation was eased: if an image required for the feeling was not there before your eyes, you could put it in. The great advantage of the landscape technique was that you could adjust the images and arrange the relationships between them in such a way that the 'scene' would stand for the feeling just as vigorously as it stood for a certain landscape in Nature. The picture refers 'in' as well as 'out'. The second advantage was that you were not compelled to be explicit: there was no need to supply a grammar, or to specify the relationships as they are specified in a sentence; you could satisfy your own sense of congruity and leave the rest to the audience. So we have what Santayana calls the technique of the correlative object; what Eliot called the objective correlative; where the state of mind is embodied in an objective form of words, so chosen and arranged as to stand for the internal condition, the state of mind otherwise impalpable. Those who wonder how a certain arrangement of images can stand for a state of mind, without the endorsement of a grammar, are not easily answered: we know very little about these 'correspondences', except that in some mysterious way they seem to 'work'. Analogies drawn from sculpture and music are not helpful.

Given the example of landscape painting, the poet's next step was interior or psychological landscape. McLuhan says: 'Whereas in external landscape diverse things lie side by side, so in psycho-

logical landscape the juxtaposition of various things and experiences becomes a precise musical means of orchestrating that
which could never be rendered by systematic discourse.'[1] 'Juxtaposition' is not, I think, precisely the word for what is going on,
but we can leave that question for the moment. 'That which
could never be rendered by systematic discourse' is the 'state of
mind,' always mysterious. The technique is static and simultaneous; as distinct from narrative, which is sequential and temporal. The state of mind is given as a picture, contained within a
frame of simultaneous apprehension. Instead of the 'And then
and then' of action, there is the 'Now, now, now' of consciousness. This explains the desire, in Tennyson often extreme, to
prolong the moment of consciousness, to hold the frame of the
picture for fear it will collapse. Tennyson's poetry is a Book of
Moments. The relation between one moment and the next is not
narrative, it is a relation of 'quality'; the transition obeys laws
which are musical rather than syntactical. In music we move
from one note to the next according to mysterious persuasions
of feeling and form. This applies in Tennyson; also in Eliot. Both
poets establish a landscape which corresponds so intimately to a
'state of mind' that it becomes that state, for the life of the poem.
It is worth remarking that both poets had the same tempera-
mental difficulty in going beyond these states of mind to render
states of being; what we call 'the world's body', the sense of being and character, of which a state of mind is only one part, one
moment. It was the conscientious desire to go beyond this
limitation that led Eliot into the theatre.

But there are certain differences to be enforced. McLuhan re-
lates Tennyson and Eliot as Symbolist poets, implying that in a
poem like 'Mariana' Tennyson anticipates the procedure of 'The
Waste Land'. But he leaps a crucial distinction. Here is the first
of Eliot's 'Preludes':

> The winter evening settles down
> With smell of steaks in passageways.
> Six o'clock.
> The burnt-out ends of smoky days.
> And now a gusty shower wraps
> The grimy scraps

[1] H. M. McLuhan, 'Tennyson and the Picturesque': *Essays in Criticism*, Vol. I,
p. 271.

Of withered leaves about your feet
And newspapers from vacant lots;
The showers beat
On broken blinds and chimney-pots,
And at the corner of the street
A lonely cab-horse steams and stamps.
And then the lighting of the lamps.

There is an imagined spectator, the figure whose feet are pes-
tered by newspapers. Or rather, a participant, since presumably
the relevant state of mind is his or hers. And there is a correlation, one supposes, between that state of mind and the landscape,
the occasion, the leaves, the showers; including the rhymes, the
rhythm, and the other details purely linguistic. The correlation
is not specified; we may associate the loneliness of the cab-horse
with another loneliness in the human figure, but we are not admonished to do so. We make this connexion, or we do not. The
only 'rule' is that, as the philosopher Bradley argues, in immediate experience the subject and object are one. 'I am what is
around me,' a voice in Stevens says. Eliot, Bradley's pupil,
would have it so. Hence in this Prelude subject and object are
blurred into one another, and the only point of which we are
sure is that the blur is arranged with words. Responding to this
verse, we sense that the rhyming of *wraps* and *scraps* plays a much
more positive part than it would in earlier poetry; more positive, more determining in its effect, than the presence of the
participant, whose 'your' is virtually suppressed by the insistence
of leaves, feet, and newspapers. We are to understand that the
fancies which curl about these images are not prepared to commit themselves to a finite owner. We are reading tone poetry, in
which one effect seeps into another and the full effect is the whole
meaning. In 'Mariana', on the other hand, subject and object are
still distinct. The poem consists of seven stanzas, each ending
with Mariana's lament in much the same words, a moaning re-
frain. The first stanza gives the principle:

With blackest moss the flower-pots
Were thickly crusted, one and all:
The rusted nails fell from the knots
That held the pear to the gable-wall.

The broken sheds look'd sad and strange:
Unlifted was the clinking latch:
Weeded and worn the ancient thatch
Upon the lonely moated grange.

It is natural that an inhabitant of that dreary landscape should
share its 'quality'; unless the impresario is Alain Robbe-Grillet,
who has vetoed these expectations. If this were a Prelude by
Eliot the inhabitant would be insinuated into the landscape and
left there to 'melt' into the scene. Eliot would not go beyond
this in expressing the feeling; he would blur subject and object
to that degree. Tennyson puts Mariana into the landscape, but
he does not hand over her feeling to the landscape. He tells her
feeling directly, by making her tell it in her own words:

> She only said, 'My life is dreary,
> He cometh not,' she said;
> She said, 'I am aweary, aweary,
> I would that I were dead!'

This is psychological landscape, but at a much less sophisticated
stage than in Eliot's poem. True, most of the feeling is given by
the landscape, in the sense that the feeling is contained 'in principle' in the details of the scene, the broken sheds, the moss, the
rusted nails. The effect of Mariana's words is merely to bring out
what is already implicit in the scene. But still: Mariana and the
landscape are not one and the same, subject and object are distinct. As this technique developed into the later phases of Symbolism, the human figures were secreted more and more deeply
in the landscape. In 'The Waste Land' the human figures, as such,
have disappeared: what remains is a musical arrangement of
voices, each a fragment of a state of mind. We receive the words
like notes in an arpeggio.

Most of this is implicit in Hallam's famous review of Tennyson. Specifying the main qualities of Tennyson's poetry, Hallam
mentions two which are particularly relevant. The first: 'his
power of embodying himself in ideal characters or rather moods
of characters, with such extreme accuracy of adjustment, that the
circumstances of the narrative seem to have a natural correspondence with the predominant feeling and, as it were, to be

evolved from it by assimilative force'.[1] 'Moods of character' are
states of mind. And the second quality is: 'his vivid, picturesque
delineation of objects, and the peculiar skill with which he holds
all of them *fused*, to borrow a metaphor from science, in a
medium of strong emotion'. The important perception here is
that Tennyson does not render his objects with the lucidity of
independence: he never glories in the sheer objectivity of a
thing, the sense in which it is independent of its observer. He
always holds the object in an atmosphere of governing feeling;
and he tends to make the object receive the feeling and hold it
there. He was not afraid that the object might escape or might
be lost: he was afraid that the feeling might be lost, fretful in the
void.

We may read a celebrated poem from *The Princess*:

> Now sleeps the crimson petal, now the white;
> Nor waves the cypress in the palace walk;
> Nor winks the gold fin in the porphyry font:
> The fire-fly wakens: waken thou with me.
>
> Now droops the milkwhite peacock like a ghost,
> And like a ghost she glimmers on to me.
>
> Now lies the earth all Danäe to the stars,
> And all thy heart lies open unto me.
>
> Now slides the silent meteor on, and leaves
> A shining furrow, as thy thoughts in me.
>
> Now folds the lily all her sweetness up,
> And slips into the bosom of the lake:
> So fold thyself, my dearest, thou, and slip
> Into my bosom and be lost in me.

It would be impossible to write this poem if the rules of likeness
were strict; if A had to be like B in several respects before their
similarity could be counted. Poetry has never been too stringent
in this regard, especially the poetry of the nineteenth century.

[1] A. H. Hallam, 'On Some of the Characteristics of Modern Poetry': reprinted
in Walter E. Houghton and G. Robert Stange (editors) *Victorian Poetry and Poetics*
(Boston. Houghton Mifflin, 1959), pp. 802 fol.

The rhetorical aim of the song is to establish a network of analogies, a landscape of such congruence among its parts that the
only appropriate feeling is the one implicit in the scene. Any
other feeling would be wilful. And, as the rhetoric says, any
other act. The petals are humanized ('sleeps'), as the negatives
('Nor waves': 'Nor winks') clear a space for the human imperative ('waken thou') by holding all the natural configurations in
abeyance. Where everything else is stilled, the stillness becomes
an invitation, a gentle conspiracy. Here, things which have no
verifiable connexion are nevertheless connected in the music of
feeling. 'The fire-fly wakens': so, 'waken thou with me'. This
impression of a conspiracy among the natural forms is given
partly by the coincidence of syntax and rhythm, suppressing the
differences liable to arise between them in a more liberal use of
language, when words are given their head. Everything is subor-
dinated to the 'persuasion' of the scene. In the same way the relation between the earth and the stars, erotic because the stars are
the shower of gold in which Zeus visited the imprisoned Danäe,
is an 'open' invitation all the more vivid because it is directed in
one sentence. The sentence implies that the correlation is as
reasonable as grammar. This is quite different from Verlaine's

> Voici des fruits, des fleurs, des feuilles et des branches,
> Et puis voici mon coeur, qui ne bat que pour vous. . . .

because here the fruits, flowers, leaves, and branches are detached
from the lover as gifts are detached from their donor: they persuade only by their propriety as gifts. They do not incriminate
the feeling. In Tennyson's song the invitation to 'slip into my
bosom' is already anticipated by the fact that the lily has willingly
slipped into the bosom of the lake. Lilies are always right. The
atmosphere of silence and hush is part of the scene; it is also the
strongest part of the persuasion. But again the links are specified.

A more complicated rhetoric is at work in one of the later
poems in In Memoriam which describes the breaking of new life
with the coming of Spring. A poem so ridden by loss and death
is bound to develop a rhetoric of rebirth if only because it must
keep itself going. Up to the end of this poem the description
seems to be 'pure': but then Tennyson associates it with his own
sense of loss:

>   . . . and my regret
> Becomes an April violet,
> And buds and blossoms like the rest.

Presumably he effects this translation because he needs to do so. But what is implied; and in what sense does the regret share in the budding and the blossoming? Tennyson has handed over the regret to its determination without the chosen figure; its fate is now the fate of the flower. But he is not quite prepared to see this happen, or to let it happen too completely, so in the next poem he tries to retain the regret within the form of the concept:

> Is it, then, regret for buried time
> That keenlier in sweet April wakes,
> And meets the year, and gives and takes
> The colours of the crescent prime?
>
> Not all; the songs, the stirring air,
> The life re-orient out of dust,
> Cry thro' the sense to hearten trust
> In that which made the world so fair.

Here rumination has the effect of keeping the regret under the poet's direct control: this would not be possible, or at least would not be certain, if the feeling were to be handed over to the image without any guarantee of safe keeping. Anything might happen. In the next stanza the stir is embodied in the image of Hallam's face shining upon the poet:

> Not all regret: the face will shine
> Upon me, while I muse alone;
>   And that dear voice, I once have known,
> Still speak to me of me and mine.

So the final effect of handing over the feeling to the landscape, the regret to the violet (to the extent that this is done) is that the purposive intimations of renewal flood back into the human relationship, making that, in turn, more positive; a matter of shining and speaking. One of the more daring features of the Symbolist procedure, in its later development, is that once the feeling has been consigned to the image it has, in a sense, left the poet's hands and must take its chances in the new idiom. It must take the risks of the image. Just as the image has a life of its own, the feeling is now implicated in that life, at whatever cost. The Symbolist poet is willing that this should be so: his confidence is based on the belief that poetry is, after all, a magical transaction, the imagination a magical power. This is why it is easy to think of Eliot's early poems as if they were charms, runes, or spells. If we find it harder to think of Tennyson's poems in this way, the reason is that those poems lack the concentration, the peremptory quality of Eliot's: they are not prepared to trust their magic.

Tennyson is willing to do a lot for the 'state of mind', then, which is the occasion and the instigation of the poem; short of doing everything. Browning was wrong, I think, when he implied that Tennyson was not really interested in such matters. If both poets were to describe the situation of an unfaithful medieval knight, he said, 'I should judge the conflict in the knight's soul the proper subject to describe; Tennyson thinks he should describe the castle, and the effect of the moon on its towers, and anything *but* the soul.'[1] Browning did not allow for the intimate relation that Tennyson would establish between the knight's soul and the castle with the moon shining upon its towers. Indeed, Tennyson would describe that landscape in such a way, fraught with such soulful cares, that it would hardly be necessary to reflect upon the knight's soul at all. He would, indeed, reflect upon it; as Eliot would not.

I am arguing that if we look ahead from Tennyson to Eliot, with an agreed glance at the French Symbolists, we see that the state of mind is more and more deeply secreted in the landscape, the 'scene'; and the withdrawal of comment and reflection. We also see, as part of the same fact, a movement toward the embodiment of meaning, rather than its 'expression'. Meaning is more and more daringly embodied in pure forms, in the 'romantic image'—to use Frank Kermode's term—the image which holds its own counsel, keeps its own silence. Stevens tells, in an extremely lucid piece of prose, that one day he went into the Carré Gallery in New York to see an exhibition of paintings by Jacques Villon. 'I was immediately conscious,' he says, 'of the presence of the enchantments of intelligence in all his prismatic material. A woman lying in a hammock was transformed into a

[1] Browning, *Letters*, edited by T. L. Hood (London. Murray, 1933), p. 134.

complex of planes and tones, radiant, vaporous, exact. A teapot and a cup or two took their place in a reality composed wholly of things unreal.'[1] By 'unreal' Stevens normally means 'imaginative', subject to extreme pressure of imagination, so that what happens in the painting is a formal miracle, a transformation. Stevens delights in this transformation because, as he says elsewhere, the world about us would be desolate but for the world within us. He ascribes little or no value to those teapots and cups, except that they have made themselves available for transformation; they have allowed themselves to be killed, so that a miracle might take their place. Indeed, Stevens is never happy until the transformation is complete; as complete as possible, shall we say, given the disability that in words it can never be absolutely complete. Once the transformation has taken place, we have a new form, in which the history of the things that went into it has been lost: presumably we feel that history, but silently. At this point the teapots, cups, and the woman herself have been translated into consciousness, 'a complex of planes and tones'. Stevens reports that, in Villon's case, the complex was 'radiant, vaporous, exact', as if to console the sluggish who wonder sometimes whether the transformation is always a gain. And he would remind us, like a good formalist, that we cannot reasonably regret the loss of what we have never had, those teapots, those cups, that woman; we have had them only as memories, at best, images evocative of other more tangible teapots, cups, and women. If the dispute persists, one asks the poet what he means by 'exact' in his praise of Villon's transformations; radiant, yes, vaporous, yes, but why 'exact'? At this point the argument is likely to become unruly.

We may generalize a little. In nineteenth-century English poetry there were some poets who thought that they could best deal with matter by transforming it into spirit, teapots into consciousness. But this decision was invariably hesitant; no poet was prepared to go as far as Baudelaire. Tennyson was not ready to opt for the autonomy of spirit and the corresponding impoverishment of matter. Dissociated, he still yearned for unity. He was not willing to say that the only reality is spirit; or (a statement equally large) that spirit is identical with mind. The modern philosophy of mind is an attempt to endow the life of the disso-

[1] Stevens, *The Necessary Angel* (New York. Knopf, 1951), p. 166.

ciated spirit with the direction and force of action. Tennyson remains locked in feeling, the moodiness a sense of being neither
fish nor flesh.

The likeliest way-out is offered by Clough; to live with the
given, and make the reasonable best of it. When Clough advised
Alexander Smith to strengthen his poetry by copying out passages of good prose, notably Goldsmith's prose, he spoke on behalf of certain Augustan values which he found seriously absent
from contemporary verse. Most of the new poems Clough read
seemed to him effeminate, fanciful, precious. His own commitment, as Bagehot said of another poet, was to work upon stuff.
The certainty of green peas, which Bagehot elsewhere invoked,
was more consoling to Clough than to Tennyson. Clough's
poems sound as if he had subjected his idiom to the test of prose,
copying it out, perhaps, before allowing it to aspire to the condition of poetry. Tennyson's poems give the impression that he has
not read much prose, or much of the best prose. This is why his
medium seems particularly intractable when he tries to think in
verse, and often miraculously apt when a mood is to be released
in moody words.

Here is the last stanza of Clough's poem, 'The Music of the
World and of the Soul':

> Yea, and as thought of some beloved friend
> By death or distance parted will descend,
> Severing, in crowded rooms ablaze with light,
> As by a magic screen, the seer from the sight
> (Palsying the nerves that intervene
> The eye and central sense between);
> So may the ear,
> Hearing, not hear,
> Though drums do roll, and pipes and cymbals ring;
> So the bare conscience of the better thing
> Unfelt, unseen, unimaged, all unknown,
> May fix the entranced soul 'mid multitudes alone.

It is clear that while Clough mediates between the two musics, he
acknowledges the experience of both: he does not shame one in
the sight of the other. This is the prose of the poetry. In 'The
Comedian as the Letter C' Stevens speaks of Crispin gripping
'the essential prose', savouring rankness 'like a sensualist':

As being, in a world so falsified,
The one integrity for him, the one
Discovery still possible to make,
To which all poems were incident, unless
That prose should wear a poem's guise at last.

The one integrity for Clough is the density of the actual, the
indisputable life of what is there. If, in verse, he commits himself
to the essential prose, it is in the hope, never brashly conceived,
that this prose may wear a poem's guise at last. It is part of
Clough's moral sense, a mode of his scruple, that he allows both
musics their freedom. Both are given a range of life which corresponds to them in the vigour of the images. Appropriately, the
resolution of the poem is achieved when both musics are in-
audible. Or rather, when the second music is heard in the soul,
the 'central sense', and the images are dissolved in trance. The
'bare conscience of the better thing' is a magnificent phrase to
render this state; since the whole world of the senses is stilled, the
conscience is bare and the experience is rich in intimations of
value, the 'better thing'. This is partly the effect of the negatives,
'Unfelt, unseen, unimaged, all unknown': strangely, these words
retain the feeling, seeing, knowing, and imagining, but they retain them in memory, and memory points them on their way.
The condition is given as trance because it is attention intensified
to the highest degree and 'fixed' there. This is Clough's way of
redeeming his quietude from the taint of indifference. The relation between the 'essential prose' of Clough's commitment and
his sense of the world's body is clear enough; his reluctance to
dissolve the rankness of the world in consciousness. He is always,
in Stevens's phrase from another occasion, 'a florist asking aid
from cabbages'. He would have found great difficulty in adopting the Symbolist ways.

If Tennyson is the first point at which the Symbolist ways become audible in English poetry, we should make one or two
distinctions. Never as thoroughgoing as Valéry or Eliot, he
moves in their direction. In his poems things run the risk of losing
themselves; the feeling in the landscape, the landscape in the
words: only the words survive. Everything, good or bad, is part
of the process; matter is urged not to insist. Indeed, one of the
reasons why thoughts of Evolution proved so engaging, years

before Darwin, is that already the imagination was pressing things toward higher and higher forms, more and more subtle manifestations. Tennyson will find it easy to say,

> Arise and fly
> The reeling Faun, the sensual feast;
> Move upward, working out the beast,
> And let the ape and tiger die.

The fluidity of Tennyson's poetry often takes this form: if it is a question of direction, then the answer is 'upward', away from the ape and tiger, but it is rarely an insistence or even an aspiration. This is why McLuhan's word 'juxtaposition' won't do; because it implies a sharp edge. McLuhan first uses the word to describe Pope's way with the couplet, where one figure, one situation, is sharply set against another, like the Elizabethan double plot. The great merit of the double plot is that one and one are more than two: but the lineaments of each plot have to be distinct, before they overlap. It is like metaphor, which depends upon the temporal fixity of its referents. Swift, who distrusted metaphor, is in this sense metaphorical, featuring a sharp deployment of perspectives: he commands his effects by fixing things in the positions he assigns; if they were to slide into one another, the effects would be spoiled. But Tennyson's poems are metonymic rather than metaphorical; a distinction allowed, I am glad to find, by René Wellek and Austin Warren in their *Theory of Literature*: 'Metonymy and metaphor may be the characterizing structures of two poetic types—poetry of association by contiguity, and poetry of association by comparison.' In *The Palace of Art* the corridors are devised to stand for certain states of mind, to contain them 'in principle': the states are widely different in cast, but they are not juxtaposed one against another. They are not set off; and they are reconciled, perhaps too easily, by the soul that receives them. Tennyson is never interested in setting one state of mind against another; in this he differs from many Symbolists including Joyce in *Ulysses* and Eliot in *The Waste Land*. He is not engaged in irony, comparison, satiric 'placing'. His special mode is 'all we flow from, soul in soul'; one feeling staining another, neither definable apart from the stain.

5

The Human Image in Yeats

Yeats: a poet intensely and often painfully preoccupied with the irreconcilable claims of Soul and Body; 'body and soul/ Estranged amid the strangeness of themselves'. Intensely and painfully, because being a poet he was driven toward images of 'wholeness', unity, and 'perfection'. It seemed impossible to realize 'Unity of Being', that state in which 'all the nature murmurs in response if but a single note be touched'. Indeed, by the time he came to write the second Book of *The Trembling of the Veil*, he had modified that demand. I now know, he said, 'that there are men who cannot possess "Unity of Being", who must not seek it or express it. . . . They must await that which lies beyond their mind . . . the man of science, the moralist, the humanitarian, the politician. . . .' In 'King and no King' he had written:

> And I that have not your faith, how shall I know
> That in the blinding light beyond the grave,
> We'll find so good a thing as that we have lost?
> The hourly kindness, the day's common speech,
> The habitual content of each with each
> When neither soul nor body has been crossed.

There were many moments in which Yeats thought—or hoped against hope—that everything would be fulfilled in the accords of a distinguished human body; that the body, in splendid animation, would certify an undissociated unity of being, like the transfiguration which Ribh conjured at the tomb of Baile and Ailinn. Yeats often recited harmonious parables like 'The Three Bushes'; and perhaps he was drawn toward the alchemists because their object was—in Jung's summary—'to produce a *corpus subtile*, a transfigured and resurrected body, i.e. a body that was at the same time spirit'.[1] This would relate his meditations upon unknown thought to the woman Homer sang and both to whatever 'unconditioned' state was his God-term for the time being. But more soberly he named the body a dissociated and dying animal.

This is Yeats as patient. As agent he sought to heal himself: first, by lamenting the lost harmony, invoking a great-rooted chestnut tree that suffered from none of man's dissociations. And again: with a dramatist's instinct he broke down the crux into its two conflicting parts; thereafter interpreting experience, as his 'condition' prodded, now in terms of Soul (or Spirit), now in terms of Body (or Nature). The crux was a complex and unmanageable simultaneity: Yeats replaced it, imperatively, by a more tolerable scheme of successiveness. He resolved a contradictory 'yes-no' situation by setting up a plot that developed from 'yes' to 'no' and vice versa.[2]

In *The Wanderings of Oisin, Crossways, The Rose*, and *The Wind among the Reeds* Yeats located the Spirit in a realm of picturesque sorrow with 'numberless islands', 'many a Danaan shore', and a 'woven world-forgotten isle'. In those books whatever mode of existence is identified with the Spirit is protected from the critique of Body or Nature. Those early poems are a long and intermittently beautiful 'yes' to the Spirit; but the Spirit is abused, maimed, because torn from the Body. In later years and with different materials Yeats often said 'yes' to the Spirit; under the guise of Mind, for instance, as in 'All Souls' Night':

> Such thought—such thought have I that hold it tight
> Till meditation master all its parts,
> Nothing can stay my glance
> Until that glance run in the world's despite
> To where the damned have howled away their hearts,
> And where the blessed dance:
> Such thought, that in it bound

[1] Carl Jung, *Psychology and Alchemy*; translated by R. F. C. Hull (London. Routledge and Kegan Paul, 1953), p. 408.
[2] Cf. Kenneth Burke, 'Mysticism as a Solution of the Poet's Dilemma': in Stanley Romaine Hopper (editor), *Spiritual Problems in Contemporary Literature* (New York, Harper, 1952), pp. 95 f.

> I need no other thing,
> Wound in mind's wandering
> As mummies in the mummy-cloth are wound.

In this poem Yeats praises those adepts who, like Florence Emery, meditate upon unknown thought and repudiate the Body:

> What matter who it be,
> So that his elements have grown so fine/the fume
>   of muscatel
> Can give his sharpened palate ecstasy
> No living man can drink from the whole wine.

Ours are 'gross palates'. This is one situation, one act in the plot. Its counterpart is the Crazy Jane series in *Words for Music Perhaps*.

The year is 1929. Yeats is recovering from an attack of Maltese fever. Behind him, or so he fancies, are the world of politics, the Irish Senate, and 'a sixty-year-old smiling public man'. He writes to Olivia Shakespear from Rapallo: 'No more opinions, no more politics, no more practical tasks.' Joyful riddance: it is a prosperous moment. Sixty-four years old, Yeats feels new strength and sexual energy returning to his body. He is impelled to have recourse to that 'nature' (in bodily terms) from which he had withdrawn, estranged, to a more gracious world of pure Mind. Now he withdraws again, provisionally, not only from pure Mind but from a 'practical' scene of disillusion. Ridding himself of a practical world he reduces his scene accordingly: he identifies his will, provisionally, with the urges of the body in revolt, giving it—for protection and definition—the name 'Crazy Jane'.

It is a simplification on Yeats's part, and therefore an evasion. Indeed, each of Yeats's books of poems is a strategic simplification, a trial account of his universe devoted not to the entire complex truth but to a particular bias which is dominant for the time being. Some are phoenix books; others, turtle books; what one longs for is the mutual flame:

> Heats remote, yet not asunder;
> Distance, and no space was seen,

In the Crazy Jane poems Yeats for the time being places as much
trust in the bodily (a turtle, surely) as Racine in the greatly passionate, or Wordsworth in the greatly sensitive. The bodily imperative is the 'myth' of the Crazy Jane poems, corresponding to
the anthropological myth of 'The Waste Land'.

   Words for Music Perhaps; the words are for music, not because
they are to be sung, but because their burden, like that of the
ballad, belongs to the folk. The context has 'the body's poten-
cies'—Lawrence's phrase—as its prime motive.

   The connotations are important. It is 'that foul body' in
'Those Dancing Days are Gone', but this does not mean—as a
recent critic maintains—that Yeats 'identifies the physical, cor-
poreal aspects of love with that which is foul', or that in his later
poems, going one better, he 'regards the sexual act as mostly
beastly'. Quite the opposite. There is a curious tone in those
Crazy Jane poems:

>   Come, let me sing into your ear;
>   Those dancing days are gone,
>   All that silk and satin gear;
>   Crouch upon a stone,
>   Wrapping that foul body up
>   In as foul a rag:

The body is not foul. What is foul—here—is its decay, its loss
of power, mainly sexual ('the vigour of its blood'). Six days before writing this poem Yeats had rendered that bodily power in
'Crazy Jane Grown Old Looks at the Dancers':

>   God be with the time when I
>   Cared not a thraneen for what chanced
>   So that I had the limbs to try
>   Such a dance as there was danced—
>   Love is like the lion's tooth.

Again in 'Mad as the Mist and Snow' the winds are foul because
they testify to decay. In 'All Souls' Night' the years are foul because they wear away Florence Emery's beauty. Indeed, Yeats
uses the word when he has in mind sheer mutability. A difficult
case is 'Crazy Jane Talks with the Bishop':

>   I met the Bishop on the road
>   And much said he and I.

> 'Those breasts are flat and fallen now,
> Those veins must soon be dry;
> Live in a heavenly mansion,
> Not in some foul stye.'

The choice is offered as if it were unanswerable; the Bishop, as rhetorician, has no time for the Gidean problematic. Here, of course, 'foul' is censorial, and we expect the Bishop to be whipped for his cliché. Crazy Jane accepts the word and its challenge:

> 'Fair and foul are near of kin,
> And fair needs foul,' I cried.

There is also, she claims, the God of Love; and he has rights, a trim decorum, and his own special mansion. And the term he proffers—since two can play the rhetorical game—have a sanction prior to that of the Bishop's God, because they are certified by the axioms of the body and by 'the heart's pride':

> A woman can be proud and stiff
> When on love intent;
> But Love has pitched his mansion in
> The place of excrement;
> For nothing can be sole or whole
> That has not been rent.

A devotee of Blake, she has the last word.

She has the first word in 'Crazy Jane on the Day of Judgement', and here her interpretation of love has a wider circumference than usual. Indeed the Crazy Jane of this poem encompasses the three great dramatic roles through which, as Richard Ellmann has observed, Yeats voiced his conceptions. First, she is the Seer:

> 'Love is all
> Unsatisfied
> That cannot take the whole
> Body and soul';

the Victim:

> 'Naked I lay,
> The grass my bed;
> Naked and hidden away,
> That black day';

finally, the Assessor:

> 'What can be shown?
> What true love be?
> All could be known or shown
> If Time were but gone.'

The poem is intensely moving because it is willing to test the possibilities of growth and extension in a conception of love based on the bodily imperative. Crazy Jane's speculations do not go very far, and anything like an Incarnational view of the body is as far removed from her as from Yeats himself at any point; but in this poem there is an urge to face radical questions which are often evaded in *Words for Music Perhaps*. This book is devoted to a partial view of things: Crazy Jane has a deeper idea of love than Jack the Journeyman, but she is less urgently engaged in refining this idea than in knocking down Aunt Sallies like the Bishop. In the later 'Supernatural Songs' Ribh plays a similar role; not so much enacting the whole as insisting upon the part which, he asserts, the Christian view discards; 'the phallic consciousness', again Lawrence's phrase:

> Natural and supernatural with the self-same ring are wed.
> As man, as beast, as an ephemeral fly begets, Godhead
> begets Godhead,
> For things below are copies, the Great Smaragdine Tablet
> said.

Crazy Jane and Ribh are propagandists, speaking half-truths by vocation. They may be more humanely 'right' than the Bishop, but they are just as severely dissociated as he, and the poetic metaphor is just as far beyond their grasp. If the speaker in 'All Souls' Night' is a Paleface, Crazy Jane and Ribh are Redskins— to use Philip Rahv's famous terms; countering the 'sensibility' of *The Tower* with their own 'experience'. But the experience is raw, and therefore equally vulnerable to irony.

Yeats wanted his 'Poems for Music' to be 'all emotion and all

impersonal'. On 2nd March 1929—the day on which he wrote
'Crazy Jane and the Bishop' and 'Crazy Jane Grown Old Looks
at the Dancers'—he referred to the poems: 'They are the opposite of my recent work and all praise of joyous life, though in the
best of them it is a dry bone on the shore that sings the praise.'
Joyous life in this book is life in which the prime commitment
is to the body. Everything else may change or be dissolved, but
not that.

Until now we have been discussing the book as Yeats's 'self-
expression'. But it is necessary to add another context, involving
the persuasive relation between the poet and his audience.

Yeats 'believed in' none of the public, institutional faiths. But
he needed their authority, their momentum, or at least authority
and momentum from similar sources. And he was a spectacular
rhetorician. So he used each of the public faiths whenever he
felt that one of its patterns of insight was specially relevant to the
feeling of the poem. He may have been drawn to these local
'allegiances' by sensing a purely formal congruity between the
pattern in the 'public' structure and the pattern implicit in the
private feeling. This would account for the Way of the Cross in
'The Travail of Passion', to certify feeling akin to its own; or the
figure of the Guardian Angel in 'A Prayer for My Son'. Similarly in the Crazy Jane poems the bodily imperative is a 'public'
pattern of experience, with the force of public authority, complete with dogmas, rites, mysteries—and these by universal
assent. The great advantage of the bodily imperative as a source
of verbal communication is that it is prior to all conflicts of
thought or belief; it under-cuts the contentious levels of experience. In lofty moments Yeats would invoke the Great Memory
as the source and means of communication, and he would speak
beautifully under its sign, but there would always be something
problematic in its operation. The human body was more reliable; indeed, the body was the only universal Church to which
Yeats would belong.

We have described a strategic simplification and called it—
harshly—evasion. And we would suggest that a great mind
which has recourse to such a strategy must harbour severe misgivings, knowing that it omits so much, condones so much dis-
tortion. That is why one has the feeling, reading the later books,
that very often Yeats is adopting certain roles not to protect

himself from tourists but because he fancies himself in the parts;
like the 'character part' of the lusty old man or the ruthless neo-
Fascist. A new and distressing kind of picturesque, this leads to a
certain hardening of the arteries in such a poem as 'News for the
Delphic Oracle'. Here is part of the first stanza:

> Man-picker Niamh leant and sighed
> By Oisin on the grass;
> There sighed amid his choir of love
> Tall Pythagoras.

Porphyry's Elysian Fields are very like Yeats's Islands of Forget-
fulness, and Yeats—sly old virtuoso—can now jeer at both.
With the same virtuosity he can laugh at the equestrian Inno-
cents:

> Straddling each a dolphin's back
> And steadied by a fin,
> Those Innocents re-live their death,
> Their wounds open again.

The last word is Yeats's: he offers it, surely, as critique:

> Foul goat-head, brutal arm appear,
> Belly, shoulder, bum,
> Flash fishlike, nymphs and satyrs
> Copulate in the foam.

Touché. Yes, but isn't it, itself, in a weak position, despite the
bodily imperative and the sophisticated accent? The poem has
ended, but one could envisage a fourth stanza (by Dante) in
which the Old-Yeatsian heaven of the third would be shown
for the vulnerable thing it is. The critique is valid enough as far
as it goes, but not valid enough to justify the tone, the shrill ex-
hibitionist mockery. The Yeats of the Last Poems did not often
laugh in the tragic joy of Lear and Hamlet; his laughter is too
shrill for that. The apocalypse of these poems is a willed tumult,
the poet goading himself into the role of a randy old man to
repel the temptations of a laureate old age. (But there are great
humane exceptions to this rule, such as 'The Circus Animals'
Desertion', 'An Acre of Grass', and 'Beautiful Lofty Things'.)
   This shrillness in Yeats's late work issues, I think, from those

misgivings which I have mentioned. In *Words for Music Perhaps,
A Full Moon in March*, and many of the *Last Poems* Yeats's
strategic simplifications landed him in a false position; hence the
strident tone.

He soon got tired of Crazy Jane, though, perhaps acknowledging the limited range of her insight. He used her once again,
innocuously, cursing puny times and a world bereft of Cuchu-
lains.

Words for Music Perhaps—a final comment before we look at
other human images in Yeats—is a valuable book because it
enables us to re-enact a movement of feeling downward into the
limited, finite thing. The movement is touching in itself, in its
compulsions and embarrassments; only the most sullen reader
could fail to be moved and disturbed by this partial image of the
human condition. The pathos of the book is that when Yeats had
reached down into the finite Body there was little he could do
with it; he saw no means of penetrating the finite without
transcending it and thereby destroying it, as Roderick destroyed
Madeline, in a rage for essence. The trouble was that he could
not value the human body in itself; only when it agreed to wear
a bright halo of animation.

It is painful dialectic. The poet for whom plenitude of being
is everything finds himself kicking several of man's faculties out
of the way in his rage for essence. The devotee of 'perfection'
bows before fragments. In his most perceptive moments he
knows that it is a desperate expedient, that even his Byzantine
eternity is artifice:

> It seems that I must bid the Muse go pack,
> Choose Plato and Plotinus for a friend
> Until imagination, ear and eye,
> Can be content with argument and deal
> In abstract things; or be derided by
> A sort of battered kettle at the heel.

If you reduce a human being to his consciousness, and then provide a diet of unknown thought, argument, and abstraction, you
must face the risks involved; attrition, emaciation, a desert of
mummies. Time and again in *The Tower* Yeats prays for a
kinder unity:

O may the moon and sunlight seem
One inextricable beam,
For if I triumph I must make men mad.

But that book is a little too engrossed with its own exposure to allow much consideration for other people; apart from a few chosen friends, the rest are given as hot-faced bargainers and money-changers. And what can we say of the monstrous crudity, the sheer vulgarity, of 'Mrs. French,/Gifted with so fine an ear'? Grant that Yeats's position was difficult, perhaps impossible. 'All Souls' Night' was written under the sign of body-wearied Plotinus; as in the fourth *Ennead*, the dying animal of 'Sailing to Byzantium' is here dead, a mummy, and the 'soul' moves from its prison of diminished being. But in Yeats it has nowhere to go; the poet could not make anything of Plotinus's belief in the later stages of emanation toward the One. Hence the desperate stratagem, six years later, of Byzantium.

'All Souls' Night' is almost a test case for the hazard of the human image. It is a thrilling poem; we are at once thrilled and shocked to find Yeats driving himself into such a terrifying corner. The position itself—we feel at once—is untenable. It is unnecessarily dissociative. Mind—as Philip Wheelwright puts it —'does not stand alone: it exists intentively in relation to objects and it exists dialogically in relation to other selves'.[1] So the intensity of 'All Souls' Night' amounts to this: a stern mind denying the most serviceable relations in a humane life, and holding this denial 'to the end of the line'. If intensity were enough, this poem, this action, would be one of the greatest achievements in modern literature, and we would assent to it without reservation and find in it none of the wilfulness which disturbs us now. But intensity is not enough, and may well serve no other purpose than to assure us that we exist.

Does this matter? Or is it the fury in the words that matters, and not the words?

The received opinion among readers of Yeats is that the classic poems are in *The Tower*. And yet by comparison with *The Wild Swans at Coole* the human image in that spectacular book is curiously incomplete; remarkably intense, but marginal;

[1] Philip Wheelwright, 'The Intellectual Light', *Sewanee Review*, LXVI, 3, Summer, 1958, p. 411.

a little off-centre. Does this matter? Yes, it does; intensity is not enough. It matters greatly that *The Wild Swans at Coole* is at the very heart of the human predicament, groping for values through which man may define himself without frenzy or servility.

This book is concerned with the behaviour of men in the cold light of age and approaching death. The ideal stance involves passion, self-conquest, courtesy, and moral responsibility. Yeats pays the tribute of wild tears to many people and to the moral beauty which they embody; the entire book is rammed with moral life. Most of the poems were written between 1915 and 1919, and it is significant that those were the years in which Yeats was perfecting his dance-drama; because the dancer was the culmination of the efforts which Yeats made in *The Wild Swans at Coole* to represent the fullness of being as a dynamic action. Frank Kermode in his *Romantic Image* has discussed the role of the dance, in Yeats's poems, as the embodiment of that image, and more recently he has suggested the kind of dancer Yeats had in mind. We know from *The Death of Cuchulain* that it was not the dancer painted by Degas, their chambermaid faces distressed him when he wanted something 'timeless'; and clearly their glamour was a little low for his taste. Loie Fuller's dancing, Mr. Kermode argues, had precisely the connotations Yeats demanded: 'She is abstract, clear of the human mess, dead, and yet perfect being, as on some Byzantine floor: entirely independent of normal action, out of time.'[1] It is beyond dispute that Yeats and many of his artistic contemporaries were fascinated by this dancer; and yet the description does not seem quite in keeping with the dance-climaxes of Yeats's own later plays, which do not try to evade time at all. The Yeatsian dance seems much more severe, much stricter than the Symbolist dance of Loie Fuller. We should recall the description of the ideal dancer which the Old Man provides in *The Death of Cuchulain*: 'the tragi-comedian dancer, the tragic dancer, upon the same neck love and loathing, life and death'. This is much more Yeatsian, I think, than the dancer of Mr. Kermode's description. It is also much more in keeping with the human image of *The Wild Swans at Coole*, which has nothing in common with the bodiless,

[1] 'Poet and Dancer before Diaghilev': *Partisan Review*, XXVIII, I, January–February 1961, p. 75.

timeless vision of Loie Fuller. It would seem very strange if
Yeats, after *The Green Helmet*, were to present fullness of being
in an image itself timeless and bodiless. Indeed, the dance was a
powerful image precisely because it was committed to body; an
apt equivalent in our own time is the dance-drama of Merce
Cunningham or Martha Graham, which glories in the physi-
cality of the body, in its muscular and nervous experience, in the
resistance of the ground itself. Yeats's dancer is never allowed to
circumvent the body or to grow wings.

In 'The Double Vision of Michael Robartes' the girl who
dances between the Sphinx and the Buddha dreams of dancing
and has outdanced thought; which I take to mean that in her
Action is not distinct from Vision but is Vision itself formulated. The moral equivalent of this is a certain nonchalance or
recklessness, Castiglione's *sprezzatura*, a certain high daring;
mastery, rather than singularity, to cite Valéry's distinction. As a
gloss we may quote a few sentences from Buber's meditations
upon Nijinsky:

'The decisive power in the development of the dance was
neither play nor expression, but what bound them and gave
them law: magic. That is the response to the chaotic and
furiously inrushing happening through the bound, lawful movement, through movement as form. The bound binds.'[1]

Above all, it must be dynamic, this ideal behaviour; it must
not be complacently picturesque. In T. S. Eliot's later poems this
ideal condition appears a little static; the poet may say, 'at the
still point, there the dance is', but there is very little energy in
that dance, and we have to exert some goodwill before we can
register it at all. In some of Wallace Stevens's poems the ideal
condition is given as a still life—a blue woman, in August, registering grape leaves and clouds—someone sitting in a park
watching the archaic form of a woman with a cloud on her
shoulder. These are handsome moments, and we are free to
relish them. But Yeats knew that they are at best provisional, at
worst evasive; in his greatest poems static effects denote a
failure of being.

The Wild Swans at Coole is committed to action; not to
thought or concept or feeling, except that these are essential to

[1] Martin Buber, *Pointing the Way*, translated by Maurice Friedman (New York.
Harper, 1957), p. 23.

the full definition of action. We are to register action as the most scrupulous notation of human existence, far more accurate, more 'creatural', than thought or concept—which are simplifications; far more comprehensive, too. Action is silent articulation of experience. Yeats's dancer has outdanced thought, summarized thought in a pattern of gestures. Her dance is an act of desire toward the God-state, or God-term; the dancer strives toward an 'essential' human image, an image of dynamic perfection freely formulated—fulfilled—at the end of the body-line. This is probably what Yeats meant in the well-known letter which he wrote a few weeks before his death, in which he said, 'It seems to me that I have found what I wanted. When I try to put all into a phrase, I say, "Man can embody truth but he cannot know it." ' Truth is embodied in the figure of action, the dancer for whom meaning is embodied in gesture and gesture the only expression there is. Thought is not enough; even the 'thinking of the body': the most accurate annotation is that act which outdances thought and sums up human potentiality in gesture.

In *The Wild Swans at Coole* the dance which engrosses Yeats is the dance of the self and anti-self. In 'Ego Dominus Tuus' the Yeatsian speaker says:

> I call to the mysterious one who yet
> Shall walk the wet sands by the edge of the stream
> And look most like me, being indeed my double,
> And prove of all imaginable things
> The most unlike, being my anti-self
> And, standing by these characters, disclose
> All that I seek. . . .

The appropriate gloss is from 'Anima Hominis': 'Unlike the rhetoricians, who get a confident voice from remembering the crowd they have won or may win, we sing amid our uncertainty; and, smitten even in the presence of the most high beauty by the knowledge of our solitude, our rhythm shudders.' Add to this that Art is a vision of reality: in the artist this vision is animated by his own passion, and in the passion his rhythm shudders. This is the dance, the ecstasy, man and daimon feeding the hunger in one another's hearts.

It is also dialogue, the fruitful grappling of self and anti-self. Hence the number of poems in *The Wild Swans at Coole* in which the structure is 'dialogical' and the animation is the rhythm of speech. One of the finest examples is 'The People':

'What have I earned for all that work,' I said
'For all that I have done at my own charge?
The daily spite of this unmannerly town,
Where who has served the most is most defamed,
The reputation of his lifetime lost
Between the night and morning. I might have lived,
And you know well how great the longing has been,
Where every day my footfall should have lit
In the green shadow of Ferrara wall' . . .

This is the mutual flame. A poet, in weariness, voices a natural demand, claims the reward of the rhetorician; quarrelling with others, he makes a rhetoric, strong if a little sullen. He is in the condition of earth, the 'place of heterogeneous things', as Yeats calls it, and he is admonished by his phoenix, the spirit of fire 'that makes all simple'. The common ground between them is the human world, which includes Castiglione's aristocrats as well as 'the people'. The poet prolongs the dispute by setting up a conflict between the purity of a natural force and the definitions of the analytic mind; but the dispute is helpless. The real dispute, the real dialogue, is under the words, in the meeting of phoenix and turtle, the leaping of his heart at her words, the sinking of his head abashed. This is the poet's quarrel with himself. If we feel that the proper response to this poem is intimacy and assent, the reason is clear: the poem commits itself to the human situation, to the specific occasion of dialogue. Its acknowledgement is complete. Time, place, and circumstance, the facts of the case, are the ground of the poem's action: from these issues the idiom, certified speech. It is sometimes argued that Yeats's rhetoric is the imperious kind, that his swans are never swans but symbols conniving with a tangible form. There are a few poems in which the case might be urged. But in the great middle poems the images are palpable to a degree that hardly applies in another modern poet: the houses are houses, the people are people, and if a certain emblematic resonance accrues to them in the poems it is precisely because they are deemed significant and that significance is historical. Yeats lived in an eventful time: when he sought images of value and force he found them there, in events, in time. His phoenix is a historical woman and remains so even when she is identified with Helen of Troy; she never loses her authenticity.

Yeats's spokesman in 'Ego Dominus Tuus' justifies his tracing characters upon the sands instead of imitating the great masters: 'Because I seek an image, not a book.' Thought is not enough, though the poet will sometimes fancy otherwise in *The Tower*. The image he seeks is described by Robartes in 'The Phases of the Moon': at the fourteenth phase 'the soul begins to tremble into stillness, to die into the labyrinth of itself':

> All thought becomes an image and the soul
> Becomes a body.

The body and the image, I assume, are the dancer and the dance, dynamic, indistinguishable, the final gesture in the dialogue of self and anti-self.

My argument, to bring these matters to a conclusion, is that in *The Wild Swans at Coole* the balloon of speculation is brought into the shed of common experience: in this book more radically than elsewhere Yeats takes 'the living world for text'. We have to realize this before we can register the impassioned gravity of its later pages.

Perhaps this explains why the poems in *The Wild Swans at Coole* seem peculiarly 'central' to our experience. The burden of meaning has been placed firmly where it belongs, in people, and in the acts that embody their values. The book is an anthology of represented lives in which private vision becomes incarnate in public action; Lionel Johnson, John Synge, George Pollexfen, Robert Gregory, Solomon and Sheba, Iseult Gonne, the anonymous and classic fishermen—and many more. The poems speak to us directly, to our sense of the human predicament; and in the last reckoning this is a more reliable mode of communication than the Great Memory or even the Body. The human image in this book is at once sweet and serviceable; it hides behind no platitudes that it can see; it does not feel called upon to take possession of the world or to set up as God. It acknowledges human limitation and tries to live as well as possible under that shadow. The image chimes with our own sense of the 'creatural' situation; it is continuous with our own unspectacular experience in its assent to common occasion.

It is intriguing to note that one such occasion, the poem 'Her Praise', was written in 1915, the year in which Eliot wrote Prufrock's more famous love song. It was *Prufrock* that brought in the new age, defining the new tone. In recent years many of the younger poets have been labouring to avoid the melody that Eliot established; often picking up snatches of an older tune and reciting them again. Many of the best poems in the past few years are closer to 'Her Praise' in idiom and feeling than to *Prufrock*. There are several poems in *For the Union Dead* in which Robert Lowell, speaking in his own voice, recalls the old poetry rather than the new; recalls Yeats, to be precise, and Hardy, and E. A. Robinson. This is not a matter of spotting influences. But it seems clear that the books which are likely to be important to the new poets, Yeats's *The Wild Swans at Coole*, Stevens's *The Rock*, among a possible list, will urge the poet toward the common life of feeling, verifiable in common terms. 'J. Alfred Prufrock,' Hugh Kenner has observed, 'is a name plus a Voice.'[1] Not a character, not a person. Like Tiresias he is 'the name of a possible zone of consciousness where the materials with which he is credited with being aware can co-exist'. It seems essential to Eliot's purposes, in the early poems, that he should reduce a man to his consciousness, throw away the human being he began with, and ponder the remainder as a detached possession. The encounter of man with man, the I-Thou without reduction, was alien to him. Hence the famous cultivation of invisibility. But in 1919 Yeats wrote:

> Now days are dragon-ridden, the nightmare
> Rides upon sleep: a drunken soldiery
> Can leave the mother, murdered at her door,
> To crawl in her own blood, and go scot-free;
> The night can sweat with terror as before
> We pieced our thoughts into philosophy,
> And planned to bring the world under a rule,
> Who are but weasels fighting in a hole.

And a few years ago Robert Lowell, in a love poem, 'Night Sweat', said:

[1] Hugh Kenner, *The Invisible Poet* (New York. McDowell, Obolensky, 1959), p. 40.

Poor turtle, tortoise, if I cannot clear
the surface of these troubled waters here,
absolve me, help me, Dear Heart, as you bear
this world's dead weight and cycle on your back.

This is what I mean by continuity of feeling. Eliot found it difficult to address himself to anything but the detached consciousness: hence, as I have argued elsewhere, his equation of sanctity
with the extreme reaches of consciousness: nothing else was real
to him. But to Yeats and Lowell everything else in man is just as
real as his mind. In 'Soft Wood' Maine is real, the wood is
painted white, and the air makes it whiter. We can believe these
things, as we believe in George Pollexfen while reading 'In
Memory of Major Robert Gregory'. The continuity of feeling
between Yeats and Lowell implies that we live in the world as
finite people, not merely zones of consciousness. Words alone
are not, after all, certain good; as Yeats discovered.

6

Yeats and the Living Voice

For better or worse the high poetry of this century has pro-
ceeded on Symbolist lines; the poetry we agree to call 'modern'
in a sense in which *Prufrock and other Observations* is modern and
Three Taverns is not. The modern poet deals with experience by
treating it as a plane surface upon which selected images are
placed in silent juxtaposition: he takes his bearings from the
landscape painting or the visual field, where images are ranged
about like flags on a military map. Visual metaphors, visual analogies; the crucial moment is the moment of vision, when all
the images are held in focus by the poet's imagination. Indeed,
it is characteristic of Symbolism to identify Imagination with
Vision: it was Milton's alleged lack of visual imagination that
distressed Eliot in a famous encounter. The Symbolist poet
assumes that meaning is available as a visual pattern, often a pattern imposed by the imagination. This accounts for our sluggish-
ness in coming to terms with poets who live by a different
allegiance; as Whitman's allegiance—a point already urged—is
contact, and Yeats's is action. Marshall McLuhan has argued that
the invention of the printing press and the corresponding change
from an oral to a typographic culture have specialized our modes
of knowledge; our minds work by seeing meanings as we see
black marks on a white page without hearing the sounds for
which they stand. The evidence is not fully convincing; there
are problems. But it is hard to refute. In our present context it
would link silent reading, spatial analogies, the promotion of
sight over its four sensory colleagues, the book as a solid object
rather than a transcript of speech, the poem as a well-wrought
urn.[1] There is clearly a direct relation between this aspect of

[1] Marshall McLuhan: *The Gutenberg Galaxy* (London. Routledge and Kegan
Paul, 1962), cf. Rilke: 'Ur-Gerausch': *Das Inselschiff* (Leipzig), I (1919), 14–20;

Symbolism and the primacy of the 'closed system' as the modern image of knowledge. If we feel that a certain play by Pinter or Albee is 'untrue', that is, morally nasty, a libel against life, it is very difficult to say so; because the prevailing meaning of 'true' is 'consistent with its own terms'. Truth is the law which obtains within a closed system. The play is true in that sense; but it may be damnably false, a travesty, in the old sense.

A further word about the assumptions of Symbolism. The traditional poets invariably assumed that the grammatical structure which we call the sentence was an excellent instrument for the representation of reality. Composing a sentence was an act of faith, in one sense; you dedicated yourself to the proposition that the mind could deal with experience in that way by directing a flow of energy through a subject, a verb, and an object. If this seemed too rigid, you could complicate the report by bringing one sentence to bear upon another. The Symbolist, by and large, rejects this belief. Valéry is a case in point. The assumption that generates all his writings on literature and art is that a bourgeois demon resides in grammar and syntax and must be defeated. Syntax and grammar are always on the side of the common man because they serve his purposes. The poet must therefore use all his sceptical intelligence to thwart this demon, twisting the language into configurations from which there is no 'practical' escape. Valéry also argued that the daily forms of language try to impose themselves upon the poet by insinuating the attitudes they imply: again the true poet will defeat the attitudes by resisting the grammatical forms. There are several possibilities. He can pretend to take the attitudes seriously while using them as grist for his mill. He can deny commitment in the

reprinted in Rilke's *Gesammelte Werke* (Leipzig. Insel–Verlag, 1927), Band IV, pp. 285–94. Translated by Carl Niemeyer in Rilke's *Primal Sound and Other Prose Pieces* (Cummington, Mass. Cummington Press, 1947), pp. 33–8.

'At a certain time when I was beginning to concern myself with Arabian poetry, in whose origin the five senses seem to have a more simultaneous and more equivalent share, it first struck me how dissimilar and sporadic is the contemporary European poet's use of these talebearers, only one of which—sight—overcharged with perception, continually engulfs him. How small in contrast is the contribution of the inattentive hearing, to say nothing of the indifference of the remaining senses, which, functioning discontinuously and apart, exert themselves only in their own conveniently confined territories. And yet the finished poem can come about only on condition that the world, simultaneously grasped by these five levers, appear under a given aspect upon that supernatural plane which is precisely the plane of poetry.'

words by locating expressiveness in the 'presence' which is the poetic form; in the *being* of the poem as a force beyond its *meaning*. He can exalt the uselessness of art. He can deflect the reader's attention from the stubborn reference of the words. He can push poetry toward the condition of music, thereby defeating the aims of the practical world. The ideal poetic language is a systematic deviation from the daily forms and it is carried on with subversive intent. The poet can also resort to parody: by pretending to speak in sentences he can parody the pretention of their structure, as Eliot does so often. When the visionary Tiresias says, near the end of 'The Waste Land':

> A woman drew her long black hair out tight
> And fiddled whisper music on those strings. . . .

it would be foolish to ascribe even a notional existence to this woman or to conclude from the use of the past tense that she might have been encountered thus engaged in London or Vienna. If we take her as a domesticated version of the maenad in the 'Ode to the West Wind' or perhaps as one of the mermaids in 'Prufrock', this is as far as we should presume upon her reality. Indeed, the best comment upon her is that passage in *Modern Painters* in which Ruskin distinguishes between the true grotesque and the false grotesque which he finds in the griffin on the Temple of Antoninus and Faustina at Rome:

'A fine grotesque is the expression, in a moment, by a series of symbols thrown together in bold and fearless connection, of truths which it would have taken a long time to express in any verbal way, and of which the connection is left for the beholder to work out by himself; the gaps, left or overleaped by the haste of the imagination, forming the grotesque character.'[1]

Ruskin goes on to say that this is the third form of the grotesque, 'art arising from the confusion of the imagination by the presence of truths which it cannot wholly grasp'. And he argues that this is a noble form. We should not doubt him. It would be unwise to assume that Eliot's imagination was confused by the presence of truths which it could not wholly grasp. The nobility of the figure is beyond dispute; its nature remains opaque. The black-haired woman is a correlative object and therefore an important point on an emotional map. She is not in any sense veri-

[1] John Ruskin, *Modern Painters* (London. Allen, 1910), III, pp. 100-2.

fiable: she has emblematic status in the landscape of the poem, but no other status. She is an event within a closed system. The words set up a network of associations, organized with great daring, and the network is engrossing as rhythms may be engrossing, but it refers to nothing; it constitutes the only reality there is, for the life of the poem. To the extent that the words 'work', we are the music while the music lasts. The bold and fearless connexion of the words has far more to do with their internal resources, the relation between one vowel and another, assonance, and so on, than with anything 'there'. So this poetry is not essentially different from the systematic deviations encouraged by Valéry's aesthetic. (Not by Valéry's own poems, incidentally.) In fact, it works on the same assumption, that the traditional grammar of sentences is merely a mental category, one of many, and that it has no special qualifications in the confrontation of human life. Poets like Valéry resent these categories and resist their bourgeois influence. For proof, they point to the chaos of actual life. Hence the Symbolist poet disengages his poem from all responsibility to quotidian life by making it an object, an icon, a mobile floating free and pure in air. He demands, in the medium of words, the same degree of freedom which is accorded, in stone, to Barbara Hepworth or Henry Moore. When he proceeds from one thing to another, the movement is subject to his own laws, and these are much more permissive than those of logic, syllogism, grammar, or plot. In 'The Fire Sermon' when the woman puts a record on the gramophone and Eliot gives, as the next line, a famous sentence from *The Tempest*, 'This music crept by me upon the water,' the only law at work is that of association, one music calls to another from a different moral world. The meaning of the passage is whatever happens in the reader's mind when he holds these two situations together, simultaneously, for contemplation. The lines mean as a sculpture means, by constituting an autonomous event for which the artist takes full responsibility. We cannot say that the procedure is either right or wrong, but we can say that it is arbitrary. We can also say, more generally, that the characteristic hazard of the Symbolist poet is that, as Yeats said of someone, he is helpless before the contents of his own mind. If you make language as independent as possible; if you think of it as a poor relation to music and hope to improve it by cultivating musical manners; you can never do this as thoroughly as the musicians, and you are unlikely to do much better than the Pure Poets. Indeed, Symbolism is merely Pure Poetry writ a little larger. The characteristic Symbolist frustration is the discovery that music and poetry are different; that words will drag their daily reference into the purest mansions of your poetry.

The only other alternative, it would seem, is to acknowledge a reality not yourself, not your Supreme Fiction, a reality independent of your consciousness. You can even acknowledge that it was there before you came and may survive your departure. After these acknowledgements it is much easier to think of language as an instrument by which a man mediates between himself and a world not himself; an instrument in the service of a reality that is not linguistic. If you go so far you will probably value the mental categories and share the allegiance that frames a sentence. This constitutes an act of faith, and there is no point in minimizing its implications. In the third Book of *Endymion* Keats speaks of 'the feud/'Twixt Nothing and Creation'. If we hold this phrase beside the history of modern Symbolism we see that for the Symbolist poet there is, strictly, Nothing; or rather, nothing but the human imagination, the strictly creative power. So that the poet becomes God, creating out of nothing. Wallace Stevens's poem, 'Another Weeping Woman', speaks of

> The magnificent cause of being,
> The imagination, the one reality
> In this imagined world. . . .[1]

and another Stevens poem, 'Tea at the Palaz of Hoon', invokes ointment, hymns, and the sea only to say

> Out of my mind the golden ointment rained,
> And my ears made the blowing hymns they heard.
> I was myself the compass of that sea:
>
> I was the world in which I walked, and what I saw
> Or heard or felt came not but from myself;
> And there I found myself more truly and more strange.

This is Stevens in one of his extreme moments, and it does not prevent him from having other moments in which he makes at

[1] Wallace Stevens, *Collected Poems* (London. Faber and Faber, 1955), p. 25.

least a provisional act of realist faith. In the fifth Part of 'The
Comedian as the Letter C' he arranges that Crispin will discover for himself that

> The words of things entangle and confuse
> The plum survives its poems.

Crispin lays aside the rebellious thought, he will rest in the decision not to set up as God or to challenge God. But the tendency
of Symbolist poetry is to assume, not that the plum survives its
poems, but that the very existence of a plum depends upon the
goodwill of the poet and the hospitality of the poem: the poet
invents a plum and gives it housing room in his poem, as God
created man from nothing but divine goodwill and made a
world in which man might live. This is the real difference between the Symbolist poet and the poet for whom reality, such
as it is, is 'given'. Stevens is the kind of poet who, when faced
with an 'either-or' situation, opted for 'both'; he could not bear
to relinquish any mode of the imagination, any possibility of the
mind; hence he preferred a dozen provisional beliefs to the imperative of a single belief, largely because the first arrangement
gave his imagination more work to do. (But we will return to
Stevens later in the book.)

Yeats's part in this dispute is our theme. True, he flirted with
the theory of Symbolism and made some attempts to understand it with the aid of Arthur Symons, but it was always an
alien tongue. Besides, he had his own way of clearing spaces in
which he might live. In his later years he recognized that Symbolism was a foreign device and he rejected it, notably in some
of his last letters to Dorothy Wellesley. His chief objection to it
was that it tried to disengage itself from time and history. But I
would argue that the force which kept Yeats from joining the
modern Symbolists was the persuasion of a native culture which
he loved and hated and only barely understood.

We need not make this a chauvinistic occasion. On the other
hand it is clear that Symbolism and the Irish tradition run in
opposite directions. For one thing, Symbolism is visual; Irish
literature is oral. Symbolism creates a mystique of the Book:
Irish literature transcribes a world of sound. Symbolism aspires
to the fixity of the sculptured object, freeing itself from responsibility to people, places, and things; Irish literature is devoted to

these, and content to survive in a long memory. In 'Literature and the Living Voice' Yeats said:

'Irish poetry and Irish stories were made to be spoken or sung, while English literature, alone of great literatures, because the newest of them all, has all but completely shaped itself in the printing-press. In Ireland today the old world that sang and listened is, it may be for the last time in Europe, face to face with the world that reads and writes, and their antagonism is always present under some name or other in Irish imagination and intellect.'[1]

That was in 1904, and it explains why Synge went to the Aran Islands, to listen, to move in a world of sound. It also explains why Joyce's greatest gesture of repudiation was not his leaving Dublin; it was his determination to put everything into a *book*, and to make that a more bookish book than any book had ever been.

Yeats was not prepared to do this. He wanted, after all, a relation to a specific people. In 'All Souls' Night' he would invoke

> Such thought, that in it bound
> I need no other thing,
> Wound in mind's wandering
> As mummies in the mummy-cloth are wound . . .

but he knew that this security was available only to the dead and that the living are unappeased. And like Synge he chose the living world for text. Think how often he envied those strong, simple men like Thomas Davis and John O'Leary who spoke directly to the Irish people by offering them strong, simple images. Think how often this problematic poet tried to write a ballad, a strong, simple story to coax into life those capable of responding to it. That he never had a genuine touch for the ballad makes his devotion to it the more remarkable. As early as 'The Ballad of Moll Magee', as late as 'Colonel Martin' he reached for a direct relation to a simple audience. And think how often he revelled in those situations in which people are gripped by the same image: it might be a revolution, a speech, or a meeting of the Galway races:

---

[1] Yeats, *Explorations* (London, Macmillan, 1962), p. 206.

> There where the course is,
> Delight makes all of the one mind,
> The riders upon the galloping horses,
> The crowd that closes in behind. . . .

Yeats would try to achieve a similar cohesion in his own poetry by offering his sense of life in massive archetypes; the fisherman, the beggar, the fool, the hermit, the hunchback, the saint, the lover. On those occasions he would take his bearings from the Irish folk-tales provided for him by Lady Gregory and Douglas Hyde, where charm, magic, and prophecy run together. In 'Ideas of Good and Evil' he says: 'Whatever the passions of men have gathered about, becomes a symbol in the Great Memory, and in the hands of him who has the secret it is a worker of wonders, a caller-up of angels or of devils.' And to complete this he says: '. . . that literature dwindles to a mere chronicle of circumstance, or passionless fantasies, and passionless meditations, unless it is constantly flooded with the passions and beliefs of ancient times.'

For this reason, he says further, the Celtic element has again and again 'brought the "vivifying spirit" of "excess" into the arts of Europe'.[1] The general argument may or may not be true. What we should emphasize is simply this; that Yeats found in Celtic folk-tales a great 'excess', a free range of the imagination, a flow of passionate experience, incorrigibly temporal, which he feared was lost in modern literature. We tend to smile, these days, at Yeats's traffic with legendary heroes, and yet our smile is idle and a little vulgar. When Yeats spoke of magical events he invoked and praised all those possibilities of the spirit for which there is no other explanation than the passion that incites them; and it was the passion he revered. By comparison, he thought his own time puny and timid, the work of the counting-house, except when it flowered beyond prediction in a great act, like the Easter Rising in 1916.

If we agree that Yeats's poems are concerned with the possibility of a completely human life—which he often invoked as Unity of Being—then the importance of the Irish tradition to that concern becomes clear. The old Irish stories are the speech of person to person: once that convention is established there is

[1] Yeats, *Essays and Introductions* (London. Macmillan, 1961), p. 185.

no limit to the range of imagination, fantasy, recklessness. The stories transcend the bounds of realism as easily as they invent a character, but it is always a human invention, even when they revel in linguistic exuberance. Indeed, we can put this more directly. An oral culture commits itself to the human situation in a sense that Symbolism tries to evade. It assumes the integrity of the Person and the validity of temporal life: it has no interest in the inscrutable silence of Symbolism. What Yeats missed in modern literature, besides 'excess', was 'emotion of multitude', a resonance of feeling which is primitive and fundamental. The modern well-made play or poem could have everything necessary for high art, he said, except emotion of multitude: unless it somehow touched and stirred that deep, primitive sense of life, it was bound to be meagre, superficial.

I am arguing that Yeats sought emotion of multitude and excess and found them in Celtic legends and never released himself from the human images they sponsored. If he revered the aristocratic hauteur it was because this was the nearest gesture he could find in history to the excess he found in legend. This partly explains one of the chief differences between the poems of Yeats and of Eliot. If we think of characteristic poems by Eliot, we can easily imagine them as paintings, or sculptures, or string quartets: this is what we mean, after all, when we say in some desperation that 'The Waste Land' has Cubist form. But Yeats's characteristic poems are cries, laments, prayers, stories, legends, rebukes; human sounds rather than objects. This does not mean that he neglected to 'make' his poems. It means that the making of a poem, for him, largely consisted in making the sounds more and more responsive to a human occasion, real or imagined. In the 'General Introduction to My Work' he said that he tried to make the language of his poems 'coincide with that of passionate, normal speech'. 'It was a long time,' he said, 'before I had made a language to my liking; I began to make it when I discovered some twenty years ago that I must seek, not as Wordsworth thought, words in common use, but a powerful and passionate syntax, and a complete coincidence between period and stanza.'[1]

We must try to be more specific about this. Yeats wanted a language capable of registering the full life of man; body and

[1] ibid., p. 521.

soul, matter and spirit. He might have wished for a better reality than the one proferred by his senses, but he laboured with the given, with 'the sigh of what is'. The human situation, to Yeats, is the place of long memory, where values are audible from generation to generation. This, indeed, is Tradition.

Tradition as Voice. Eliot spoke of Tradition as if it were a visual field upon which the great works of the past figure as 'monuments'; it is his own word in 'Tradition and the Individual Talent'. The genuinely new work that makes a difference is then inserted, placed on the field, and it alters the map; the entire configuration is changed. A man takes intellectual possession of his tradition, then, by inspecting it and taking in a simultaneous impression of the monuments laid out on the ground. But Yeats thought of tradition in quite different terms; as a choir of voices in which the new voice is heard. The values of the past are not seen or inspected, they are heard, passed along through the generations in story, song, and rhyme. A race is unified because the passions of its people have gathered around a few images. The continuity of these passions is the emotion of multitude. This is what Tradition means, the concert of passions and the images that engage them. The individual talent is the 'excess', the flare of personality.

This explains why Yeats resorted to the drama. There is no more accomplished form for the representation of human life as a fully engaged experience, with all the faculties working at full stretch. Drama is the imitation of an action, we are told; action, not vision or consciousness. It is committed to the body, to gesture, to the paradigm of conflict, to beginning, middle, and end. It cannot easily reduce itself to a single faculty; or if it does, the reduction is immediately clear. Drama works by the justice of rival voices; it does not favour the fixed point of view. (And we recall again from the 'General Introduction' Yeats's remark: 'I hated and still hate with an ever growing hatred the literature of the point of view.') But above all, drama presents human life in the image of bodies in animation: in that sense it is the most human art. We often think that Yeats's plays are impossibly rarefied: we think this until we see them well played, and then we find that except for the very earliest plays they are much more resilient, much harder than their literary reputation has suggested.

Indeed, it is quite wrong to think of Yeats's plays as if they were translations of Maeterlinck; just as it is wrong to think that his dealings with the Japanese Noh drama were merely exotic intellectual excursions. The fact is that he wanted a form of drama which would be simple, direct, stark, and which would get rid of the 'furniture' of the modern well-made European play. He wanted to throw out the furniture, the mimicry, the busy acting. But he was always certain that drama is true because it is dynamic; it is the dynamic element which bridges the gap between consciousness and experience. This is what he had in mind in that passage in 'The Irish Dramatic Movement' in which he wrote:

'There are two kinds of poetry, and they are commingled in all the greatest works. When the tide of life sinks low there are pictures, as in the "Ode on a Grecian Urn" and in Virgil at the plucking of the Golden Bough. The pictures make us sorrowful. We share the poet's separation from what he describes. It is life in the mirror, and our desire for it is as the desire of the lost souls for God; but when Lucifer stands among his friends, when Villon sings his dead ladies to so gallant a rhythm, when Timon makes his epitaph, we feel no sorrow, for life herself has made one of her eternal gestures, has called up into our hearts her energy that is eternal delight. In Ireland, where the tide of life is rising, we turn, not to picture-making, but to the imagination of personality—to drama, gesture.'[1]

That was in 1904, the year in which the Abbey Theatre tried to restore 'Cormac's ruined house'.

I would bring a few things together at this point. Yeats's commitment to an oral culture held him to people, place, and time. His commitment to Tradition as Voice was a feeling for the roots of things, memory, familial metaphors, all those continuities which persist in change. His commitment to drama was an assent to time and limitation.

There is much to be said about these and other commitments, and even more about their relation, one to another. I would emphasize only one point. Eliot's poems, in which we share the poet's separation from what he invents, tend to present the essential figure of life as paradox; the simultaneous presence of incompatible things on the field of life, these being resolved by

[1] *Explorations, supra*, p. 163.

the religious faith that transcends them. Yeats's poems tend to present human life in the mode of drama, conflicts in place and time; value resides in the conflict, not merely in the victory. Hence, among other advantages, Yeats can free himself from the obsession with the transience of things which is one of the burdens of a visual culture. Eliot's poems concede that life may offer a few dazzling moments in which time stands still, but everything else is, as one of his poems says, 'a waste sad time stretching before and after'. In Keats's great Ode permanence is conceded to the nightingale's song; natural processes work benignly, it seems, in favour of birds, while man languishes, worn down by the hungry generations. This is very much the note of a visual culture. When Keats says of the nightingale's song:

> The voice I hear this passing night was heard
> In ancient days by emporor and clown. . . .

those to whom tradition is a 'speaking' from father to son will protest that there are also human continuities audible in precisely this way from generation to generation. In visual cultures it is very difficult to feel the continuities from one generation to another, because so much feeling is overwhelmed by intimations of waste and decay. Within an oral culture it is easier to reconcile oneself to the temporal, the limited, the finite, because these are the very conditions of Voice. In this sense, 'all lives that has lived'. Indeed, the best 'answer' to Keats's 'Ode to a Nightingale' and its image of man's fate is Yeats's 'Meditations in Time of Civil War'. When Yeats looks at Sato's gift, the sword five hundred years old, he is just as deeply moved as any other qualified spectator from any culture, but he does not see it as an emblem of man's transience. In fact, the continuities figured in Keats's bird-song are shown as proceeding, in time, from father to son; so that instead of the temporal appearing a poor second to the permanent, its characteristic quality is a continuous splendour. Thinking of the sword, Yeats says:

> In Sato's house,
> Curved like new moon, moon-luminous,
> It lay five hundred years.
> Yet if no change appears
> No moon; only an aching heart

Conceives a changeless work of art.
Our learned men have urged
That when and where 'twas forged
A marvellous accompliment,
In painting or in pottery, went
From father unto son
And through the centuries ran
And seemed unchanging like the sword.
Soul's beauty being most adored,
Men and their business took
The soul's unchanging look;

which means, I suppose, that men and their business or the pro-
ductions of Time, if only they are sufficiently 'accomplished',
have as much of Eternity's splendour as we can conceive or desire: enough is enough.

This is not, in Yeats, a flood of sentimentality, because he
knows that the cost of man's achievement is high. In 'Two
Songs from a Play' he says:

Everything that man esteems
Endures a moment or a day.
Love's pleasure drives his love away,
The painter's brush consumes his dreams;
The herald's cry, the soldier's tread
Exhaust his glory and his might:
Whatever flames upon the night
Man's own resinous heart has fed.

But if the price is high, Yeats is prepared to pay it; and even
when he thinks of human life as a wound, he rarely irritates it.
A typical moment is the little poem 'Consolation', from the sequence 'A Woman Young and Old':

O but there is wisdom
In what the sages said;
But stretch that body for a while
And lay down that head
Till I have told the sages
Where man is comforted.

> How could passion run so deep
> Had I never thought
> That the crime of being born
> Blackens all our lot?
> But where the crime's committed
> The crime can be forgot.

This tone is unusual in modern literature, which rarely forgives and never forgets the crime of death and birth. One has only to think of the energy D. H. Lawrence had to expend in driving his readers to acknowledge the law of temporal limits. Indeed, a good text to put beside Yeats's antinomies of day and night is Lawrence's *Apocalypse*, especially that part in which he gives a free-wheeling gloss upon the two 'witnesses' of *Revelation*. He says that they are 'rivals, dividers, separators, for good as well as for ill'; they are 'the rivals within a man's own very nature', they give 'the two alternate forms of elemental consciousness, our day-consciousness and our night-consciousness'. They are witnesses to life, Lawrence says, because 'it is between their opposition that the Tree of Life itself grows, from the earthly root'. And all the time, he says, 'they put a limit on man. They say to him, in every earthly or physical activity: Thus far and no further. They limit every action, every "earth" action, to its own scope, and counterbalance it with an opposite action. They are gods of gates, but they are also gods of limits: each forever jealous of the other, keeping the other in bounds. They make life possible; but they make life limited.'[1]

   This is very much in Yeats's idiom; the acknowledgement of conflict within the single state of man, and at the same time the further acknowledgement that value resides in the conflict itself. Eliot, in these circumstances, would tend to resolve the dispute by direct appeal to a higher authority: Yeats made most of his poems from the dispute itself. Think how often, in Yeats's poems, the antinomies of day and night are featured as rival claims upon our feeling; in a poem like 'Father and Child', for instance:

> She hears me strike the board and say
> That she is under ban
> Of all good men and women,
> Being mentioned with a man

[1] D. H. Lawrence, *Apocalypse* (London. Secker, 1932), pp. 146-9.

That has the worst of all bad names;
And thereupon replies
That his hair is beautiful,
Cold as the March wind his eyes.

But a rivalry of this kind is resonant only when the human situation is acknowledged as valid, in and through and despite its transience. If the human situation is deemed illusory or a mere construction of the human imagination, such rivalries are meaningless.

We need a poem, to bring these speculations into order. And, after that, we must tackle those poems, two especially, which would seem to undermine my general argument about Yeats. For the first poem I choose 'Coole Park, 1929', not one of Yeats's most imperious performances but for that reason one of his most characteristic poems. Like many of Yeats's poems it 'moralizes' a landscape—the swallows, a sycamore, a lime-tree, the great house itself. We think of it as an eighteenth-century mode of poetry, and this is proper especially if we think of the tradition inherited from such poems as Jonson's 'To Penshurst', the verse letters, and so on. In this tradition there is a direct relation between the ascription of beauty and the acknowledgement of truth and merit; as the handsome scene at Coole Park is the place of great deeds, the fine things done and thought and said within the house, 'a dance-like glory that those walls begot'. As in 'The Municipal Gallery Revisited' and 'In Memory of Major Robert Gregory', the 'genius of the place' is given through the people who visited or lived there; Douglas Hyde, Yeats himself, Synge, Shawe-Taylor, Hugh Lane, and the great lady herself:

They came like swallows and like swallows went,
And yet a woman's powerful character
Could keep a swallow to its first intent;
And half a dozen in formation there,
That seemed to whirl upon a compass-point,
Found certainty upon the dreaming air,
The intellectual sweetness of those lines
That cut through time or cross it withershins.

The certainty found upon the dreaming air is the 'accomplishment' invoked in 'Meditations in Time of Civil War', a splendour flowing through the generations into a house, a person, a deed, a thought. And the lines cut through time not to destroy it but to mark its possibilities, like a flare. In a difficult poem, 'Stars at Tallapoosa', Wallace Stevens posits lines 'straight and swift between the stars' which have nothing at all to do with the sea-lines or the earth-lines; we think of them as pure acts of the mind, performed by man for his pleasure and because he must. But the lines that Yeats praises are continuous with the earth-lines and the sea-lines, they are these articulated in speech, grace, and accomplishment. And lest this be lost through a breach of tact or a failure of memory, Yeats introduces a qualified witness, of a later generation, to remember what should be remembered:

> Here, traveller, scholar, poet, take your stand
> When all those rooms and passages are gone,
> When nettles wave upon a shapeless mound
> And saplings root among the broken stone,
> And dedicate—eyes bent upon the ground,
> Back turned upon the brightness of the sun
> And all the sensuality of the shade—
> A moment's memory to that laurelled head.

The shade is Hopkins's 'dapple', Whitman's 'drift', Stevens's 'Summer', the 'dark declivities' in another poem by Yeats himself; it is the plenitude of things. And the sensuality is the 'brown hair over the mouth blown', in a poem by Eliot, or the 'love's play' in another poem by Yeats. And both the shade and the sensuality are in time and place.

We are given this through the speech of the poem; common speech sharpened to an aristocratic grace, in keeping with Yeats's belief that the best things in life come from the peasant and the aristocrat. It is a commonplace that the high literature of the twentieth century has set itself to undermine the assumptions of the middle class. This is one of the reasons for which many high poets have repudiated common speech. Yeats approved of the object but not the means. He criticized the middle class by showing its members a common speech tempered to a new strength. But he gave nothing away. He would not hand over to the 'hot-faced bargainers and money-changers' the language they had wounded; he would show the healing properties of intelligence and grace. From the peasants he would learn 'emotion of multitude'; from the aristocrats, 'excess': and he would bring those values into a common speech which would shine with a new resilience. If the new speech rebuked the old speakers, all the better: this is what fine speech is made to do:

> You gave, but will not give again
> Until enough of Paudeen's pence
> By Biddy's halfpennies have lain
> To be 'some sort of evidence',
> Before you'll put your guineas down . . .

And later in the same poem:

> Let Paudeens play at pitch and toss,
> Look up in the sun's eye and give
> What the exultant heart calls good
> That some new day may breed the best
> Because you gave, not what they would,
> But the right twigs for an eagle's nest.

In pitch and toss the players look up at the pennies and then down at the ground. In another poem Yeats would praise the 'lidless eyes that face the sun'; and the prefatory poem to *Responsibilities* says, 'Only the wasteful virtues earn the sun.' Whoever looks directly into the sun is an aristocrat of feeling if not of birth; the wasteful virtues are the fine 'excess'. So Yeats is using an uncommonly fine common speech to rebuke those who treat common speech as their own property and abuse it accordingly.

I have argued that 'Coole Park, 1929' is a typical Yeats poem; what is true of this poem is true of the vast majority of his poems from 'Adam's Curse' to the very last pages of the great book: these poems choose the living world for text, they are poems of place, time, memory, voice, conflict, personality. I do not find there a single poem in which Yeats releases himself from these obligations: he never composed a Supreme Fiction. That he occasionally wished to do so, I would not deny: the poems that spring to mind at once are, of course, the two Byzantine poems.

I have argued on another occasion[1] that the best way to read Yeats's *Collected Poems* is to think of it as dramatizing a great dispute between Self and Soul; Self being all those motives

[1] Denis Donoghue and J. R. Mulryne, ed. *An Honoured Guest* (London. Edward Arnold, 1965).

which tie one to earth and time, Soul being the freedom of imagination transcending the finite. The dispute was never resolved. Yeats would lend himself to one side or the other, but always with misgivings, knowing the cost of severance. This is my chief quarrel with those who would read the Byzantine poems as if they were written by Wallace Stevens: these poems are not parables about the free imagination; they are poems about the dispute of Self and Soul at a time when old age and approaching death seem to vote resoundingly for Soul.

'Sailing to Byzantium' begins with the old man leaving the world and human life, looking back at the sensuality of the shade; partly in wonder, partly in pathos, partly in self-pity. In the second stanza the Self is separated from Soul, as Dublin—shall we say—is separated from the 'holy city of Byzantium'. The third stanza is a prayer to the new household gods to destroy the antinomies of day and night, resolving everything now in 'the artifice of eternity'. (Yeats still knows the limitations of this device; if it is eternity it is also artifice.) The last stanza is a furious promise, as if in atonement for all the selfish motives of a temporal life:

> Once out of nature I shall never take
> My bodily form from any natural thing,
> But such a form as Grecian goldsmiths make
> Of hammered gold and gold enamelling
> To keep a drowsy Emperor awake;
> Or set upon a golden bough to sing
> To lords and ladies of Byzantium
> Of what is past, or passing, or to come.

I wonder if it has been noted what a curious song the bird is to sing; almost as strange as the motto given to us by the figures on Keats's Grecian urn. We are out of nature, in Byzantium, in eternity, and yet the burden of the song is 'what is past, or passing, or to come'; Self-topics, with a vengeance. Kenneth Burke takes these lines to mean 'that "nature" becomes tyrannously burdensome, once the poet, having made himself at home in "grace", finds that it has been withdrawn'.[1] Nature is his term, I think, for Self, and Grace for Soul. I read the passage differently, on the principle that Yeats never made himself at home in Soul

[1] Kenneth Burke, *A Rhetoric of Motives* (New York. Braziller, 1955), p. 317.

and dragged the Self with him even into Byzantium. The last
lines seem to be a turning-back to the world of time, joining up
again, incipiently, with the sensual music of the first stanza.

   In the later poem, 'Byzantium', a poet, half in sickness, thinks
of death. But since death is by definition beyond experience he
cannot do much with it, so he finds relief and some dignity in an
engaging fancy, the neo-Platonic décor of death. And because
he is at least an amateur dramatist he wants to give his images the
thrust of action and event; hence his recourse to Dante and the
guides. For the time being, the chosen affiliations are identified
with Value, and an attempt is made to disengage these from the
'fury and the mire of human veins'. The poet's choices are tem-
peramental and suitably 'aesthetic', but once entertained they
keep the needs of the occasion at bay and work up an impressive
energy. Because they have an imposing lineage they are self-
perpetuating, and Yeats goes along with them. The feelings engaged call for the High Style, not because they carry the freight
of doctrine but because the occasion is featuring a ceremonial
event, a large showing. Officially, Yeats is opting for the moonlit dome, and he tries to work up a corresponding severity, if not
'disdain', for 'all that man is'. The second stanza begins,

> Before me floats an image, man or shade,
> Shade more than man, more image than a shade;

thus giving us the terms of an ascending sequence, spiralling toward Byzantium. Later in the poem we will be given another
set of terms, distinguished in precisely the same way: for man,
shade, and image we are now to read bird, handiwork, and
miracle:

> Miracle, bird or golden handiwork,
> More miracle than bird or handiwork,

and in any event we are directed thus beyond the natural condition. But this needs a certain pressure, and the second stanza includes one dangerously vatic moment which the style can barely
hold: 'I hail the superhuman; I call it death-in-life and life-in-
death.' But the meditative trance continues with a second version of moonlit disdain. In the third stanza the flames on the
Emperor's floor are distinguished from their counterparts in the
natural world, which otherwise they would dangerously re-

semble; similarly the dance and the 'agony of trance'. And then, thinking of the dolphins that carry the human souls to the next world, Yeats 'makes the mistake' of adverting to their 'mire and blood'. Now immediately the dispute of Self and Soul, which seemed to have been resolved by transcendence, breaks out all over again. As I read the poem, this is the saving stanza, as the poet turns his gaze back and out to the sea of human life and the pity of the whole thing rushes into the rhythm, 'That dolphin-torn, that gong-tormented sea.' For me this act certifies the drama, and without it I would assent to the play only slug-gishly, for most of it is indeed a performance, however impres-sive. This mode of poetry is not the highest, because it can hardly have the sublimity of prophecy and anything less, on such an occasion, is bound to be a little fanciful. 'Byzantium' is a more spectacular poem than 'Sailing to Byzantium', but it is not as fine, as coherent or as just. This is not because the later poem is more dependent upon its handsome symbols but because it com-mits itself to its presumptive form at a stage somewhat short of moral understanding. It is as if 'Byzantium' were a very late draft for a poem never quite completed. Yeats is saying rather less than he seems to claim, making spectacular play with the heuristic possibilities of the symbols. The poem, in short, is weak in moral syntax. Perhaps this explains our hesitation, if we hesi-tate. The play is spectacular but heady, somewhat hysterical. A chosen tradition plays an important part in the poem, supplying most of the symbols and most of the feeling, but the function of the traditional lore is largely honorific and picturesque; most of it is present to make up a distinguished gathering. The tradition does not test, because there is not enough to test, not enough to criticize, not enough Fact to put to the measure of Value. The domes, bobbins, cocks, and dances reverberate imperiously, and Yeats draws wonderful music from these traditional instruments, but the tradition does not finally grapple with the individual talent. This is why 'Sailing to Byzantium' and—to choose an-other—'Vacillation' seem to me better poems, poems of reality and justice.

To bring this discussion toward a conclusion, there is one important qualification which I should make. I am arguing that Yeats was a much more rooted poet than we have allowed, and he was much more rooted in the oral tradition of Ireland than we have been prepared to acknowledge. We often think that he was barred from the resources of Irish culture because he did not know the Irish language. And we think that the Irish tradition was itself severely damaged when Irish ceased to be the daily language of the majority of Irishmen. Admittedly, the Irish oral tradition was not a 'going concern' at the beginning of the twentieth century: Yeats was not Homer, with all the resources of a native tradition immediately available to him, ready for his hands. And of course the continuity of the Irish oral tradition was gravely undermined by the reduction of the Irish language to minority status. But the loss of the language, though tragic, did not mean that Irish culture was totally destroyed, that Irish memory was broken, or that the old Irish world was blocked off. Partly as a result of work done by the nineteenth-century scholars, translators, folklorists, and anthologists, a great deal of the Irish tradition persisted. To put the matter bluntly: Yeats got from Irish sources what he needed for his poems; a sense of roots, a feeling of continuity, a sense of communal values issuing in speech and action, 'the dialect of the tribe'.

7

The Old Drama and the New

I

In 1920 and 1921 William Archer gave a course of lectures at King's College, London, under the title *The Old Drama and the New*. The lectures were published under the same title in 1923, with slight alteration to fit the printed page. So we may take the note of exhilaration as indicating a particularly happy occasion: Archer was to announce a renaissance in the drama. The old drama was magnificent in its own way and, in every other way, very bad; unreal, bombastic, absurd. But now, centuries later, the drama had sloughed off its absurdities and come to know itself. It is difficult to explain Archer's enthusiasm for a new art which revealed itself in such plays as *Mid-Channel, Candida, The Voysey Inheritance, The Tragedy of Nan*, and *The Silver Box*: we can only report the fact. We might also say that *The Voysey Inheritance* and *Candida* were so far superior to the plays which Archer had seen in his early days in London as to induce the feeling that they must be masterpieces. In 1897, several years after Janet Achurch's performance in *A Doll's House*, Archer was still complaining of 'The Blight of the Drama'. What he said about it is what Arnold said, that modern English drama was primitive, a provincial thing. In 1874 Henry James remarked the tawdriness of the drama in England and America, and especially the 'oppressively high moral tone', as he said, of plays 'replete with aesthetic depravity'.[1] By these standards it was easy to welcome *The Voysey Inheritance*. But Archer was not merely praising some new plays: he had a larger aim.

'We all know the meaning of "imitation," ' he says,[2] with a

[1] Henry James, *The Scenic Art* (London. Rupert Hart-Davis, 1949), p. 13.
[2] William Archer, *The Old Drama and the New* (London. Heinemann, 1923), p. 4.

degree of certainty we are unlikely to share. Indeed, he uses his
terms with some complacency. He speaks of 'the faithful repro-
duction of the surfaces of life'. The business of drama is 'to look
life straight in the face'; 'to hold a plain, unexaggerating, un-
distorting mirror up to nature'. The metaphor has the prestige
of long standing, but we recall an aphorism of Malcolm de
Chazal: 'A mirror has no heart but plenty of ideas.' The new
drama, Archer says, 'though barely a century has passed since it
definitely disengaged itself from the heterogeneous elements
which had so long overlain it, has already a long list of masterpieces to its credit; and who can doubt that the future belongs
to it?'

The immediate answer is: T. S. Eliot; whose first thoughts on
drama were conceived to refute Archer. Behind Archer there
was the figure of Lamb, whose *Specimens* enforced a distinction
between drama and literature. Eliot found the distinction accepted by Archer in one way, by Swinburne in another. Swinburne thought that plays were really literature, Archer thought
that a play need not be literature at all. But it was unnecessary to
refute Swinburne: Archer was the real danger. He is the alien
presence discernible behind Eliot's *Dialogue on Dramatic Poetry*
and the essays on Elizabethan drama. Eliot tries to show that
Archer's view of drama is superficial and vulgar. One of the
speakers in the *Dialogue* says that Archer 'knew nothing about
poetry' and therefore did not understand that 'the greatest drama
is poetic drama'.[1] In the 'Preface to an Unwritten Book' on
Elizabethan drama Eliot is obviously replying to Archer when
he says that 'the great vice of English drama from Kyd to Gals-
worthy has been that its aim of realism was unlimited'. But for
an imputation of discourtesy it would be necessary to say that he
had Archer in mind when he remarked that 'since Kyd, since
Arden of Feversham, since *The Yorkshire Tragedy*, there has been
no form to arrest, so to speak, the flow of spirit at any particular
point before it expands and ends its course in the desert of exact
likeness to the reality which is perceived by the most commonplace mind'. The next words are 'Mr. Archer'. Eliot is moving
toward a theory of drama in which the essential thing is not to
express passion but to contain it: hence the necessity of an
imperative convention, to contain the flow of feeling, drawing

---

[1] T. S. Eliot, *Selected Essays* (London. Faber and Faber, 1932), p. 50.

a circle, as Eliot says, beyond which the dramatist 'does not trespass'. Where Archer implied an evolutionary progress from the Ancients to the Moderns, Eliot countered that 'the Elizabethans are in fact a part of the movement of progress or deterioration which has culminated in Sir Arthur Pinero and in the present regiment of Europe'. That was in 1924, when it seemed to Eliot that what drama needed was also what the world needed, a form to be 'imposed upon the world of action'. The lack of such a form sent Eliot to the Greek drama when he took his first steps as a playwright. Meanwhile he attacked Archer on every feasible occasion. Realistic drama, he said, is drama 'striving steadily to escape the conditions of art', handing itself over to the actor.

This is not merely a local dispute. It is part of its time. Eliot is expressing in one idiom what Yeats and other poets expressed in their several idioms, a contempt for the middle-class audience and the actor-manager, a revulsion from the modern well-made play, an appeal to art, form, rhythm, convention. Much earlier, James criticized *Hedda Gabler* for a lack of 'free imagination', a lack of 'style'. And he wrote again of Ibsen: 'I feel in him, to the pitch of intolerable boredom, the presence and the insistence of life.' James said many things of Ibsen, and much of his report is appreciative, but he could not rid himself of the feeling that in Ibsen's plays the relation between art and life is somehow wrong, there is not enough artistic force to constrain the insistent life. The rift between the public theatre and the artist who thinks of life as an unwritten poem is complete.

I have suggested that we cannot use Archer's terms without misgiving. Eliot's terms are far closer to us, mainly because we are his pupils. There is an extraordinary sentence in the 'Preface to an Unwritten Book' which reveals the majesty of his intention. He proposes to 'define and illustrate a point of view toward the Elizabethan drama', but not merely as an essay in taste. 'It should be', he says, 'something of revolutionary influence on the future of drama.' Eliot wanted to alter the direction of drama as he would alter the direction of poetry. It is clear that in the drama he has failed. After Eliot we know the limitations of realism; we recognize the 'desert of exact likeness' when we feel the sand. But Yeats had already warned us of that desert. Besides, the alternatives to realism have their own limitations.

Eliot's own theory of drama is vulnerable. He speaks of plays as if they were receptacles for poems, anthologies of dramatic lyrics. I cannot recall that he has ever discussed the structure of a play in detail: it is always a matter of the word, a phrase here, a couplet there. Indeed, the differences between Eliot and Swinburne in this regard are slight: both men are 'verbalists'. Neither had any inkling of a *poésie de théâtre* (in Cocteau's phrase) in which the poetry consists of the whole composition and the words are the last grace of the dramatic rhythm. Eliot thought that the main job was to get rid of the realistic play: there would then be a place for art; that is, for words.

Mediating in the dispute, I would suggest that there is an Old Drama and that the relation between the Old and the New is not a chronological matter, but a matter of attitude and assumption. We feel that we are moving from the Old to the New when we go from Shakespeare's *Henry IV* to Pirandello's *Henry IV*, and that the chronological movement is beside the point. Or from *Coriolanus* to *The Tempest*; from *The Voysey Inheritance* to *Heartbreak House*; from *An Enemy of the People* to *Peer Gynt*; from *Waste* to *Life is a Dream*. We have a similar feeling when we think of Stanislavsky and then of Artaud. The easy explanation is that we are moving from one genre to another, and that the genre dictates the tone. But the attitude, the vision, dictates the genre.

Perhaps the first distinction between the Old Drama and the New is that the Old feeds on existence, the New ranges for essence. The Old takes things as they seem to come, the New exerts upon such things the pressure of an idea, a pattern in the dramatist's mind, and the pattern is deemed to have priority. The New capitalizes upon the ambiguities of action, acting, playing, roles, making believe; the Old assumes that acting and being are one and the same. This reflects the difference between, say, *Marienbad* and *Bicycle Thieves*. With plays as different in other respects as *Dr. Faustus*, *The Silver Tassie*, and *Man and Superman*, we feel that each play comes to us, in the first instance, as the dramatist's invention, and only thereafter is it, in varying measure, a representation of human life. These plays are answerable to the writer's imagination before they answer to anything else. It is characteristic of such plays to present man as already dissociated, a partial man, living on his nerves or his spirit: the world's body is dead. *Waiting for Godot* is a New play because it registers to an unusual degree the pressure of an idea, a hypothesis. *Mother Courage* exemplifies the Old Drama because the pressure of its idea is far less than its commitment to human life, regardless of the idea. Clearly the New Drama is more sophisticated than the Old; more intellectually provocative, more a matter of ideas and perspective. For this reason it often features the play-within-a-play, as in *Life is a Dream*; or it points up the range of possible construction, as in *The Balcony*. While the Old Drama attends to man as a personal and social being, the New dissolves these relationships or parodies them in the cause of its pattern; as in *The Insect Play*. The Old Drama assumes that the important questions are moral, the New assumes that, if they exist, they pose metaphysical problems. In the *Tractatus* Wittgenstein says: 'Everything we see could also be otherwise.' The New Dramatist answers, 'Yes, of course': the Old answers, 'Perhaps; it is not, however, otherwise.' Wittgenstein also says that if there is a Value it must lie outside happening, since happening is merely accidental. The Old dramatist recognizes accident and does not understand it but he does not assume a necessary separation of accident and value. When we lose interest in an Old play we feel that it claims to be true and that the claim is bogus: when we tire of a New play, we feel to the pitch of intolerable boredom that it is merely an arbitrary construct or a 'happening'. The New play begins by saying, 'Suppose'; the Old, by saying, 'It was like this. . . .' Hence the relation between the Old play and daily life is direct and we respond to its poignancy or its venom by linking it with our own. The relation between the New play and daily life is always indirect and often so tangential that we respond to it as to one more hypothesis among many. When the Old Drama consoles, it does so by confirming the reality, the value, of daily life: when it distresses, it does so by making that life seem insupportable. The New Drama tends to criticize daily life by ignoring it.

These are generalizations to mark tendencies, nothing more. To see them in motion we should look at a masterpiece of the Old Drama and another of the New.

II

In 1934, after the failure of *Days without End*, Eugene O'Neill left the theatre and went into the desert, an appropriate place for meditation. His career was already a success, but it was attended by an air of ambiguous achievement. The work was impressive, one play added to another, but it was not good enough. O'Neill had tried everything. He had gone to school with Strindberg, Ibsen, and Chekhov; he had taken formal lessons from the Greek tragedians, he had studied the resources of symbolism. But it was not enough. By temperament, he took his themes where he found them, in places, conditions, facts, people. He tried to give his characters a representative dimension so that they would not be merely themselves; they would acquire a glow, a quality of radiance, making them memorable. But the sum had not come out right. The more he put into the plays, the less they retained. Making his characters more than themselves, he made them less than anybody. The more elms he added, the harder to believe in the desire. So he went into the desert and, eight years later, wrote *Long Day's Journey into Night*.

This is to put the matter with extreme simplicity. But we know little of those desert years, and even if we knew much more it would not help us to see the difference between the masterpiece and the earlier plays. But if we think of *Long Day's Journey* in association with *The Moon for the Misbegotten*, which deals with some of the same material much less effectively, we can make a start. The main difference between *Long Day's Journey* and the earlier plays is that now, in a far deeper sense than before, O'Neill has committed himself to his own experience. In many of the early plays he had 'used' that experience, and he would do so again; we can assume that Harry's Bar and its patrons in *The Iceman Cometh* are recalled rather than invented. But it is one thing to use an experience and another to commit oneself to it. When O'Neill used his experience in the early plays he suborned it for local colour, and sometimes to point a moral he recited a tale from memory; but it never seemed profound enough until he adorned it. There had to be something more, a bonus; so the experience had to be amplified, or raised to a higher degree. Usually he tried to turn five into ten by adding dark intimations, as in *The Emperor Jones*. But in

Long Day's Journey he commits himself to his experience without demanding that the return should double his investment. Valéry said that the Gods give poets the first line of the poem for nothing, but it is up to the poets to carry on from there, to find a second line that harmonizes with the first and doesn't disgrace its supernatural partner. In the early plays O'Neill would not leave the first line alone, he would always pester it to go beyond its contract. In *Long Day's Journey* he 'let be': the Gods had given it, let it be so. He had only to commit himself to it, and proceed from there. In *The Moon for the Misbegotten* he returns to the experience of James Tyrone, but now he has lost faith again, he reverts to the old way, adds a few myths, a few clichés, and spoils the play.

The characters of *Long Day's Journey* are people to whom something once happened. It is worth saying this before remarking that for the rest of the play nothing happens. Mary, a convent-educated girl who might have become a nun, fell in love with a romantic actor. Tyrone, the actor, was once praised by Edwin Booth, but he sold his soul to a popular 'vehicle' and killed a notable talent. Jamie, a brilliant boy, was expelled from college. Edmund, the failed poet, once took to the sea and discovered its freedom. These events are now over; the pain and sweetness of their recollection remain, imprisoning their victims in corresponding images of value and desire. When Edmund is drunk he reverts to the sea, now inordinately heroic in his Conradian memory. In Shakespeare Tyrone finds the standard by which he condemns himself, the nobility which makes everything else seem sordid. Jamie's decadence is shamed in the sight of a greater decadence, in the poems of Baudelaire, Dowson, Wilde. Mary retreats to her father's house, a heaven-haven in memory. Nothing will happen; we are not watching *Ghosts* or *Hedda Gabler*. These people will not break away into freedom or romance, open wide the windows: there are no wild ducks. The Tyrones look back, or yearn back, to the first colours of life. Fate gave them the first line of their lives for nothing, but they have not carried on from there in the same glad spirit, they have not written their poems. So an action is begun, and the victims suffer its consequences. We know that under certain auspices it is possible to equate Action and Passion. Thomas's first speech in *Murder in the Cathedral* urges this equation:

They know and do not know, what it is to act or suffer.
They know and do not know, that action is suffering
And suffering is action. Neither does the agent suffer
Nor the patient act. But both are fixed
In an eternal action, an eternal patience
To which all must consent that it may be willed
And which all must suffer that they may will it,
That the pattern may subsist, for the pattern is the action
And the suffering, that the wheel may turn and still
Be forever still.[1]

Thomas can transcend the dichotomy of action and passion by equating them, appealing to the higher term, the will of God, which reconciles them. But when the higher term is missing, or when the identification with the will of God is refused, the terms split apart. There is a passage in *Little Gidding* which ponders this situation; when action and passion split apart, we are told, action becomes mere motion:

Where action were otherwise movement
Of that which is only moved
And has in it no source of movement—
Driven by daemonic, chthonic
Powers.

This is an accurate description of *Long Day's Journey*. For these characters there is no higher term to resolve or contain the passion: this is the degree of their exposure. They are driven by what O'Neill elsewhere calls 'the Force behind'. Mary can forget the present pain by remembering the pleasure of her childhood, but the cost is that she cannot remember anything else; her recession to childhood is thus 'fated': 'None of us can help the things life has done to us. They're done before you realise it, and once they're done they make you do other things until at last everything comes between you and what you'd like to be, and you've lost your true self for ever.'[2]

It is hard to think of this play as a tragedy if we insist upon tragic heroes and roles which they assume with a more or less steady march into the future. Unless we are prepared to admit the tragic spirit when the motives are ambiguous and barely

[1] T. S. Eliot, *Collected Plays* (London. Faber and Faber, 1962), p. 17.
[2] Eugene O'Neill, *Long Day's Journey into Night* (London. Cape, 1956), p. 53.

conscious, we must look for another name. But this is hardly necessary. Northrop Frye has been discussing Tragedy in terms which suit our present occasion. We come close to 'the heart of tragedy', he says, 'when the catastrophe is seen, not as a consequence of what one has done, but as the end of what one is'. Hence 'the Christian original sin, the medieval wheel of Fortune, the existentialist's "dread" are all attempts to express the tragic situation as primary and uncaused, as a condition and not an act, and such ideas bring us closer than Aristotle's flaw (*hamartia*) does to the unconscious crime of Oedipus, the unjust death of Cordelia, or the undeserved suffering of Job'.[1] In O'Neill's play 'the Force behind' has so arranged things that the characters are what they are; and, being what they are, they are driven along those fateful lines. Harold Rosenberg distinguishes between a personality and an identity in terms which clarify *Long Day's Journey*. A character in a play has an identity when there is a role available to him and he is sufficient to take it up. He is a personality where no role is available or he is insufficient to it.[2] We find this situation so often in daily life that we are not surprised to see it in the theatre. Hamlet at the beginning of the play is merely a personality: however richly endowed, he is insufficient to the only role he is offered, the Revenge Hero. Later, after his return from England, he becomes an identity; he is now sufficient to the role, and identified with it. In *Long Day's Journey* the tragic condition is the fact that no roles are available to these particular people. So, even if they have very few qualities, the qualities they have are in excess of their occasions; they are spiritually unemployed. The play is saved from tedium by the fact that we don't know, at any moment, whether the several uneasy factors given at the start will be kept apart and separately disposed, or whether they will be brought into sinister conjunction. 'And then life had me where it wanted me,' Tyrone says: the action of the play is the action of Fate in doing this, getting these people where it wants them.

This is where the idea of Original Sin is relevant. For the local ills of life O'Neill often implies specific cause; cause in

[1] Northrop Frye, *Anatomy of Criticism* (Princeton. Princeton University Press, 1957), pp. 282 fol.
[2] Harold Rosenberg, 'Character Change and the Drama': *Symposium*, Vol. III, July 1932: reprinted in Irving Howe (editor), *Modern Literary Criticism* (New York. Grove Press, 1958), p. 70.

heredity, childhood, society, and so forth. But there is a residue
of pain and evil for which no historical cause can be assigned. It
might be argued that O'Neill's presentation of this evil in social
and biological terms is a secular version of the Christian belief in
Original Sin. According to this belief we inherit a categorical
guilt; in O'Neill's version we are never free from the evil of being born and the second evil of being the children of our parents.
The argument might be extended. When O'Neill gave up his
Catholicism, he did not shed the secular patterns of that faith.
He could not be a Pelagian, denying Original Sin: he continued
to believe in evil and guilt as categorical conditions. The Christian believes that Christ and the Church mediate between that
guilt and his own soul; that Christ's sacrifice was accepted for
that end. If you give up the Christian faith and yet retain belief
in a secular version of it, you must find some other means, some
mediation between yourself and the inherited guilt. There is no
evidence that O'Neill solved this problem, and every evidence
that it plagued him. The only way out was to assume an universal determinism and live under its shadow.

I suppose the main feature of Determinism is the transfer of
motive and decision from the personal agent to the scene in
which he acts. And its first effect is to surround the terms 'agent'
and 'act' with limitations more or less severe. We are deter-
minists if we feel that the 'real' decision is taken elsewhere, that
human choice merely 'seems', that the moving Force is more or
less indifferent to personal will. A classic statement is Strindberg's Preface to *Miss Julie*; especially that passage in which he
lists the several factors which combined to drive the heroine
toward disaster:

'I see Miss Julie's tragic fate to be the result of many circumstances: the mother's character, the father's mistaken upbringing
of the girl, her own nature, and the influence of her fiancé on a
weak, degenerate mind. Also, more directly, the festive mood
of Midsummer Eve, her father's absence, her monthly indisposi-
tion, her preoccupation with animals, the excitement of dancing,
the magic of dusk, the strongly aphrodisiac influence of flowers,
and finally the chance that drives the couple into a room alone—
to which must be added the urgency of the excited man.'[1]

[1] Strindberg, Preface to *Miss Julie*: *Plays*, translated by Elizabeth Sprigge
(Chicago, 1955), pp. 94-8.

If we take these factors together, we must assume a 'scene' which incorporates them in sinister fellowship. The theatre is peculiarly powerful in giving an impression of such a scene. Indeed, Strindberg is a master of this impression only a little more authoritative than O'Neill, as a master is more authoritative than his pupil. Let us say that the gift of impression is common to both, and in good measure. In *Long Day's Journey into Night* the unease in the personal factors is intensified by a corresponding unease in the 'scene' itself. Much of this is expressed by Mary, reasonably enough because the scene presses upon her more virulently than upon anyone else. So she says, over and over, that where she is is not her home, that she has never had a home since she gave up her first home to marry James Tyrone; since then she has been living in one-night-stand hotels and rooming houses; and now in a dreary summer-house which could never be home. There is no question of escape. Even in alcoholic dream Mary can only think of merging herself with the fog. 'I really love fog,' she says. 'It hides you from the world and the world from you. You feel that everything has changed, and nothing is what it seemed to be. No one can find or touch you any more.' Edmund takes up this theme later on, finding his release in the fog and the sea. 'The fog and the sea seemed part of each other,' he says. 'It was like walking on the bottom of the sea. As if I had drowned long ago. As if I was a ghost belonging to the fog, and the fog was the ghost of the sea.' And, outside the play for a moment, we recall Baudelaire's release in the London fog, where the harsh grip of man and his environment, subject and object, is eased.

There is no release from the hours and the days, Samuel Beckett says in his commentary on Proust, thinking of life as a bad habit. And there is a passage in 'Dance and the Soul' in which Valéry speaks of the intrinsic tedium of life and the compulsive lucidity of judgement. Both texts are relevant to O'Neill's play. One of the speakers in Valéry's dialogue names the only escape-routes; madness, drunkenness, the diverse intoxications of love, hate, greed, and power. But there is also the intoxication of action, which is most beautifully fulfilled in the Dance. Now the other speaker, Phaedrus, says: suppose a man wanted to stop being clear and, instead, to become 'light'; suppose, trying to be infinitely different from himself, he attempted to 'change his

liberty of judgment into liberty of movement'.[1] Socrates in-
terrupts to say that this would be everything, definitive and
magisterial. The unity of the Dance is not a modern invention,
though we think of Valéry and Yeats among its most loyal
students. We may call it an escape by the high road. In O'Neill's
play there is no escape from the terrible lucidity of judgement.
Each character knows the others with frightful accuracy; drunk
or sober they speak the truth. They could only save themselves
—and each other—by forgetting; and this is impossible. So they
lacerate one another; this is the form of their care, and of their
love. This is one of the many respects in which O'Neill's play is
superior to Edward Albee's *Who's Afraid of Virginia Woolf*, a
play which resembles the first in a few superficial ways. The
main difference is that Albee's play is a labour of hate: hate is not
only its material but its motive. O'Neill's play is a work, as he
says, of 'old sorrow, written in tears and blood'. The characters
tear each other to pieces because their care and love are exacer-
bated by a continuous piercing judgement: so they jerk in and
out of dialogue, twitching back and forth.

The figure the play makes in our minds, then, is a painful
rhythm of loss and gain, the gain less than the loss, until in the
end, it seems, the loss is irrevocable. Mary's regression to childhood, her slipping away from life, is the major cadence within
which lesser cadences in the same form are defined. When she
comes down the stairs carrying her wedding-gown and babbling
of Sister Martha, the drunken Jamie says: 'The Mad Scene. Enter
Ophelia!' This is the greatest regression, but the play is vivid
with smaller versions; as when Edmund says, 'It felt damned
peaceful to be nothing more than a ghost within a ghost.' If this
rhythm seems relentless, it is because it is introduced at the start
and played over and over again, with different materials, different
combinations of feeling and sound. The climax is its musical
conclusion. In that sense the principle of the cadence is inescapable, even though the precise form of its embodiment cannot, at
any moment, be anticipated. It is as if the cadence were, like the
guilt, categorical and we have merely to wait for each of its
manifestations: but we do not know when any will come.

This is how O'Neill's theatre-poetry works; it is a matter of

[1] Paul Valéry, *Selected Writings*, translated by Dorothy Bussy (New York. New
Directions, 1950), p. 195.

structure, rhythm, cadence, coming from life and flowing back
into life again. It is not, in the first instance, a verbal matter. The
easy thing to say of O'Neill is that he cannot write. He said it
himself. Edmund, O'Neill's *persona* in *Long Day's Journey*, has a
long drunken speech about his experiences at sea. The style is
high, a hectic mixture of Conrad, O'Neill, and Melville. At the
end, Tyrone, the silent audience, says: 'Yes, there's the makings
of a poet in you all right.' And Edmund says, sardonically: 'The
makings of a poet. No, I'm afraid I'm like the guy who is always
panhandling for a smoke. He hasn't even got the makings. He's
only got the habit. I couldn't touch what I tried to tell you just
now. I just stammered. That's the best I'll ever do. I mean, if I
live. Well, it will be faithful realism, at least. Stammering is the
native eloquence of us fog people.' We take Edmund at his
word; he is not a failed poet for nothing. And we accept the
identification of Edmund and O'Neill. It is easy to agree that
O'Neill lacks the finesse of words which we find in Yeats, Eliot,
Mann, or—to shame him further—Shakespeare. There are many
speeches in O'Neill's plays in which he tries to conceal the
stammer by recourse to the high style and the high bravado. But
Long Day's Journey is a poetic play because of the coherence of
its elements and the depth at which the coherence is achieved.
The elements are not, in the first instance, verbal; they are movements of feeling, gestures, relationships, the things that Yeats
called Life when he invoked two rival 'ways', the other being
Words. It is the urgency and coherence of these elements that
makes the play poetic. What we demand of the words is that
they will not shame the feelings placed in their charge: everything else is a bonus. If Shakespeare writes like an angel and
O'Neill stammers like poor Poll, this is a fair measure of the
difference between them; but it should not blind us to the fact
that O'Neill has something of that poetic and theatrical sense
which prompted Shakespeare, in *Macbeth*, to bring in the
Porter's scene immediately after the murder scene. If we put the
two men irrevocably apart, it is only after putting them, in this
respect, together. The impact of *Long Day's Journey* comes from
finesse certainly not verbal but, to a high degree, formal, a finesse
of structure; so that the excitement of waiting to see whether
the ingredients are combined in an innocent or a catastrophic
way goes along with a formal excitement; what Charles Morgan

calls 'the suspense of form', the latency of form until the form is eventually fulfilled. The form, it is hardly necessary to remark, acknowledges a life which is neither formal nor linguistic.

It is difficult to suggest this formal coherence and impossible to prove it: we can point to words on a page but we can only imply the presence of forms, sequences, and rhythms which are verbal only in one of their manifestations. In the first Act, for instance, we are given, within the first few minutes, several 'question marks', sources of unease, any one of which might develop into a major issue. Most of these have small beginnings. Mary is nervous, she has eaten little breakfast; there is the gap between her nervousness and the bluff heartiness of James Tyrone. Why have the two boys stayed behind in the dining-room? There is talk of McGuire and the Wall Street swindlers. Edmund has 'a bad summer cold'. Mary has just come back, and perhaps she is 'her dear old self again', as Tyrone says. Perhaps; perhaps not. Then there is Jamie, who, if Mary's confidence is well placed, will 'turn out all right in the end'. Another 'perhaps'. Behind these areas of trouble there is the fog. Gradually as the first Act proceeds these questions are developed in more salient order. Some, like McGuire and Wall Street, recede a little, and the feeling begins to gather around two questions: Mary's nervousness and Edmund's illness. There will be more of Jamie's squalor later on, and Tyrone's afflictions will be pursued, but just now the feeling begins to converge. And then we are ready for the second Act. None of this is straightforward: the noise you hear is not a steady march from one situation to another; the characters come and go. But this, too, is part of the emerging cadence. These people are not to act; they are to be acted upon, they behave. So it is vital that we feel the behaviour and sense the cadence; and they allow us to do so because they repeat the essential modes of their behaviour. That is why we see so many instances of Tyrone's miserliness, or Mary's nervous retreat: if identities are certified by the precision of the roles they sustain, personalities can only be divined by the rhythms of their behaviour. We are accustomed to this kind of poetry, not because we find it regularly in O'Neill but because we find it regularly in Chekhov. Eric Bentley has pointed out in his study of *Uncle Vanya* that 'what makes Chekhov seem most formless is precisely the means by which he achieves strict form—namely, the series of tea-drinkings, arrivals, departures, meals, dances, family gatherings, casual conversations, of which his plays are made'. 'His method,' Bentley says, 'is to let both his narrative and his situation leak out, so to speak, through domestic gatherings, formal and casual. This is his principle of motion.'[1] I would prefer to call it his dramatic rhythm and to say that his special device is to let the private feeling slip out from the gaps in the public occasions; as in the second Act of *The Three Sisters*, the social occasion in Prosorov's home. Chekhov has the kind of resource in the theatre which Eliot has in his early poems; the power to make human feeling jump the gaps between the words. We are accustomed to this power in Chekhov and Eliot, but we have had little cause to expect it in O'Neill, whose normal effects have been intolerably broad. And even now, when we look back on his career, we do not find there a pattern of sustained development, the blunt instrument becoming finer with use. That special gratification is not available. But there is another gratification, not as rich but rich enough, when a writer suddenly confounds us by producing a splendid work. John Crowe Ransom once remarked of *The Thinking Reed*, a novel by Rebecca West, that the book excelled 'in a form so rare that hundreds of efforts must fail in order that one may be successful'. It is never clear why the wastage must be so great. If we reduce the number of failures to decent proportion we can make the same remark of O'Neill's play. Before the arrival of *Long Day's Journey* there was little enough to be said about O'Neill except what Mary McCarthy said, that the poor man had a writing problem as other people have a money problem or a job problem. Even Eric Bentley, who spent many years trying to like O'Neill, found his patience exhausted by the effort of producing *The Iceman Cometh*. And yet, after all, we have a masterpiece of the Old Drama, proof that the thing can be done.

III

Danton's Death is based on fact, on history. It could be produced as a straight history play. But it is a masterpiece of the New Drama, none the less.

To begin with, the play issues from an imaginative figure, al-

[1] Eric Bentley, *In Search of Theater* (London. Dobson, 1954), p. 353).

most an idea, more directly than from the French Revolution. Its first irony is the implication that while the stage is occupied by great historical characters doing famous deeds, the truth of things is private, locked within the self. No significance is ascribed to the given world, the daily life, or even to the historical facts. It is like Chekhov's implication, but much more extreme. In the first moments of the play Julie, Danton's wife, tries to cheer him up and at the same time to bring him back to personal values: 'You know me, Danton.' 'Yes,' he answers, 'that's what they call it. You have dark eyes and curly hair and a delicate complexion and you always call me "dear Georges". But'—and he touches her forehead and eyelids—'what about here, and here? What goes on behind here? No, there's nothing delicate about our senses. Know one another? We'd have to crack open our skulls and drag each other's thoughts out by the tails.'[1] We are not to expect, after this, a strong relation between man and man, man and society, man and anything but himself. Samuel Beckett has spoken recently of 'the farce of giving and receiving', his answer to any intimation of a relation between one thing and another. In *Danton's Death* life is similarly bereft. We live, if we do, by dressing up in borrowed robes. This has no significance; it has nothing to do with playing a role. In the second Scene role-playing is parodied by the drunken Simon, an actor, miming the good Roman. Immediately after, the mob prepares to hang a gentleman; then he is freed, he has made a joke. The next scene is Robespierre's harangue, in which the relation between cause and effect, motive and deed, is just as oblique as in Simon. We are reminded that in *Waiting for Godot* time is passed in similar obliquities, all arbitrary, 'good' only because they last their own length. Beckett's characters do not even go through the motions of expecting reasonable things to happen; they assume that nothing will happen; hence their sad freedom to do what they like is subject to the qualification that there is nothing they particularly like. They cannot prefer one thing to another.

The source of the malaise in *Danton's Death* is the feeling that the human condition itself is radically defective, a sad mistake;

[1] Georg Büchner, *Gesammelte Werke* (Zurich. Artemis-Verlag, 1944), p. 9. Translation by Carl Richard Mueller, *Plays* (New York. Hill and Wang, 1963), p. 3.

as Danton says in the second Act: 'I'm disgusted with it all; why must men fight one another? We should sit down and be at peace together. I think there was a mistake in the creation of us; there's something missing in us that I haven't a name for—but we'll never find it by burrowing in one another's entrails, so why break open our bodies? We're a miserable lot of alchemists!'

This is a typical moment in the New Drama. In *Danton's Death* as in *Deathwatch* the self twitches and squirms within a circle which is, once for all, closed. In *Waiting for Godot* Estragon says, 'We always find something, eh, Didi, to give us the impression that we exist'; and Vladimir answers impatiently, 'Yes, yes, we're magicians.' In these plays, if the self is a construction of one's own imagination, it is a magical thing; but if the magic does not work, the alchemy fails, there are no other resources. So Danton turns back upon himself, defeated and bored, guilt-ridden, dying with ennui. Many of his speeches sound as if they were transcribed from *Oblomov*; with this difference, that at least Oblomov has Zakhar and Agafa Matveevna. When Camille tries to rouse Danton, to make him take notice, Danton turns away the appeal with a sigh and a weary smile. If France is to be left to her butchers, why not: 'What does it matter whether they die on the guillotine or of fever or of old age! But there's still something to be said for leaving the stage with a good spring in your step and a fine gesture and hearing the applause of the spectators behind you.'

So life becomes an epigram, a graceful phrase. But after a few smiles he bursts out, for the last time: 'Finally—my God, I can't hold it in any longer!—finally it isn't worth the trouble, life isn't worth the effort it costs us to keep it going.' Partly this is guilt; partly, a leak in the universe. The magic has failed. 'We're only dolls,' Danton says. 'What are we but puppets, manipulated on wires by unknown powers? We are nothing; nothing in ourselves.' Henry James said that Ibsen's plays deal with 'the individual caught in the fact'; but the individual is an individual and the fact is a fact. The shapes are clear. In the New Drama the shapes are never clear, the fact is dubious, and the individual is a function of something else, a doll sent spinning by unseen hands. *Danton's Death* is a play about magic; the magic that failed.

Another version of this, in parody, is St. Just's speech to the Assembly in Act 2, Scene 7, where he appeals to 'Nature' as an emblem of the state. Nature has no scruple, she does what she wants to do, regardless of man. If the ingredients of air are changed, if a volcanic eruption takes place, so be it, Nature goes to her business. This being so, why should those who guard the State hesitate to do what is needed, however bloody the means? 'Shall an idea not have equal rights with the laws of physics in regard to annihilating that which opposes it?' St. Just refers to the march of the world as a great sentence: many words are necessarily bloody, the 14th July, 10th August, and 31st May are like punctuation marks. In the same way, Danton no longer lives in a world of motives and actions: his actions are finished, his words have released themselves from responsibility, and a shadow between words and deeds lies over the entire play. In Act 2, Scene 10, Mercier points the moral: every phrase is a man's death-rattle; follow up your words to the point where they become flesh, then look about you and count the corpses. Danton agrees, lugubriously remarking that today they work only in flesh. Later, Barrère urges St. Just to an autonomous rhetoric in which every comma has the force of an upraised sword and every full-stop is an execution. In these New plays the shadow between words and deeds is inescapable. Beckett's comedy is incited by the thought that 'where there is nothing' there is always a word. 'A word from me and I am again,' says the voice in *Comment C'est*: 'we're talking of words, I have some still'. This is the motto of the New Drama in one extremity. 'Words have been my only loves, not many,' says the voice of an abandoned work in Beckett.[1] And in *Endgame*, when Clov threatens once again to leave Hamm, saying, 'What is there to keep me here?', Hamm answers with bleak precision, 'The dialogue.'

At this extremity the difference between the Old Drama and the New is the difference between Greek tragedy and Senecan tragedy in Eliot's formulation. 'Behind the dialogue of Greek tragedy,' he said, 'we are always conscious of a concrete visual actuality, and behind that of a specific emotional actuality.' But in the plays of Seneca, 'the drama is all in the word, and the word has no further reality behind it.'[2] Shall we say, more briefly,

[1] Samuel Beckett, *From an Abandoned Work* (London. Faber and Faber, 1958), p. 28.
[2] T. S. Eliot, *Selected Essays*, p. 68.

that in Greek tragedy we are conscious of people speaking and acting; in Seneca, we are conscious of words being spoken? In the New Drama the freedom of words is taken either as hilarious or as the last jibe of Fate. The great merit of words is that they kill time: their great limitation is that time thus killed is meaningless. If *Danton's Death* reminds of us *Death's Jest Book*, the reason is that Büchner and Beddoes are both New dramatists, pained by the vision of things falling apart. Words are useless, the magic fails, but there is nothing else. 'Words are the only defence of the mind against being possessed by thought,' Elizabeth Sewell says in *The Field of Nonsense*, but the observation cuts both ways, the trouble has two parts. 'The observer infects the observed with his own mobility,' Beckett says, glossing Proust; insisting later that 'the only world that has reality and significance is the world of our own latent consciousness'. In fact, we have an embarrassment of desolate riches; words and consciousness. If these are insufficient, there is only silence. In his later books Beckett's voices long for a silence that always defeats them. Danton says, late in the play, that he wants silence, nothingness, rest. When Philippeau answers, 'Peace is in God,' Danton counters, 'In nothingness': 'Sink yourself into something more peaceful than nothingness, and if the ultimate peace is God, then God must be nothingness. However, I'm an atheist. Damn whoever said: Something cannot become nothing! The pitiable fact is that *I am something.*'

This is one of the great moments in the play, a classic moment in the New Drama. It is easy to say that this is merely Danton's longing for the tomb. True, but it is a classic moment because it arises so beautifully, so logically, from the co-ordinates of the New. Given the assumptions on which this drama is based, it is hard to avoid an occasion on which a character begs for utter dissolution. This desire is at once individual and generic. Carried to a logical extremity, consistent with its own terms, the New. Drama issues in nothingness. To recognize this, on Danton's part, is an act of imaginative propriety. The deepest misery in the New Drama is the thought that Something cannot become Nothing. 'We're all of us buried alive,' Danton says. And yet he cannot die: 'I can't die, no, I can't die.' Near the end, at the guillotine, he invokes Nothingness again: 'The world is chaos. Nothingness is the world-god yet to be born.' (Das Nichts ist der zu gebärende Weltgott.) Being, Nothingness, to stop, to go on;

these are the terms of the New Drama, pushed far. Man in these plays is the man-o'-war bird, a shock to romantic geneticists; a bird which gets its food from water and must live near a river should not have plumage that easily becomes waterlogged. In that condition the bird cannot fly, its legs are too weak. But it is often in that condition. Something went wrong with the arrangements. Büchner's most desolate man-o'-war is Wozzeck, crazed by his condition: then, death by drowning. Wozzeck is simply there; as Heidegger said that the condition of man is to be there. He is not a character, not a personality, not an identity; he is the point of intersection where all the shadows meet. Indeed, he is no more a character than the Belsen Doctor and the pervert Captain who drive him deeper into madness, goading him as Pozzo goads Lucky. They are all projections of Büchner's imagination, and if they foreshadow the ministers in the con- centration-camps, this is easily explained; any figment of an autonomous imagination is bound to be verified, sooner or later, given world enough and time.

The shape of *Danton's Death* is simple and beautiful. Danton the hero of the Revolution has withdrawn, recalled now only as the stain of the present recalls earlier stains. The play begins at the end of March 1794, when the great deeds have left only their guilt. From now on, the hero declines into silence, with death as the grave he longs for. 'I love you as I love the grave,' he says to Julie in the first moments of the play, giving the gist of it almost before it begins. But the deeper love swallows the human love. So the juxtapositions are set in motion: action, passion, nothing; deeds, words, silence. There will be a few gestures, sudden ex- plosions, but nothing can halt the diminuendo of Danton's life. If the play seems wonderfully unified and, for that reason, poetic, it is partly because of the richness of its texture; but mostly, it is because it animates and appeals to our sense of that rhythm, that diminuendo, one of the perennial rhythms of life, Büchner exerts enormous pressure upon his dramatic image, making it his own, beyond dispute of possession, but he makes his persuasion bear upon us through our sense of this rhythm. The nearest conceptual translation is determinism, but this is useless because it does not convey the rhythm clearly enough. To come a little closer to it, without going back into the play itself, there is a remarkable letter in which Büchner writes to his fiancée: 'The individual is mere foam on the wave, greatness a mere accident, the sovereignty of genius only a puppet-play, a ridiculous struggling against an iron law; to recognize it is our highest achievement, to control it, impossible.'[1]

There is a sense in which Danton lives by this idiom, as the connoisseur of a life in which he no longer acts. He can only taste, reject, translating these gestures into words. He does these things because he must. But there is no impression, in the play, that any value resides in them; no talk of 'our highest achievement'. Danton goes beyond Büchner in extremity: he finds no value in knowledge, even when he possesses it; it is merely another thing. The rivalry of knowledge and action is an incorrigible assumption in modern literature; the next assumption being that consciousness is the only good. But Danton has gone far beyond this stage. Too bored to act, he exercises his consciousness only in the same spirit of necessity which he ascribes to getting up in the morning. In Act 2, Scene 5, he stands at the window, at night, saying: 'Will it never stop? Will the light never soften and the noise die away? Will it never be dark again and still, so that we needn't look at and listen to each other's ugly sins?' In its lyric way this is far bleaker than Beckett. Even in extremity Beckett's voices extract an uncertain gaiety from the sounds they make, while conceding in sober moments that no sound is as sweet as a total silence. *Danton's Death* would be a demoralizing play if it were written in accordance with its hero's official stance. The fact that it is a deeply moving and invigorating play is partly due to Danton's pervasive 'presence', the impression that there could be nothing more 'positive' than the conscience which reduces his life to nothing. Danton is the conscience by which he has judged himself, before the play begins, and the presence by which everything else is now to be judged: he is heroic in the measure of those attributes he has disowned. So his nihilism is entirely consistent with the vitality of the play in which he lives; and this vitality goes along with the formal coherence which makes the play poetic. The juxtaposition of private and public worlds, earth and the void, deeds and words, assertion and scruple: these are the terms in which the theatre-poetry lives. We say that the play is a remarkable

[1] *Werke, supra*, p. 235. Translation by J. P. Stern. See his *Re-Interpretations* (London. Thames and Hudson, 1964), p. 95.

achievement of style, if we mean the power, the reverberation, with which the elements of the play cohere.

IV

In suggesting a distinction between the Old Drama and the New I have avoided taking extreme examples, such as the *Henry IV* of Pirandello and the Shakespeare history-play. Indeed, in a dim light the two plays examined might easily be thought to be of the same kind. What divides them is the different network of assumptions on which they are based. Stated baldly, these would be enough to cause a quarrel in any gathering. Indeed, the hostility cannot be evaded, however delicate the form in which the values are embodied. But in these plays the hostility does not seem to obtrude. I can only think that the nature of drama itself is somehow a cause of peace; by building conflict into the very nature of drama, the art seems to allow for radical dissension without leaving us in warlike mood. In poems and novels a basic disagreement in substantive values is an inescapable cause of distress. But in drama the juxtaposition of rival voices fosters an impression of justice; by contrast, poems and novels often seem one-sided and authoritarian. I can account for this impression in no other way. This is why we find it easy to entertain Tourneur and Ibsen, Büchner and O'Neill, Pirandello and Shakespeare, in the same theatre. It may also account for the persuasiveness of the 'dramatic' theory of literature; that the speaker in a poem is like a character in a play, and we attend to him to enable us to imagine modes of being different from our own. Dramatic patterns which we seek in non-dramatic poetry are far more engaging than literary patterns sought in drama; we feel that the former are somehow 'on the right lines', while even the perceptions issuing from the latter have an air of fabrication. This may have something to do with what Eliot called 'a kind of doubleness' in the poetic drama, 'as if it took place on two planes at once'.[1] Eliot was thinking of Marston, but he was responding to an impression, I think, characteristic of the greatest drama; that it does not run on a single line. The form of drama is a chord, not a monotone. The Old Drama seems to me sounder in principle than the New; its substantive values warmer, more

[1] T. S. Eliot, *Selected Essays, supra*, p. 229.

humane; less dependent upon an imperious imagination. But the New Drama is objectionable only when it is a monotone, when the case is 'rigged' so wilfully as to be unjust, when the other possible voices are silenced. It is hard to avoid this impression in thinking of New plays like *The Birthday Party* and *The Room*, where the possibilities of life are arbitrarily reduced to a monotone and the imagination is never forced to criticize itself. The justice of rival voices, the 'doubleness' of *Danton's Death*, is the moral counterpart of its theatre-poetry; where all the elements, disparate in themselves, wonderfully cohere.

8

Action is Eloquence

One of D. H. Lawrence's finest stories is 'Odour of Chrysan-themums'. One of John Crowe Ransom's finest poems is 'Pre-lude to an Evening'. In both, action is eloquence; eloquence is the depth and coherence of the action. And again; in both, words alone are *not* certain good.

'Odour of Chrysanthemums' begins with a coal-train coming from Selston and a woman walking toward Underwood. The woman, standing aside, is 'insignificantly trapped' between the train and the hedge, thus prefiguring the much more deathly trap later on, the 'mouse-trap' in the coal-pit where a man, Walter Bates, is smothered to death. This first scene is dusk, an in-between time, the birds are scared off by the noise of the train and when the train passes the scene is one of abandonment, stagnation. The miners coming out of the pit are 'shadows', diminished. There is a cottage, 'three steps down from the cinder-track'; in the little garden there are flowers, apple-trees, and pink chrysanthemums like clothes hung on bushes—a seemingly in-nocent image to be tested later when the chrysanthemums are linked to alien experience; for the moment, the flowers are handsome in our minds. At this point the scene is dominated by Elizabeth Bates, Walter's wife: she is five months pregnant, 'im-perious', 'set', mistress of silence, disillusionment and pertinacity. We are to think of her, in a preliminary image, as part of the imperious, possessive world of daylight; separated from the dark, intimate world of the pits. Her life is an ode to Duty; she protects her children and possesses herself. When her little boy John tears at the chrysanthemums and drops the petals on the ground she rebukes him; then she breaks off a twig of the flower and puts it in her apron-band, it is her possession, her trimming, it adorns her. Her father, an engine-driver, stops his engine when it reaches the cottage; Elizabeth gives him tea, bread and butter and enough conversation to rebuke him for his intention of marrying again. There is talk of Walter who has 'another bout on', hitting the bottle in the 'Lord Nelson'. When Elizabeth goes back into the cottage she begins the long, angry wait for her husband: darkness settles down, 'uncertain', Elizabeth's daughter Annie comes home from school, and they have their tea in gloom, anger, and fear. Annie sees the flower: 'Don't they smell beautiful!' But her mother rejects it now: 'No,' she said, 'not to me. It was chrysanthemums when I married him, and chrysanthemums when you were born, and the first time they ever brought him home, drunk, he'd got brown chrysanthemums in his button-hole.' Marriage, birth, drunkenness, sorrow, and later on death itself: the chrysanthemums are life itself, their odour the smell of life: Annie rushes to receive it, Walter wears it, but Elizabeth will have it only if it embellishes her. In the kitchen the wait continues; the children try to escape into their 'play-world', Elizabeth has no escape except in recrimination. 'He'll come home when they carry him'; and he does. 'He can lie on the floor'; and he will. 'I know he'll not go to work tomorrow after that'; and he won't. The children are sent to bed; Elizabeth goes to look for Walter, but tentatively and with the delicacy of her station; Walter's old mother comes to keep her forlorn company. Walter has been hurt: 'a lot o' stuff come down atop 'n 'im'. In fact, he is dead. The colliers bring his body into the cottage, into the parlour: 'There was a cold, deathly smell of chrysanthemums in the room.' He is stripped, laid out, washed. Elizabeth looks at him:

'In her womb was ice of fear, because of this separate stranger with whom she had been living as one flesh. Was this what it all meant—utter, intact, separateness, obscured by heat of living? In dread she turned her face away. The fact was too deadly. There had been nothing between them, and yet they had come together, exchanging their nakedness repeatedly. Each time he had taken her, they had been two isolated beings, far apart as now. He was no more responsible than she. . . . And her soul died in her for fear: she knew she had never seen him, he had never seen her, they had met in the dark, and had fought in the dark, not knowing whom they met nor whom they fought. And now she

saw, and turned silent in seeing. For she had been wrong. She
had said he was something he was not; she had felt familiar with
him. Whereas he was apart all the while, living as she never
lived, feeling as she never felt.'[1]

This is not yet the end of the story, but we may pause here to
make a few comments.

The roots of the story are given, by implication, in 'Notting-
ham and the Mining Country', where Lawrence describes his
origin, the life, the mines. The pit, he says, 'did not mechanize
men'.[2] In fact, the miners working underground achieved a
strange intimacy, 'a contact almost as close as touch, very real
and very powerful'. This persisted even above ground, where the
miners lived 'instinctively and intuitively', caring little about
duty and competition, continuing their fellowship in the pub.
This mode of life set the colliers apart from their wives, daylight
people concerned with welfare, hard facts, the home, the children. The rift was exemplified in their attitude to flowers: the
miner loved his garden, his flowers, with something of the
artist's love, not at all possessive; contemplative, rather. But the
women, Lawrence says, love flowers only as possessions: 'If they
see a flower that arrests their attention, they must at once pick it,
pluck it. Possession! A possession! Something added on to *me*!'
This perception, rooted in Lawrence's own early life, is the
source of the present story; the conflict figured in such terms as
male and female, darkness and daylight, acknowledgement and
possession, intuition and reason. But Lawrence exemplifies this
conflict so deeply, imagines it with such density of reference,
that it becomes, in the first instance, irrevocably itself: at a later
stage, in the second instance, it is free to join with other stories by
Lawrence to form a general theme. The 'idea' is contained in the
'image'.

So much so, that we are forced to revise the terms of the conflict: for one thing, to speak of a conflict between intuition and
reason and to find it enacted in 'Odour of Chrysanthemums' is
only part of the truth. The other part is Lawrence's attempt, in
'Odour of Chrysanthemums' and other stories, to redeem con-

---

[1] *English Review*, Vol. VIII, June 1911, p. 433: collected in *The Prussian Officer,
and Other Stories* (London. Duckworth, 1914).

[2] *New Adelphi*, Vol. III, June–August 1930, pp. 255–63, 276–85, 286–97: collected in *Phoenix*, edited Edward D. McDonald (New York. Viking, 1936).

sciousness, late as it was. On the principle that the corruption of the best is the worst, Lawrence felt that consciousness was in urgent need of redemption and that, till redeemed, it would go on sinning. Sinning against life. This partly explains why a terminology of redemption, expiation, and victimage is almost forced upon us when we read Lawrence. His victimage was a 'descent' into the rudimentary, the primitive, the aboriginal, the bodily, the 'natural'; an incarnation, on the assumption that this is where 'nature' resides, that nature is good, that good is natural, and that the right consciousness is both natural and good. It also explains why Lawrence's use of the taboo-words is in line with the redemptive motive generally and, specifically, with Christ's motive in regard to the woman taken in adultery. Finally, it suggests why the image of Christ is so potent in Lawrence's work and why, in hours of apparent failure, it was upon this image that Lawrence turned his wrath.

To return to the last moments of this story. 'Odour of Chrysanthemums' is a confession, an examination of conscience, a prayer for forgiveness, then a walk from the confessional toward the street, feeling that whatever can be done has been done and that it may or may not be enough. Upon Elizabeth the death of Walter and her vision of him lying naked and inviolate have had at least the effect of changing her attitude; the new attitude, given incipiently at the end of the story, is a conversion, a turning toward new images of value. We are made to feel that her submission to life will carry her away from 'death', even with the burden of her 'fear and shame'. The story is therefore, indeed, life-enhancing, and Walter is a correspondingly proper sacrificial victim; because it sends Elizabeth into life again under better auspices. And it liberates the reader in an analogous way, by exemplifying an instance of moral possibility. Lawrence's 'attitude' is transferred to the reader and, with it, a correspondingly vivid intention of action. The story ends:

'At last it was finished. They covered him with a sheet and left him lying, with his face bound. And she fastened the door of the little parlour, lest the children should see what was lying there. Then, with peace sunk heavy on her heart, she went about making tidy the kitchen. She knew she submitted to life, which was her immediate master. But from death, her ultimate master, she winced with fear and shame.'

The note is balance; a poise between two recognitions, but not a slick antithesis. Yet there is no constriction, the feet of the prose do not drag. Life will prevail until death prevails; in the meantime we live. Hence the tone is at once subdued, modest, and firm; as if to summarize the kind of experience which teaches, from which one learns. The diction is bare, because on the one side there is privation which will yet have to be turned to good account, and on the other there is Elizabeth's former sensibility, now recalled with shame as a bogus possession. Hence there are no metaphors, no analogies, no similes; if Elizabeth is to move out into 'life' she must do so honestly and with proper caution: there is no question of a sudden plunge into the life-stream, a merger with the life-force. Most of the effect in this passage depends, therefore, upon the syntax, which will have to be strong enough to direct Elizabeth into life and yet not boisterous, since the fateful achievement of that life is to be uppermost in her mind. So the syntax must figure a sense of radical loss consistent with the possibility of life. This is why the phrase, 'lest the children should see what was lying there', does not put a distance between Elizabeth and her husband; rather it dramatizes, with a proper apprehension, the distance always between them and now irrevocably there. The conversion itself, the turning toward life against the pressure of failure and death, is featured in the commitment to action; fastening the door, tidying the kitchen. These are the 'new' actions, corresponding to the old ones, such as the denial of the chrysanthemums, the rebuke administered to her father, and so on. The new actions are what they are, they have no strings attached: like the corpse itself, in Elizabeth's new eyes; 'After all, it was itself.'

Hence the merits of 'Odour of Chrysanthemums' are Lawrence's merits when his art achieves its own distinctive measure. These are, in brief, a remarkable sense of life, a willing commitment to the vitality of fact, a refusal of pedantry or fuss, a sense of proportion and balance among the rival claims. When he falls from this high grace the signs are equally clear; he browbeats the reader, lays a heavy hand upon the symbolism, loses measure in stridency. But in 'Odour of Chrysanthemums' it is part of Lawrence's great tact that the flowers remain flowers; they lose none of their floral nature while they serve the symbolic purposes of the tale. This is the coherence of the story; its reality and justice.

Ransom's poem exists in two versions; the original poem, written nearly thirty-five years ago, and the revised version, notably altered in 1962.[1]

The first version is a poem of eight quatrains. A man, who has been out in the world, is coming back to his wife and children. It is bound to be a difficult homecoming, because he is of a demanding turn of mind and he is about to stake a claim to his wife's soul: she must share his experience, his vision, however dreadful both. On his way home he is rehearsing a speech for the occasion. In rough paraphrase it goes somewhat as follows. 'Do not force me to give myself in to you, to the home, the children, the warmth. I have been away, I am tired, perhaps ill, but the illness cannot be cured by the domestic arts, it is too deeply part of myself. These images are monstrous to you, but you must expose yourself to them, adopting them, if for no other reason than that they are mine. So: even if the fancy is extreme and bizarre, image a confusion of dream and reality, night and day. And think that the images which have frightened you in your sleep are irrelevant, nothings, phantoms which die when you awake. Imagine now that you are giving out the oranges, the children are there, and yet you feel, with me, in the sunny room an invisible evil, preparing to strike. You are afraid: fear is part of the apparition. So you attend to your chores, but you are holding yourself apart from them: you are listening for the sounds of fear and evil. And now it is evening; you are like a waning moon, I am like Orestes, accusing the Eumenides which are now neither mine nor yours but ours. You and I are confronting the Furies; so that even if the children are hungry you will only smooth their heads, absent with me in my experience. And we meet there in the body of our fear, our evil.' There the poem ended, and it remained in that form for many years: Ransom was busy with other things. But gradually the poet came to dislike his poem. He has recently given us his reasons. The poem became, he says, 'disagreeable' to his ears, not because he tired of

<hr />

[1] The first version is given in *Selected Poems* (London. Eyre and Spottiswoode, 1947), p. 62. The second is given in *Kenyon Review*, Vol. XXV, No. I, Winter 1963, pp. 70–1; followed by Ransom's commentary, pp. 72–80. Poem and commentary are collected in the new and enlarged edition of *Selected Poems* (New York. Knopf, 1964), pp. 99–111.

its rhythms or its diction or its syntax, but because he came to think of it as a 'vindictive' poem and of its hero as 'a villain'. At the same time he wanted somehow to redeem his hero, and he was reluctant to delete him from the official record: there was clearly something in him worth preserving. So the poet took up the privilege of tinkering with the poem, altering a phrase here and there, until it became clear that he must extend the story itself. He would redeem his hero by allowing him to change; the story would go on until the speech attained a more equable accommodation, a finer justice. So he added four stanzas, as if the man, recanting, were to say: 'I would have my return a magnificant occasion, like Ulysses to Penelope. Our intimacy would not destroy my fear, rather capitalize upon it. But as I approach the house I hear a huge "No!": and I prefer to think that it is my own refusal rather than yours. I will have no tricks, no stratagems of fantasy. Indeed, I have been a prodigal husband, an even more prodigal father. I went away to escape from the knowledge of good and evil. Now I am disfigured. But every step I took has sent me back. Now I am here I will preserve the scruple of silence, because words have incited my revolt, my treason. I will creep back into the fold, making no demands except upon myself. And now in the room you "shine" on our children and this is, like the children themselves, "good".'

To moralize this a little: we are to think of husband and wife, 'one flesh', as *Genesis* says, but retaining two distinct affiliations. The wife's role is perennial, her identity and her role are one and the same: her allegiance is tribal, fundamental, varying little from generation to generation. The husband is a man of his time, a modern with the distinctly modern experience of evil. We think of him, perhaps, when Henry James invokes the 'imagination of catastrophe', when Gide propounds an *acte gratuit*, when Stevens speaks of the 'connoisseur of chaos', when Picasso describes a modern painting as a 'horde of destructions'. He is a David compelled to invent Goliaths because he must, because the image of evil must be, as Stevens says in another context, of the nature of its creator. What he brings with him, back from the world, is evil and a vision of evil; it is a contamination, he is 'the tired wolf/Dragging his infected wound'. His first desire is to make his wife share this condition: in this consists his 'villainy'. But we may risk another interpretation. The husband does not wish to be enveloped by the domestic order, his wife's order: he wants to oust that order and to replace it by a corresponding 'disorder', on Stevens's famous principle which says that 'a great disorder is an order'. The new disorder will enforce itself because it is great enough to do so: it is not a modern condition for nothing, it has grown up in a hard school. At this point the husband is propounding an Existentialist ethic: the great disorder must be daring, personal, a categorical exposure. The new condition cannot work by rote or routine: children learn by rote the Kings of France and this is innocent enough but a man puts away childish things, at whatever cost. The great disorder is perhaps Jacob wrestling with the angel.

It is perhaps worth mentioning that Ransom redeems his hero by making him an artist and allowing him to make his evil his *materia poetica*. The villain was always a modern man; now he becomes something of a poet, and the evil of his villainy becomes his *donnée*. We recall James's admonition that we must concede to the artist his *donnée*. Ransom mentions that two texts were implicated in the circumstances which prompted him to change his poem; Charles Coffin's study in the theology of *Paradise Lost* and Kenneth Burke's study in the rhetoric of religion. I am almost led to think that a third text has been forgotten; the myth of Philoctetes, which Edmund Wilson recited again some years ago as *The Wound and the Bow*. The implication of art and neurosis; neurosis the disease, art the cure; neurosis as the material of art; this is the relevance of the myth, in modern translation. In Ransom's revised poem the husband is not forced to disown his vision; rather, to contain it. The man will not impose it upon his wife: as Ransom says, 'he will not ask of her the impossible'. The artist has his wound; the wife has her own allegiance and—it is conceded—her tribal right to it. As a fruitful woman the wife has her own *donnée*; in the creation of children he has collaborated with her, but this is thereafter a domestic world. Ransom says again of the husband: 'if he desires her favours he will have to take them not on his terms but hers, which will stipulate that he must share the responsibility for the children'. And this is just. The artist will live with his neurosis as well as he can, but he must not demand that the infection be caught by his wife—or his readers: that is one of the happier offices of his art, to assimilate the neurosis and let the poor artist

live. The artist comes to accept this, but only at a late hour. The
first lines in the new section of Ransom's poem are:

> I would have us magnificent at my coming;
> Two souls tight-clasped; and a swamp of horrors.
> O you shall be handsome and brave at fearing.

The syntax makes it clear that the magnificence is theatrical as
well as erotic: this husband wants that swamp of horrors just as
keenly as the embrace; hence the two phrases, poised against
each other for an effect at once dramatic and pretentious. And
the applause in the last line is offered as if to a tragedienne in the
throes of a metaphysical shudder. But three stanzas later the
artist's will has been contained: the tragic décor is waved aside,
and the scene is now, willingly, domestic:

> I am here; and to balk my ruffian I bite
> The tongue devising all that treason;
> Then creep in my wounds to the sovereign flare
> Of the room where you shine on the good children.

And Ransom says, in gloss: 'There will be many interims yet
when he will be out in the free world again, busied in his own
way professionally. But every time he takes his leave he will
have said to them and himself: I shall return.'

If now we place Ransom's poem—the revised version—beside Lawrence's story: both are concerned with 'familiar and
familial situations'. Both assume that human relationships are
the places where vivid things happen; as here in a conversion the
wife, in Lawrence's story, turns toward the dead husband and
then toward life itself; and there, in Ransom's poem, the husband turns toward his living wife and thereby toward life itself.
The conversion, the turning, is the action, the soul of the drama.
If we ask again why Ransom changed a poem that had been received for many years as one of his most compelling works, the
answer is easy: he sought Reality and Justice in a single poem.
The first version had at least enough reality to mark its presence
in the landscape of modern poetry: but Ransom was not satisfied
as to its justice, its responsiveness to the possibility of things. The
new version would not disown the reality, but it would continue the fable until the claims of justice would be answered.

The strictly verbal part in these arrangements is small, because both Ransom and Lawrence are entirely free from the gross superstition of the Word. Erich Heller, discussing Hegel, speaks of 'the ambition of the human mind to dominate reality to the point of usurping its place', melting the flesh of reality in the aesthetic fire. And he shows that in the tradition of poetry that leads from romanticism through Baudelaire, Mallarmé, Rimbaud, and Valéry to Rilke's *Duino Elegies* and the *Sonnets to Orpheus* 'external reality has no claims any more to being real': 'The only real world is the world of human inwardness. The concrete form of this reality is the poem in its pure absoluteness. *Gesang ist Dasein.* Song is existence. . . . Imagination is reality.'[1]

The theme is inescapable in modern literature. In the first chapter of the *Enquiry concerning Human Understanding* Hume distinguishes between two kinds of moral philosophy: the first 'considers man chiefly as born for action'; the second considers him 'in the light of a reasonable rather than an active being'. It is enough to say here that from Schopenhauer to Valéry, Eliot, and Beckett modern literature has tended to yield up the terminology of action and to commit itself more and more desperately to the terminology of consciousness. This is another version of Heller's theme. Think how many modern writers, like Conrad Aiken, find their chief labour in the conversion of experience to consciousness. Admittedly the terminology of action has had a cruel passage in the twentieth century; so much so that many artists have seceded from that idiom altogether. And yet one of the crucial functions of literature today is to keep alive in the imagination a terminology that is woefully frustrated in the arena. Meanwhile the desperation that lies under the brightest images in modern literature is the result, I suggest, of two factors: the loss of the terminology of action; and the fear that the remaining idiom, the terminology of consciousness, is a blind alley, a delusion, a falsification, at best a fiddling accompaniment to the burning of Rome. Hence, among many illustrations; the frustrated parody of action and purpose in the fiction of Beckett; the equation of consciousness with an embattled virtue in the later poems of Eliot; the notion in Valéry that poetry is a rival world exhibiting an entrancing purity of mind and purpose; in

[1] 'The Realistic Fallacy': *The Listener*, Vol. 53, pp. 888–9, 19th May 1955; revised version printed in George J. Becker (ed.): *Documents of Modern Literary Realism* (Princeton. Princeton University Press, 1963), pp. 591–8.

Schopenhauer, the aspiration toward the condition of music as a relief from the bond of will and the torment of meaning. Near the end of the third Book, 'The World as Idea', Schopenhauer glorifies music as being entirely independent of the phenomenal world; a mode of ultimate expressiveness without commitment. In this spirit life is lived only as a significant spectacle; the spectacle a way of passing the time, the significance a consoling suggestiveness upon which one is not impelled to act.

Of course there is always a temptation to deal with life by making it an object of consciousness; and this can be innocent enough if the consciousness is a mode of acknowledgement. But very often the next step is that consciousness becomes the end, of which experience is the means, grist to the mill. One reason for this step is that, as Stevens implies, it is of the nature of the mind to take it. Another reason is that aesthetic answers are often more coherent than moral answers; more coherent because 'purer'. Problems intolerable in morality are often understandable if we translate them into aesthetic terms. (Sri Ramakrishna, asked why if God is good He allows so much evil in the world, answered: in order to thicken the plot.)

Lawrence and Ransom press us from 'consciousness' to 'acknowledgement' and thence toward 'action'. 'Odour of Chrysanthemums' and 'Prelude to an Evening' welcome the recalcitrance of 'external reality' and respond to it with the imagination of acknowledgement. So different in many respects, they are alike in this, that even when they want to change the ordinary universe they do not seek to dissolve it or to transmute it into words. The *world* differs from the *word* in a thousand ways, all perhaps represented by the difference of one letter; but one letter is enough.

9

Williams, a Redeeming Language

To teach, to delight, to move: Cicero's three 'offices'; a formula sufficiently flexible to sustain most discussions of literature, especially the basic considerations.

When William Carlos Williams died we knew that his entire work was now given into our hands and that we should have to make what we could of it. He had spent his life trying to bring new things into the world, poet and obstetrician, to give exact names to things long obscured under old misappellations. Now the work was over, if not done. We had the impression that the work would persist as a moral force in the world, that it would be an inspiration to young writers, and yet that it was incomplete. It would not have been completed even if he had lived many more years. Already, he had written far too much, too many poems dashed off on the assumption that anything is a poem if you say it is. Williams lived by profusion, often by waste: he corrected one poem by writing another. He thought that if one were a poet, the genuine article, anything that came from one's typewriter would be poetic. The result is that while some of his poems are miraculously fresh and true, very few of them have the finality of, say, Eliot's early poems, or Tate's. In Williams the relation between one poem and another, like the relation between language and perception, is based on the assumption that, over the course of a long life, the hidden unity will emerge. This is what we mean when we say that he trusted his own magic: he was like a witch doctor, he never knew how the magic worked, but he was always confident that it would. Thinking of his common style we think of a river insecure in its banks: failure must be treated gently because it is the defect of his quality. So we respond to his sincerity when we hear his cry.

But in the early poems of Eliot and the *Seasons of the Soul* of Tate, the question of sincerity never arises: or the question has been answered in the language, the form. We are often goaded into saying that Williams's failures, because they are so rich in stance and intention, are worth more than the successes of lesser men, but this goes too far. One day we shall have to separate the grain from the chaff and gird ourselves to throw the chaff away.

To teach: a basic duty, to have something to say. Williams had plenty to say, mostly about the fate—not too complex—of being an American; but also about things, words, history, women, and 'the poem as a field of action'. Much of this has been against the grain: hence his sentences, more often than not, are strokes of an axe; hence also his refusal to lay down the axe, even when urged to do so by consideration of friendship, urbanity, diplomacy, or the hesitation of English readers. He tried to show what it was like to be alive in a town in New Jersey; not merely the high moments, but the daily feeling of being there. He wanted to say that it was possible to be alive there, without loss of humanity or face. This explains why he wrote so much; to give the feeling of roughage and ballast. An imaginary *Selected Writings* should retain this feeling. It might include these: 'The Widow's Lament in Springtime', 'The Hunter', 'To Waken an Old Lady', 'Raleigh was Right', 'Burning the Christmas Greens', 'To Daphne and Virginia', 'The Yachts', 'These', 'Two Pendants', 'Spring and All', 'The Bull', *Paterson*, which sinks a little after the wonderful first Book but gropes up again and finishes beautifully. There should also be space for *In the American Grain*, 'The Writers of the American Revolution', the two essays on Marianne Moore, 'The American Background', and the remarkable review of *A Draft of XXX Cantos*. And the fiction: surely the collection called *The Farmer's Daughters* is one of the finest achievements in this genre, 'Comedy Entombed' a noble work. *Kora in Hell* is a little dated now, but it has remarkable paragraphs here and there; and there are letters which are almost as good as the essays, especially those of the 'forties and 'fifties when Williams was writing to Horace Gregory, Kay Boyle, Norman MacLeod, Robert Lowell, Ezra Pound, Richard Eberhart.

I often think that Williams is best understood as a grammarian; skilled in reading the signs. He had no interest in the kind of thing that interested Stevens: philosophy, ontology, epistemology, gorgeous nonsense of the mind; but he was engrossed in history, because he thought of history as signs, footprints, tracks in the mud, proof that someone has lived there. He was much closer to Davy Crockett than to Bergson, Berkeley, or Plato: one never thought of him as a suitable correspondent for Jean Wahl or Paul Weiss. When he saw a footprint he had no interest in the meaning of the experience as knowledge, perception, vision, or even truth: he just wanted to find the foot. If he saw a blackbird, he had no interest in the thirteen ways in which Stevens saw it: one way was enough, given reasonable lucidity. This is to say that Williams was a moralist, not a philosophic poet. If he was a little weak in consecutive thought, the reason was that he believed the pure reasoning powers had been in office too long; besides, his own mind worked best by pointing to things. This is what gives *In the American Grain* its remarkable animation. These things were done, Williams is constantly saying, and if we can only understand why they were done and the spirit in which they were done and the expense of that spirit, we can probably begin to understand ourselves. Conrad speaks, in a letter, of the silence of fact: Williams understood that silence, and listened to it; he wrote thousands of words, but he never thought them more important than fact.

Indeed, one of the deepest commitments in Williams is his piety toward things, the plenitude of things, their value in being what they are. Hence his delight in finding, in Marianne Moore's poems, that an apple remains an apple whether it be in Eden or a fruit-bowl; that it is not called upon to yield up its solid being so that it may take on the smear of mystery. True, there are no apples in those poems; Kenneth Burke's admonition is still in our ears. But the discrimination persists. We know what we mean when we say that Marianne Moore is a guarantor of being, refusing to will the actual out of existence in favour of a poetical transcendence which she would probably judge, in any case, a mess. Williams admires her for that scruple. For his own engagement with the actual, he has needed a language close to things, jumping the gap between subject and object. Above all, he needs a language to cut away the distorting *nebula* from feelings and attitudes; a language to redeem us from past fixations. 'No creed but clarity.' So he praised Marianne Moore again for wiping soiled words, removing the aureoles that have been pasted about

them, taking them bodily from greasy contexts. He has no
interest in Beauty.

For the poet, it comes back to speech: without true speech we
are doomed. Williams takes as a paradigm of failure the fall of
Sam Patch, the great diver whose body, in the supreme test,
wavered when he jumped 125 feet from the falls of the Genesee
River on 13th November 1826. In *Paterson* the themes gather:
the divorce of art from life, the defeat of communication, the
loss of perception in greasy speech, the boiling of pearls:

> I must
> find my meaning and lay it, white
> beside the sliding water: myself—
> comb out the language—or succumb.[1]

At its simplest, the language Williams must find, if the poem is
to be right, is agile in miming the thing seen, done, heard,
suffered. In its severest test it must yield the new thing made, not
the managed poem but the Invention. Williams knew that poems
quite unlike his own have been written and that some of them
are masterpieces. He knew this and took pleasure in it. But he
sought 'a new measure consonant with our day':

> . . . through metaphor to reconcile
> the people and the stones.
> Compose. (No ideas
> but in things) Invent!
> Saxifrage is my flower that splits
> the rocks.

This is where the commitments gather. Williams set out to
write the moral history of his country: he needed a certain language. Merely to arrange a duel with Europe was not enough. It
has been said that he never gave up fighting the War of Independence. True: hence his devotion to such writers as
Freneau, Poe, and Whitman. Sometimes he writes a belligerent,
noisy prose, like Melville in the essay on Hawthorne, because no
fight is ever finally won. But he was not a chauvinist. 'Because a
thing is American,' he said, 'or related to the immediate conditions, it is not therefore to be preferred to the finished product of

[1] William Carlos Williams, *Paterson* (New York. New Directions, 1946), p.
173.

another culture.'[1] What he wanted was the finished product of his own culture. To read widely in his work is to see that Williams has done something new in American literature because he saw what had to be done, and he had enough talent to know that the time was ripe. Hugh Kenner has described it, with American vigour. 'Dr. Williams is the first American writer to discover,' he says, 'not the phases of America that reflect what was in Europe, but the core of America that is itself, new, and so far unvocal.'[2] The core, the root, the source: this is the concern of *In the American Grain*, many of the essays, *Paterson*, the short stories, the novel *White Mule*. The people of Paterson move around, without understanding, inarticulate, because they do not understand their origin. Williams is concerned to show that the roots, understood, give new life. This is why he went to the unacademic bother of resuscitating Columbus, Cortez, the *Mayflower*, the founding of Quebec, Aaron Burr; why he took to the inspired cribbing of Cotton Mather, Franklin's *Information to Those who would Remove to America*, William Nelson's *History of the City of Paterson and the County of Passaic*. The same reason sent him to James Otis, Patrick Henry, William Bartram, Crévecoeur, Jefferson, Washington, wherever he could find the American spirit in human action, in men from his own time like Alfred Stieglitz. But history, lavish in explanation, does not explain everything. There is still, as part of the core, the irrational, the things we have to include to represent all we do not understand. So in *Paterson* Williams inserts a few letters which have nothing to do with the 'story', because he knows that the conscious story must be qualified by chance, casualty, the primitive and unconscious things. These are part of life and they must be brought, somehow, into the language if it is to be, as Williams says on the first page of *Paterson*, 'a reply to Greek and Latin with the bare hands'.

It all fits in. But how and where? Many readers of Williams feel that he is weak in structure, and they say that his breath is short, a matter of fragmentary epiphanies, as in 'So Much Depends'. And yet I should be surprised to find that the epiphanies are isolated, without the determination of some fine idea or

---

[1] William Carlos Williams, *Selected Essays* (New York. Random House, 1954) p. 154.
[2] Hugh Kenner, *Gnomon* (New York. McDowell, Obolensky, 1958), p. 42.

'moral universal' which, in their partial way, they enact. Recall
that it was Williams who wrote: 'It is hard to say what makes a
poem good, but if it is not in the detail of its construction, it is in
nothing. If the detail of the construction is not to the smallest
particular distinguished, the whole poem might as well be
thrown out.'[1] It is difficult to reconcile this with the big lumpkin
who, we are told, would not be caught dead in the company of
an idea. Besides, there is the constructive evidence of 'Tract',
'These', 'Dedication for a Plot of Ground', 'The Lonely Street',
'A Coronal'. In these poems we find Williams's life-long devotion to measure, craft, the resources of speech, the redeeming
language. Behind, there is his idea of culture as the density of
particular life. 'The burning need of a culture,' he says, 'is not a
choice to be made or not made, voluntarily, any more than it
can be satisfied by loans. It has to be where it arises, or everything related to the life there ceases. It isn't a thing: it's an act. If
it stands still, it is dead. It is the realization of the qualities of a
place in relation to the life which occupies it; embracing everything involved, climate, geographic position, relative size, history, other cultures—as well as the character of its sands, flowers,
minerals and the condition of knowledge within its borders. It is
the act of lifting these things into an ordered and utilized whole
which is culture. It isn't something left over afterward. That is
the record only. The act is the thing. It can't be escaped or
avoided if life is to go on. It is in the fullest sense that which is
fit.'[2] Stevens said, 'The natives of the rain are rainy men': what
Williams adds is the need of a sense of rain, a life of rain and
action. This is to say that Williams, in poems, essays, fiction,
letters, has undertaken to provide a grammar of American culture; American because he is American, a man with a stake in
the country, not because he thinks America is better than Athens
or Rome. If the grammar seems incomplete, the reason is, I suggest, that it lacks a religious dimension. Put Eliot's *Notes towards
the Definition of Culture* beside Williams's grammar and the point
is made. But Williams's achievement remains heroic in its dedication, its energy, its largesse.

[1] William Carlos Williams, *Selected Letters*, edited by John C. Thirlwall (New
York. McDowell, Obolensky, 1957), p. 318. Letter of 14th May 1953, to Richard
Eberhart.
[2] *Selected Essays, supra*, p. 157.

To delight: the ingratiation of style. Williams's best poems delight the mind because they show the continuing possibility of grace, delicacy, even when the *materia poetica* is ordinary. These poems offer a language, at its best, lithe, vivid, close to the contour of speech. They choose the living world for text, as Yeats said of Synge. So we read them as we read Chaucer, Wyatt, Fulke Greville, Jonson, Swift, Crabbe, Clough, Pound. But Williams, who was prepared to learn from anyone, needed someone nearer home; Whitman, who would sustain him in the belief that American speech constituted a new language, American as distinct from English and sometimes as opposed to English. In *The American Language*, a book Williams admired, Mencken quotes Whitman: 'The appetite of the people of These States, in popular speeches and writings, is for unhemmed latitude, coarseness, directness, live epithets, expletives, words of opprobrium, resistance . . . I like limber, lasting, fierce words.' This is part of Williams, too; his poems seek in resistance a new decorum, not to destroy the past but to place beside the past, in respect, the new thing, the invention. 'I live where I live,' Williams says, 'and acknowledge no lack of opportunity because of that to be alert to facts, to the music of events, of words, of the speech of people about me.' So the task in hand is to use this speech as the ground bass of a new measure, not only for the 'music' but for the sake of modes of being, otherwise dumb: 'It is in the newness of a live speech that the new line exists undiscovered.'

In his later years the new measure came to him, he believed, when he wrote in the second Book of *Paterson* the passage beginning

> The descent beckons
> as the ascent beckoned
> Memory is a kind
> of accomplishment . . .

So he wrote other poems in the same measure, including 'To Daphne and Virginia'. I quote a fragment to show how it runs:

> The smell of the heat is boxwood
> when rousing us
> a movement of the air

              stirs our thoughts
                  that had no life in them
                      to a life, a life in which
              two women agonize:
                  to live and to breathe is no less.
                      Two young women.
              The box odor
                  is the odor of that of which
                      partaking separately,
              each to herself
                  I partake also
                      . . . separately.

Williams counts each of these short lines as a foot. What he wants
is 'a *relatively* stable foot, not a rigid one', a foot expanded to
allow a freer handling of the measure. Williams's thought on
questions of metre and prosody is closely related to the world-
view of physics since Einstein; as one might say that the poetic
aim is to convert the mass of daily speech into energy. In the
fourth Book of *Paterson* he speaks of

              hydrogen
              the flame, helium the
              pregnant ash

and the Mendelief chart was fascinating to him because of the
magic, the alchemy, implied. He saw himself as a poet-scientist
changing one element into another, the poem a cyclotron, the
last grace, hey presto: hydrogen. So his new measure is as deeply
part of his poetry as, say, his praise of the Curies in *Paterson*. To
my ear the lines of the measure are equivalent only in duration,
and their determining factor is a movement in phrases, close to
speech, with the free movement of rhetorical stresses as counter-
point. The words have the movement of bars in music; each bar
may contain any number of syllables, in keeping with the tendency of the language 'to squeeze units into relatively equal
time spans'. The pattern gets its dynamics from the discreet use
of internal rhymes, assonance, complex alliteration, and pauses.
Thus the pause of depressed insight before the second 'separately':
as Daphne and Virginia live by weathering separate agonies.
Again:

I have two sons,
    the husbands of these women
      who live also
in a world of love,
   apart.
        Shall this odor of box in the heat
not also touch them
    fronting a world of women
      from which they are
debarred
    by the very scents which draw them on
    against easy access?

This is verse at least as well written as prose. The measure is just sufficiently positive to ensure that the writing is exact and scrupulous. It is not imperative. The pattern, once established, allows the poet to lay down the single, final word 'apart' and to have its bar filled with a pause of sorrowful recognition, without rancour. Auden says that American poetry differs from English poetry in its 'fingering'; a good word. It is the fingering which allows for that special load placed here upon 'debarred'. Williams is using a measure not to intensify but to control, to test the feeling as it meets the edge of the language; and he prefers the control to be as light as possible. This is why his best poems can be so individual, so unexpected, so quirky, without a trace of exhibitionism.

It does not particularly matter how we approach these poems; provided we approach them. It is good to meet them with a sense of their historical pressure, the sense of the weight of feeling behind them. Some readers are first attracted by Williams's personality, the impression of being at ease, informal, taking high risks: there are no Sabbaths in his week. Others simply listen to the words as they come. The 'propriety of cadence' which Charles Tomlinson admired in Williams is a constant delight. Reading him is like going through a diary, skipping here and there when the voltage of the writing is low, but marking the passages which are wonderfully charged with feeling. A passage like this, for instance, from *The American Background* is memorable for its own sake, not merely because it recalls a famous letter paraphrased in Pound's *Canto XXI*:

'It was Jefferson who, when President, would walk to his office in the mud, out of principle, and walk home again ignoring the mud, as against the others who would ride. And at the same time it was Jefferson who, recognising the imperious necessity for other loveliness to lay beside his own, such as it was, would inquire whether or not it might be possible, in securing a gardener, to get one who could at the same time play the flute.'[1]

The relation between this prose and the historical fact upon which it is based is at once close and devout. The sentences do not draw attention to themselves; they point to the density of what is there, in fact and event. Williams contributes to the fact only a sense of its meaning. The prose is imbued with this sense, but we feel it continuously along the line, it does not stop at any point to arrange the picture in its favour. It is typical of Williams that his 'effects' are movements of grammar and syntax, rather than clusters of imagery, forests of symbols, tropics of diction. Hugh Kenner has argued that in such poets as Williams and Marianne Moore we find the development of verbal resources which, for certain historical reasons, were stifled in the years in which the English poetic language acquired its character. The gist of the argument is that the main characteristics of English poetry were developed in the service of the stage: hence 'the mark of the Elizabethan drama is discernible on every subsequent English poet from Donne to Eliot'.[2] This made for a poetry of resonance, imprecision, incantation; the poem as a magnetic field, 'Empsonian'. It also had the effect of silencing certain potentialities which are clear in Chaucer and only less clear in Jonson: effects such as clarity, precision, the attachment of word to thing; a poetry to be read in daylight in the open air. It is this minority tradition, Mr. Kenner says, visible in Chaucer, Jonson, Dryden, and the Keats of the 'Ode to Autumn', which the American poets have tried to sustain. Tried; but Mr. Kenner argues that they could not do otherwise, except by a more or less perverse indulgence in pastiche. The case here is that the traditions of American poetry were transplanted from England in the eighteenth century; 'the antecedents of its present prac-

---

[1] ibid., p. 139.
[2] Hugh Kenner, 'Words in the Dark': *Essays by Divers Hands, Being Transactions of the Royal Society of Literature*: edited by E. V. Rieu (new series: Vol. XXIX: 1958) (London. Oxford University Press, 1958), p. 115.

tices date back only that far'. So the sounds of the Elizabethan drama, which reverberate in the ears of English poets, are barely audible to American poets: at least the sounds do not obtrude. So modern American poetry does not engage in 'majestic imprecision'; it is—to use Williams's own phrase—a poetry of transit. This is why Williams's poems seem bare to English readers; who read poems as a substitute for going to the theatre and therefore want to hear Shakespeare in the words, rather than Chaucer or Dante. English readers do not like poetry which says one thing at a time and says it finally; they want poems to be like mine fields, where the terrain looks innocent but you know that, somewhere out there, enormities of implication are laid at strategic points. Normally we call the strategic points 'diction': 'We are Tapers too, and at our owne cost die.' When an English poem fails, it is a heap of broken images: when an American poems fails, it is merely a remark.

To move: to bend, to persuade. The thesis of Williams's poetry, implicit in the instinct, is that the living world, despite much subversive evidence, is still a reliable text. These poems hold out for a mode of life in which consciousness, being, action, and suffering are mutually sustaining terms; not rivals. Or if any one of them is to be deemed *primus*, it is *primus inter pares*: as action is first in the life of a man like Herbert Clark, Williams's friend and hero, who devoted his entire energy to eliminate the yellow fever mosquito in the Central American jungle.

To see a little of this in *Paterson*.

A long poem in five Books, *Paterson* is compounded of many particles, including anecdotes, letters, scenes, celebrations of one thing or another deemed worthwhile because of the spirit it encloses or wastes. Like many modern poets Williams has been searching for a form in the long poem which is freer than the narrative or dramatic and yet more legal than talk or improvisation. Stevens had the same object but chose a different means, 'prolonged attention to a single subject'. (He wrote to Harriet Monroe that this 'has the same result that prolonged attention to a senora has, according to the authorities. All manner of favors drop from it'.)[1] But Stevens was a planetary poet, Williams terrestrial. In *Paterson* there are several themes, several subjects, so

[1] *Letters of Wallace Stevens*, edited by Holly Stevens (New York. Knopf, 1966, p. 230.

that a first reading gives the impression that one has been reading an intractable newspaper, laid out on eccentric principles.
But after a few readings the news begins to stay news.

Paterson is Everyman, his consciousness the Passaic River,
hardly distinct from the power of true speech. The great evil is
severance, as in the divorce of one person from another or from
his ancestors; or the divorce of language from mind; or the
divorce of a man from Nature; or the divorce of learning from
wisdom. The great good is Invention, a silent tribute to Ezra
Pound; because invention restores the broken harmonies. At the
end of the fourth Book we find a seed, a word, which takes root
in *Paterson Five* and flowers through the world of Art, notably
the art of the elder Brueghel who is praised for reading the signs
and painting what he saw. Here is a short passage from the end
of the first Book:

```
                        Thought clambers up,
        snail like, upon the wet rocks
        hidden from sun and sight—
                        hedged in by the pouring torrent—
        and has its birth and death there
        in that moist chamber, shut from
        the world—and unknown to the world,
        cloaks itself in mystery—
                        And the myth
        that holds up the rock,
        that holds up the water thrives there—
        in that cavern, that profound cleft,
                        a flickering green
        inspiring terror, watching.
        And standing, shrouded there, in that din,
        Earth, the chatterer, father of all
        speech. . . .
```

The serpent-figure is Time, watching, and Earth being the father
of all speech is our only home, the place of our mistakes and
occasional graces. So the signs are there: we are not confronted
with blankness. But, time being what it is, there is no assuranc
that reading the signs, here and now, will give us a text which
we can recite every morning and find always valid. If there is a

metamorphosis there is also a dispersal. This is not the same as
Stevens's welcome for change: it is a more stoic acceptance of
change as a fact of life, accepted even if it does not sponsor a
Supreme Fiction. This makes the last Book of *Paterson* strangely
moving. Williams's last world is not as densely populated as it
was in the old days. Much of its value is now to be found in the
artifice of eternity, the world of art:

> So through art alone, male and female, a field of
> flowers, a tapestry, spring flowers unequalled
> in loveliness.
>> through this hole
>> at the bottom of the cavern
>> of death, the imagination
>> escapes intact.[1]

Williams is still a pathfinder, but the signs are fewer, and while
he still votes in the old way for facts, women, and flowers, he
often looks now at the paths found by other men, other artists,
rather than the muddy tracks themselves. It is as if life, in those
last painful years, were verified not so fervently in the living of
it, but in art, where Brueghel gives some of the faith and energy
which Williams needs.

But the poet has not lost faith in the redeeming language:

> A flight of birds, all together,
> seeking their nests in the season
> a flock before dawn, small birds
> 'That slepen al the night with open Yë',
> moved by desire, passionately, they
> have come a long way commonly.
> Now they separate and go by pairs
> each to his appointed mating. The
> colors of their plumage are undecipherable
> in the sun's glare against the sky
> but the old man's mind is stirred
> by the white, the yellow, the black
> as if he could see them there.

[1] William Carlos Williams, *Paterson Five* (New York. New Directions, 1958),
no pagination.

And so it goes on. This is poetry as fair speech. It is certainly more American than English, a movement of translucent speech concerned far less with density than with a noiseless progression from one notation to the next. 'Passionately' may chime with 'commonly', making a point, but it is only a point, Williams does not insist upon it. This language is designed to be seen through; the object is deemed to be more important than the words. Chaucer is at home here as Shakespeare would not be at home, with 'the temple-haunting martlet' or 'the crow makes wing to th' rooky wood'. This is not to say that the lines would be better or worse if they were 'Shakespearean' rather than 'Chaucerian': it is to say that they would be different. In his review of *A Draft of XXX Cantos* Williams said of Pound and words: 'Pound has taken them up—if it may be risked—alertly, swiftly, but with feeling for the delicate living quality in them— not disinfecting, scraping them, but careful of the life.'[1] This is the phrase we need for Williams himself, for brevity and definition: care of the life.

[1] *Selected Essays, supra,* p. 111.

10

Dangling Man

I

Saul Bellow's novel, *Dangling Man*, appeared in 1944 when few readers had fiction on their minds and even dangling had to be postponed.[1] But the hero, Joseph, was neither the first nor the last victim of modern perception. The marks of his anguish are visible in much of twentieth-century literature.

The dangling man is conscious of being in an interim situation, waiting either for nothing or for a Godot answerable to his dignity and his imagination. He is in prison. His deepest feeling is a sense of displacement. He may live in a hotel, like the hero of *Seize the Day*, but, wherever he is, he feels 'out of place'. He has no contact, no roots: 'Someone had said, and Wilhelm agreed with the saying, that in Los Angeles all the loose objects in the country were collected, as if America had been tilted and everything that wasn't tightly screwed down had slid into Southern California. He himself had been one of these loose objects.'[2]

In *Dangling Man* Joseph feels himself imprisoned in one room. 'I, in this room, separate, alienated, distrustful, find in my purpose not an open world, but a closed, hopeless jail. My perspectives end in the walls.' In this situation action seeps away. The hero devotes himself to the niceties of routine in the hope of mistaking them for deep rituals. To keep up his morale he rises early, buys his cigars, drinks a Coca-Cola, and—like the victim in *Seize the Day*—is down in the lobby by eight o'clock.

These characters are more acutely aware of the symptoms of their malaise than of its cause. Henderson in *Henderson the Rain-King* hears a voice within which repeats, 'I want, I want, I want,'

[1] Saul Bellow, *Dangling Man* (London. Weidenfeld and Nicolson, second edition, 1960), p. 30.
[2] Saul Bellow, *Seize the Day* (London. Weidenfeld and Nicolson, 1957), p. 22.

but he is not sure what he wants. He is afflicted, like Eliot's image of Hamlet, with a radical disease at once vague and exorbitant. If he is articulate as well as suffering, like Bellow's Augie March, he tries to find some cause of his tumult. Augie laments that his life has no inherited images of value to set against the rush of events. Instead of the silken images of Sicilian lovers Augie has only 'deep city vexation'.[1] But prophetically charged moments are rare in Bellow's fiction: the nearest we come to them is in *Henderson the Rain-King*, where Henderson tries to talk to his faithful Romilayu who is digging his way out of the prison. 'I told that man next door I had a voice that said, *I want*.'[2]

So the dangling man feels that he has lapsed from an older, finer self. And he invents an Eden of warmth and resonance from which he has been displaced. What he retains is a scruple, an uncomfortable possession. Einhorn names it for Augie: 'But wait. All of a sudden I catch on to something about you. You've got *opposition* in you.' Augie thinks of this: 'I did have opposition in me, and great desire to offer resistance and to say "No".' Bellow's heroes share this scruple. It is easy to think of it as, simply, imagination. The exemplary imagination is always wayward, insisting upon its right to criticize, because it is like the conscience of its bearer and it will not allow him the pleasure of facility. Meanwhile, and necessarily, the heroes are painfully introspective. Wilhelm's eyes peer into the dark of himself, disliking what they see. This partly explains Henderson's sense of his own body, the huge thing, the face like Grand Central Station. A moral Tarzan with the additional burdens of imagination and conscience, Henderson is long past the stage of swinging from branch to branch. He flounders. He has no direction. All he knows now is that, somehow, he must maintain 'a sense of his own being'. Some of the obstacles come, then, from within; others from outside, often embodied in an older, more successful brother—Amos in *Dangling Man*, Simon in *Augie March*. These brothers want to help, but the only help they can imagine makes the victims mere ciphers, functions. And the hero's 'opposition' balks at this indignity.

---

[1] Saul Bellow, *The Adventures of Augie March* (London. Weidenfeld and Nicolson, 1954), p. 117.
[2] Saul Bellow, *Henderson the Rain-King* (London. Weidenfeld and Nicolson, 1959), p. 318.

It is time to ask what exactly these characters want. The short answer is: equilibrium. Or, in another version, they want to know how to live, what to do. Joseph gives a more elaborate answer: 'to know what we are and what we are for, to know our purpose, to seek grace'. When Augie sees the exiled Trotsky in Acatla he becomes enthusiastic, especially about the exile, and he thinks of the impression the man gave 'of navigation by the great stars, of the highest considerations, of being fit to speak the most important human words and universal terms'. So the search for value is not so much a search for the truth, a message, or a revelation; it is an attempt to respond to the experience of life by producing a man adequate to its challenge. Augie says at one point: 'You invent a man who can stand before the terrible appearances. This way he can't get justice and he can't give justice, but he can live.' As far as it goes, this is fine, but later, in the inflammable conversation with Mintouchian, Augie has a darker insight:

' "You will understand, Mr. Mintouchian, if I tell you that I have always tried to become what I am. But it's a frightening thing. Because what if what I am by nature isn't good enough?" I was close to tears as I said it to him. "I suppose I better, anyway, give in and be it. I will never force the hand of fate to create a better Augie March, nor change the time to an age of gold." '

The novel ends with a little self-indulgence; Augie, alone, travelling hopefully, a Columbus from Chicago reminding us that Columbus found his America. It is softer than the tone of great Comedy.

In the earlier novels the search for value was invariably the great preoccupation. In *Dangling Man* the hero surrenders, gives up the struggle on the last page, like Hans Castorp going down to the war:

> 'I am no longer to be held accountable for myself; I am grateful for that. I am in other hands, relieved of self-determination, freedom cancelled.
> Hurray for regular hours!
> And for the supervision of the spirit!
> Long live regimentation!'

In *The Victim* the search is oblique and evasive. The book is concerned with guilt, borne by Asa and embodied in his relation to Kirby Allbee. The guilt is given as a condition of Asa's being, and the best pages deal with his moral analysis and Allbee's appalling speculative earnestness. Asa is the conscience and the imagination of his race; a good man. But the novel allows external circumstance to lift his burden. It lets this Job off, makes Cordelia live to marry Edgar. The facts of the case are given as an inner condition, a mode of sensibility, but the solution is circumstantial. Allbee brings in a whore and desecrates the holy bed of Asa and Mary; so Asa can drive him away, and the guilt evaporates. It is a contrivance. In *Henderson the Rain-King* again the hero is too easily redeemed, set free with a symbolic lion cub and a child's friendship.

We can summarize this by saying that Bellow's heroes seek value, equilibrium, salvation—Henderson's word—an earthly condition in which body and soul may live. The condition, if it were possible, would allow the self a genial relation to its world. Henderson gave up hunting because it seemed 'a strange way to relate to nature'. Augie looks with anguish at the eagle which Thea is training to kill lizards. Aggression, aggression, aggression. The self will not take the offensive, it will not profit from the sufferings of others, it will return a verdict for reason 'in its partial inadequacy and against the advantages of its surrender', as Joseph says. Bellow's characters reach a dark moment in which they feel that reason has nothing to do with action. Augie's conjunction with Stella on a mountain of wet grass in Mexico is followed by the reflection that, 'After much making with sense, it's senselessness that you submit to.' Tommy Wilhelm sees himself as a man 'who reflected long and then made the decision he had rejected twenty times'.

Basically, these characters want to be assured of their own existence. Augie meditates that, 'Personality is unsafe in the first place. It's the types that are safe. So almost all make deformations on themselves so that the great terror will let them be.' The great terror takes many desolately prosaic forms, including the boredom of one day following another, the Indian file of tedium. Joseph says, 'It may be that I am tired of having to identify a day as "the day I asked for a second cup of coffee" or "the day the waitress refused to take back the burned toast", and so want to blaze it more sharply, regardless of the consequences.'

There is another demand; that a man be his own master, agent in his own action. The philosopher Clarence Irving Lewis has argued that 'a being which could not act would live out its life within the bounds of immediacy. It could find no difference between its own content of feeling and reality. There could be no self, because there could be no other-than-self: the distinction could not arise'.[1] Bellow's heroes want to choose, because their humanity depends upon the hazard of choice, but they fear that the irrational may be a categorical condition, like the air we breathe. Hence the image of dissociation. These men seek salvation within their own being and from their own resources. They find no sustenance in other people, in society. Society is what went wrong: the body politic and the world's body are bankrupt. The only mode of society which Bellow's men take seriously is the family. Augie is devoted to his family and to the idea of the Person. But he has no vision of society as a great family, in which a man might live with due autonomy while being a member of something larger than himself. And often, outraged by a society which has failed and deceived them, these characters seek moral simplicity as an entirely private possession. Henderson goes through the heart of darkness into the desert, impelled to 'simplify'.

In theory, there is no conflict between this desire and the urge to 'love'. Bellow often quotes Simone Weil: 'To believe in the existence of human beings as such is love.' This is the ground of his entire fiction. But in practice it rarely obtains. Joseph spends a lot of time pondering the difference between persons and things. In *The Victim* Schlossberg defines, for Asa's benefit, what it means to be human.[2] Henderson tells Romilayu: 'The only decent thing about me is that I have loved certain people in my life.' But there is an incorrigible vacuum between theory and practice, between profession and realization. Bellow's characters live on the assumption that belief in the existence of human beings as such must come later; after they have managed to secure a belief in their own existence. They do not take much stock in the idea that precisely by committing ourselves to the existence of other people our own existence is certified. They think that they can say 'I' before saying 'Thou'.

[1] Clarence Irving Lewis, *An Analysis of Knowledge and Valuation* (La Salle, Illinois. Open Court, 1946), p. 21.
[2] Saul Bellow, *The Victim* (New York. Viking Press, 1956), p. 146.

But all these matters are exactingly complicated by *Herzog*, the residence of Bellow's latest dangling man.

In the original *Dangling Man*, as we have seen, Joseph suffers from 'a feeling of strangeness, of not quite belonging to the world, of lying under a cloud and looking up at it'. He feels himself cut adrift from the past, living in a spectral present tense in which Tuesday is the same as Saturday because both are featureless. So we register the first difference in *Herzog*, that a verifiable past is Moses's ball and chain. But at least he has a past. Like Wilhelm in *Seize the Day*, he is 'a visionary sort of animal', but he commits himself to his own experience. Wilhelm 'had cast off his father's name', but Moses keeps the name and the image. His father and mother are dead, but they range through his story, carrying the brute weight of their existence. Moses never repudiates them. Like *The Adventures of Augie March*, this is a Jewish story, a family story. Indeed, it is closer in spirit to *Augie March* than to any of the other books, before or after. Bellow has given up the allegorial neatness of *The Victim* in preference for the richer idiom of fact and event. Equally, he has evaded the symbolic itch of *Henderson the Rain-King*: we are not required to take a course in 'the Africa within'. Herzog's experience is given to us in the same terms in which it is given to him; specific acts, casualties, and sufferings. We are not allowed to substitute a formula for the things given. Nor is he. The plot is a commitment to live through the terms of its reference: Herzog keeps going, he strikes through every proffered mask, and because God is finally Good he is eventually allowed to reach a quiet place, the rediscovered Berkshires of his spirit. Bellow has often found trouble in making an appropriate Act Five, but the end of *Herzog* is entirely convincing, Moses lying down, containing himself, feeling the strength of his quietness for the first time. Tommy Wilhelm believed that the 'easy, tranquil things of life' might still be recovered, that even yet life might be 'reduced to simplicity again'. The simplicity is realized in *Herzog*, but it is not a reduction; life is enhanced in those quiet Berkshires.

So the book is animated by Bellow's constant concern; Fact and Value, the relation between the terms; the redemption of the event, the thing done, because it is done in a certain spirit. Herzog knows that he must do a great deal of mind-work if he is to preserve his vigilance and be ready to deal with his experi-

ence as it comes to him and he goes to meet it. 'Awareness was
his work; extended consciousness was his line, his business.' But
he knows that this can't be the answer: we have been conscious
for centuries, and, look, we have not come through. The quality
of our consciousness is wrong, to begin with. We need the consciousness of appreciation, not the consciousness of possession;
the open hand, not the grip of claw. There is a long passage, late
in the book, where Herzog ponders these matters. 'Not thinking
is not necessarily fatal,' he reflects. 'Did I really believe that I
would die when thinking stopped?' This is the first sign of
health, the old body standing up to defend itself against the destructive consciousness. 'Go through what is comprehensible and
you conclude that only the incomprehensible gives any light.'
Further: 'And consciousness when it doesn't clearly understand
what to live for, what to die for, can only abuse and ridicule
itself.' The knowledge of these fundamental things is not ob-
tained in the head. It is a sixth sense, closely in touch with the
other five; or perhaps it is an ur-sense prior to any other. And if
it has a special intimacy with one of the five, it is with the sense
of touch: we come to know what to live for by touch, in the
silence of wonder. Herzog has spent much of his life abusing and
ridiculing himself, writing manic letters to men good and bad,
living and dead, for fear his mind will stop and, stopping, bring
him crashing to the ground. The turning-point comes when he
gives up the abuse and the struggle to convert experience into
mind; and simply waits. The human imagination, he says at one
point, 'starts by accusing God of murder'. It cultivates a griev-
ance. No more of that: let the dead grievances bury their dead.
Herzog has lived most of his life converting experience into
words, as if words alone were certain good: 'I go after reality
with language.' But he comes to discover that words are destructive, subversive, if sought in the wrong spirit. 'Perhaps I'd like
to change it all into language, to force Madeleine and Gersbach
to have a *conscience*. There's a word for you.'

So this is a book of genial words reaching into silence. At the
end, Herzog finds that he has said everything he needs to say, at
least for the present; there will be no more talk, no messages, no
unmailed letters to Nietzsche. Now, for a saving while, he will
live modestly among tangible things, trusting to the emergence
of light without force or pressure. So his last fictive moments are

spent among wine bottles, hats, roses, a Recamier couch, Mrs. Tuttle's broom. Forty pages earlier he wrote: 'The dream of man's heart, however much we may distrust and resent it, is that life may complete itself in significant pattern. Some incomprehensible way. Before death. Not irrationally but incomprehensibly fulfilled.'[1] This is his 'rage for order', but he discovers that he stands a better chance of finding order when the rage is stilled, and he tries to trust the world. This does not mean that he calls off the hunt or sacks his imagination; it means that he prescribes new conditions, sets a new quiet key.

There is a beautiful incident which, more than another, gives the spirit of the discovery. Herzog makes a mad dash to Chicago with a dim plan to kill his wife and her lover. He takes his father's gun and the required bullets. As he travels he works himself up to the necessary steam of venom. When he comes to the house, he looks in the back window and sees the lover, Gersbach, giving the child—Junie—her bath. It is all ordinary, almost handsome. Herzog knows that there can be no question of killing. This does not solve his predicament; his story does not become a fairytale, but it shows him that some crucial things in life have nothing to do with the higher mind-work, they simply are what they are.

So the book makes a strange and beautiful figure. The first half is all steam, mania, *angst*; energy lurching, an expense of spirit in a waste of hate and shame. Some of this is brilliantly done; especially when Herzog is brought home by the Himmelsteins and a browbeating session leaves the victim distracted. (Himmelstein is first cousin to old Einhorn in *Augie March*.) Bellow's feeling for this scene is impeccable; where the browbeater is thick, ignorant, and right while the victim is all sensibility and wrong. He is not quite as good when the scene is academic and clever; the visit of Shapiro to the Herzogs is a bright parade of highbrow lore, Moses the odd-man out, but it is unconvincing, a set piece too set in its ways.

Bellow is a man's novelist. His female characters tend to be done with far smaller resource, as in *Herzog* Ramona, given in great detail, is a piece of cardboard while Father Herzog, a brief sketch, is authentically 'there'. Bellow's prose can deal with women only when they are magisterial figures in the landscape

[1] Saul Bellow, *Herzog* (New York. Viking Press, 1964), p. 303.

of the past; and then they are nearly men. If a woman is thirty-five and about to become the hero's mistress, the chances are that she will reveal herself the product of scissors-and-paste. The reason is, perhaps, that in Bellow's fiction these women are there merely to give the hero something more to suffer; they merely add to the noise and fret of his life. And, strictly speaking, anyone could do this for him. In the novels since *Augie March* Bellow's imagination is devoted to this problem, among many; how to lure the facts into peace without denying their recalcitrance, how to reach solid ground, how to live. Women have very little to do with this part of the story: the hero's problem is now personal and representative.

I mention this limitation to suggest that Bellow's resources as a novelist, more impressive than ever, are not unlimited. But he is one of the important novelists because of the depth at which his options are made and his sense of the pressure they have to meet. This is what the novelist's integrity means, the measure of his scruple. If we think of *Herzog* as a severe examination of the modern orthodoxies in literature, the Wasteland myth and the arrogance of consciousness, we know at the same time that Bellow is not a smiling salesman selling toothpaste. His 'positives' go no further than the propriety of silence, at this time; the illness is not miraculously cured. I would not ask him to go beyond this point. But *Herzog* is important because it reveals our whining orthodoxies for the shoddy things they are; and because it urges us to try again, and try harder. The book tells us that we are infatuated with our own illness, since we deem it the proof of our integrity. But health is better than illness, and *Herzog* points to at least one possibility.

This is what the style of the book implies: it is a prose of human size, much freer than that of *Dangling Man* or *The Victim*. The early books are rigid in their parables, they live by constriction, and they exhibit a correspondingly rigid style. The style is the parable. But according as Bellow has liberated himself, more and more deeply, from the governing orthodoxies of modern literature, he has moved into richer modes of style. There is clearly a direct relation between the possibilities he sees in life and those he has discovered in his language. The eloquence of the writing wells up from the life it exhibits, the characters, events, situations: it is not an artificially induced eloquence, a merely personal invention. In the scene in the police-station, when Madeleine comes to bring Junie home after Herzog's arrest, the graph of Herzog's feeling as he watches her is drawn with remarkable exactitude: technically, it is largely a matter of syntax, beginning with the short sentences in which Herzog registers the precision of Madeleine's movements, her command of herself, the way she knows where to drop the milk-carton even though she has just entered the room. And as the thoughts incite one another, the syntax reflects the nervous gesture, the twitches of feeling. But the feelings were there before the prose; the prose 'imitates' them. Hence the change of tempo at the end, the nerves calmed; and the prose is like Mrs. Tuttle's broom, the exact and faithful answer to its occasion.

II

In the first volume of The Man Without Qualities Musil's narrative voice says of Ulrich: 'There was something in him that had never wanted to stay anywhere, but had groped its way along the walls of the world, thinking: "There are still millions of other walls." It was this ridiculous drop of Self, slowly growing cold that did not want to give up its fire, the tiny red-hot core within it.'[1] Musil's central concern is that drop of Self, deemed ridiculous only because, in this perspective, everything is ridiculous. The walls of the world are relevant only because the drop must grope somewhere. And The Man Without Qualities is unfinished because there are always millions of other walls. Young Törless and the short stories are essays in the mythology of self.

The landscape is familiar. There is the old rift between man and Nature, between motive and action, between feeling and word: let us say, between consciousness and experience. And the place is littered with broken images. The affections are estranged. 'One can't be angry with one's own time without damage to oneself,' Ulrich concedes, but the concession is theoretical. 'For a long time there had been a faint air of aversion hovering over everything that he did and experienced, a shadow of helplessness and isolation, a universal disinclination to which he could not

[1] Robert Musil, The Man Without Qualities (London. Secker and Warburg, 1961), I, 178. Translation by Eithne Wilkins and Ernest Kaiser.

find the complementary inclination. At times he felt just as though he had been born with a gift for which at present there was no function.' In Musil himself there is some evidence of a corresponding rift between the analyst and the moralist: one result is that tangible, historical things are constantly shamed in the luminous traversing of hypothesis and possibility. Musil could never believe that the fact that a thing exists gives it any precedence over things that do not.

This is his first axiom; the arbitrariness of what is. It was against his will that he lived in place and time, denying value to both. (I am reminded of Richard Wilbur's 'Epistemology':

> We milk the cow of the world, and as we do
> We whisper in her ear, 'You are not true.'[1])

In *Young Törless* the hero says: 'Things just happen; that's the sum total of wisdom.'[2] Events are interchangeable. The vulgar distinction between the indicative and the subjunctive moods is bogus. 'It's all chance,' Claudine says in *The Perfecting of a Love*.[3] Musil's characters dangle (in Bellow's sense) because they see no reason why they should attach themselves to one configuration of nature which exists rather than another which doesn't: all configurations, if they exist, are mere casualties of fact. So the encounter between character and environment which is essential, as Lukacs argues, if the potentialities of a particular individual are to be realized, never takes place. Character in Musil is merely another accident. Gottfried Benn speaks of 'the perforated self' through which Nature blows, indifferently. Musil's intimations are even more deterministic. Action is reduced to motion, things are done because they happen. We are held by habit. When habit is broken, as in a divorce, a vacation, a journey, the rush of possibility takes over, a new set of co-ordinates moves into arbitrary place, and we grope in its shadow. Claudine reflects: 'It's going to happen all over again.' The vulgar distinction between good and evil is discussed in detail by Ulrich and his sister Agathe, but the assumption is that the distinction is archaic.

[1] Richard Wilbur, *Poems 1943–1956* (London. Faber and Faber, 1957), p. 47.
[2] Robert Musil, *Young Törless* (London. Penguin Books, 1961), p. 167. Translation by Eithne Wilkins and Ernest Kaiser.
[3] Robert Musil, *Five Women* (New York. Delacorte Press, 1966), p. 168. Translation by Eithne Wilkins and Ernest Kaiser.

In one of their 'holy conversations' Ulrich implies to Agathe that the only remedy for dissociation is a great mystical conflagration in which everything will be One. There has already been a lot of talk about Utopian possibilities, images of the New Man. Sometimes this figure is represented as taking part in a 'vast sensuality with which life simultaneously satisfies all the rival contradictions in its boundless and exorbitant body'. But Musil's later work favours a mystical unity, spectacularly intimated in the relationship between Ulrich and Agathe, Osiris and Isis, the Siamese Twins. *The Man Without Qualities* is Musil's Notes towards a Supreme Fiction, the fiction that is Man.

Meanwhile, since mystical conflagrations can be coaxed but not presumed upon, Musil's characters keep themselves going with provisional gestures. Occasionally they silence the moralists by identifying the drop of Self with the Soul, handing over to the mere Body the motives and acts which, therefore, 'do not matter'. Claudine, who loves her husband, gives herself to another man, a stranger, but she assures herself that 'fundamentally it did not touch her and essentially had nothing to do with her'. This act, and other acts of the same kind, seem 'like a brook rushing along, always away from her, and her only feeling is of sitting quietly on its bank, lost in thought'. In *Grigia* the man, Homo, becomes the peasant woman's lover. 'This change that had taken place in him much occupied his mind, for beyond doubt it was not something he had done, but something that had happened to him.' This ethic of a double standard is related to an 'invisible principle' which Ulrich recalls. 'The soul of the Sodomite might pass through the throng without foreboding, in its eyes the limpid smile of a child; for everything depends on an invisible principle.' But Ulrich invokes this in some distress, because it seems to him to exude 'the sweet, sickly odour of corruption'. Later, however, he brings it back by citing a scientific metaphor: in a field of energy it is the constellation of the events which charges them with meaning, not the events themselves.

In another version of the double standard Musil implies a vaguely Darwinian ethic. Acts which strike the conventional moralist as evil are redeemed by serving an evolutionary graph. In *Tonka*, where the poor girl has died as a result of the hero's ministrations, the story ends: 'From that time on much came to his mind that made him a little better than other people, because

there was a small warm shadow that had fallen across his brilliant life. That was no help to Tonka now. But it was a help to
him.' In Musil's image of life every act is merely an essay, a sup-
position, a hypothesis, a scientific experiment: to every trial, its
own casual errors. They also serve, upon whom the germ falls.
There is something of Joyce in Musil, the Joyce to whom most
things were not allowed to matter; and something of Stevens, to
whom one war (1939–45) was merely part of a warlike whole.
Clarisse is right: 'A Man Without Qualities does not say No to
life, he says Not Yet, saving himself up.'

I have touched upon the morality of Musil's fiction because
one can easily be diverted from this consideration by the style,
the word-by-word detail, which is often brilliant and always re-
sourceful. In the short stories, in *Young Törless*, and the endless
novel, Musil moves from one word to the next by the force of a
commanding rhetoric: so that the ideas on which the fiction is
based gain a certain grandeur from the energy devoted to their
cause. The ideas in themselves are often banal. The experimental
imagination, for instance, is merely a lust for the Absolute.
Heard melodies are sweet, but those unheard are sweeter. Absolute Sound is audible only to the spirit, the soul, in those deemed
capable of this experience. Musil's characters aspire to a morality
of the Spheres. Claudine attends not to the words, but to the
sound of them. When she imagines herself belonging to some
other man, it seems 'not like betrayal but like some ultimate
marriage, in a realm where they had no real being, where they
existed only as music might, a music heard by no one, echoing
back from nowhere'. When Musil's decadence obtrudes, it is
normally this lust for the Absolute at work. Sometimes it is a
desire to do something utterly alien, and then to take the desire
into one's soul as a new and exotic possession. Claudine again:
'What attracted her in the unintelligible passage of events was
all there was in it that did not pertain to herself, to the spirit:
what she loved was the helplessness and shame and anguish of
her spirit—it was like striking something weaker than oneself, a
child, a woman, and then wanting to be the garment wrapped
about its pain, in the darkness alone.' Sometimes it takes the form
of a meta-Love, dissolving all strain. In Musil himself it appears
as a morbid conscientiousness; like Törless in his panic about
imaginary numbers in mathematics, Musil resents everything

for which his imagination is not responsible. His imperious imagination demands to play God.

Again, the arbitrariness of what is: this is an interesting debating point, but little more. It may be worth a minute or two to speculate on the relative value of the tree that exists and the something that doesn't. But it is a thin speculation, when all is said. The same applies to Musil's infinity of hypothesis and possibility: this is merely an academic exercise. The object of the exercise is to give the imagination something to do, short of actually living in the given world. Not yet! Not yet! When Ulrich is asked what he would do if he were God, he answers that he should feel compelled to abolish reality. Meanwhile he plays God by abolishing reality, so far as he can. Again, when he says that 'the Good has by its very nature become almost a platitude, whereas Evil is still criticism', we attend to him not because this is a bright idea but because we are still interested in his saying it: he is interesting for a hundred reasons, but the idea is interesting only because he has accepted it.

There are some comic possibilities here. Indeed, given these suppositions, Comedy is the ideal form of their entertainment, because it discourages the fretful note which is sometimes audible in Musil. One thinks of Borges's fiction, notably *Pierre Menard, Author of Don Quixote*: 'Menard (perhaps without wishing to) has enriched, by means of a new technique, the hesitant and rudimentary art of reading: the technique is one of deliberate anachronism and erroneous attributions. This technique, with its infinite applications, urges us to run through the *Odyssey* as if it were written after the *Aeneid*, and to read *Le jardin du Centaure* by Madame Henri Bachelier as if it were by Madame Henri Bachelier. This technique would fill the dullest books with adventure.'[1] Or Beckett. There are hundreds of hypotheses in Beckett, but they serve a sturdier purpose than essays in possibility. Watt's hope is 'to evolve, from the meticulous phantoms of his former selves, a hypothesis proper to disperse them, as often as this might be found necessary'.[2] Borges smiles at the rush of things, however arbitrary their nature and direction, and teases them with his imagination. They take it in good part. But where Borges is exhilarating, Musil is at once imperious and

[1] Jorge Luis Borges, *Ficciones* (New York. Grove Press, 1962), p. 55.
[2] Samuel Beckett, *Watt* (Paris. Olympia Press, 1953), p. 78.

glum. Beckett's comedy is possible because he has always taken
failure for granted; it is what one starts from. Life is then a
matter of passing time which would probably have passed anyway, but while it lasts there are phantoms to be dispersed. There
are some hilarious things in Musil, like the first conversation between Diotima and Dr. Arnheim about the Collateral Cam-
paign. But when the idiom of arbitrariness and possibility
asserts itself, the tone goes lugubrious, especially when Ulrich is
in full spate and the pages come like lectures illustrated by slides.
Musil's terms of reference allow him a wide range of irony, but
little nonchalance.

This is the case as long as he takes his terms literally. But the
impression persists that his greatest achievements are in the old-
fashioned way. When he writes an essay and attributes it to one
of his characters, it is not a bad essay, but it is not remarkable.
But when he is seized by the old-fashioned concerns, he writes
with great power. The third volume in the English edition of
The Man Without Qualities is largely given to the developing relationship between Ulrich and Agathe. Character may be a
tissue of accidents, morally null, but Musil attends to this relationship as if it were of the deepest significance. And it is. The
style is more compelling than ever, because there is an answering
substance, a deep engagement of the perennial interests. This
volume does not try to dissolve the world or to abolish reality.
What persists is the image of these two people. When Agathe,
pondering suicide, walks by herself to the graveyard at the edge
of the wood, we are reading great fiction, but its quality is the
old quality, it has nothing to do with the World as Idea.

Of the short stories, *Tonka* and *The Perfecting of a Love* are the
most successful. It is often said that Musil is such a mind-man
that his characters are dwarfed by their ideas: they are lost in the
brilliance of their syntax. This is not true of the short stories.
Even in *Young Törless*, while we know little or nothing of the
military school in which the events take place, the characters
emerge with their own resilience. In *The Man Without Qualities*
there is a sense in which some of the characters are puppets.
Clarisse and Walter have more point as functions of Ulrich than
as independent characters. Indeed, even with the Collateral Cam-
paign, Moosbrugger, and the rest, there is little impression of a
life moving independently of Ulrich's needs: the popular com-

parison with *Ulysses* breaks down at this point if it has not died already. But the characters in the short stories are never mere pressure points of the mind. Where a story fails, it is normally a failure of adjustment; as *Grigia* hurries to a dubious conclusion because it should have been a novel. But I keep coming back to *The Perfecting of a Love*. The title is questionable, whether *vollendung* is translated as 'perfection' or 'completion'. There is the usual implication, at the end, that Claudine's betrayal of her husband has been worthwhile: 'Yet at the back of her mind there was a shadowy memory of something she had once experienced on a day in spring; a state that was like giving herself to everyone and yet belonging only to the one beloved. . . . And from a long way off—as children say of God: "He is great"—she saw and knew the image of her love.' Her love, her husband, I assume. But while anything is possible, the notion that Claudine's love is enhanced and completed by her affaire with the bearded stranger seems to me fanciful, however experimental the ethic. Meanwhile Claudine's feelings are remarkable, and it is impossible to dissociate ourselves from them. If we could, we would say that the wretched woman is merely deceiving herself with words, trying to justify her promiscuity by dancing attendance upon it. We would also say that Musil is morally primitive, that his new morality is no morality at all. But the experience of reading the story is a much more formidable thing: it is not a matter of following the feelings, or even of entertaining them, but of wrestling with them as they emerge, moment by moment. There are books to which one listens in silence, and other books with which one argues all the time. Musil's dialectic incites the reader to a rival dialectic in his own behalf; he is not a writer whom one entertains. The reader's dialectic is his response to the prodigious stress among the words. And if he still thinks the story a conceit, he cannot dissociate himself even then. As Stevens said, 'We are conceived in our conceits.'

There is no easy solution. Musil is one of the big writers in this century: his reach is enormous. Sentence by sentence he is almost dangerously persuasive. And yet it is hard to escape the conclusion that his powers were severely restricted by a recalcitrant view of life, a weirdly dispiriting metaphysics. There was nothing exhilarating in the void of possibility in which he spent his mental life. True, he could never put a foot wrong, out there, because he would never put a foot in any direction; unless he could at the same time insist that the direction was merely provisional, not to be taken seriously. And because he would not accept the world, he would not respond to it. When he had to drink the cow's milk, he did so furtively and in outrage. It seems an unfortunate way of living in the world. Meanwhile and of necessity the world's hunks and colours—as Richard Wilbur calls them—meant nothing to him; or nothing that he could trust.

III

One of the most engaging images of dangling man in modern literature is Kenneth Burke's *Towards a Better Life*, a book of notable salience in the dispute of Art and Life.

Burke wanted to write his book as a realistic, objective novel, lively in event and character, with a palpable background in Greenwich Village. But his first efforts in this standard direction were so dismal that he reviewed his terms of reference, and concluded that the form, excellent for others, was to him a nuisance; that is, it did not allow him to write as he wanted to write. It struck him, and the lineaments of his talent seemed to agree, that any plot would answer, so long as it allowed him to indulge his favourite modes of expression. These consisted of six pivotal procedures: lamentation, rejoicing, beseechment, admonition, sayings, and invective. So his second decision was to move in reverse: to begin with his favourite stylistic gestures and to deduce from these a 'corresponding' assembly of characters and a sequence of events loosely designated as plot. As he said: '*Facit indignatio versus*, which I should at some risk translate: "An author may devote his entire energies to rage purely through a preference for long sentences." '[1]

He would let himself be guided by a sense of style to invent characters and events in which the style would be most becomingly disclosed. It would not be necessary to devise a style for his fiction: he had the style already, waiting for the fiction. In this preposterous decision he consoled himself with the thought that

[1] Kenneth Burke, *Towards a Better Life* (New York. Harcourt, Brace, 1932), p. xii.

he would at least disown the current standardized prose which
was apparently designed, like Kleenex, to be used once and
thrown away. In his own 'periwig' style the sentences themselves would be internally eventful, contrived with so much
stylistic scruple that the absence of newsworthy events would
pass unnoticed. Hence Burke's prose is exciting as a good sonnet
is exciting, by offering a proliferation of verbal events sufficient
to engross the most demanding reader. Thus the author hopes to
entrance a reader who would otherwise be satisfied only by pictures of war and mayhem, and to send him back to daily life
with his lust for excitement somewhat stilled.

To begin with, it was essential to put the reader in a proper
mood for the reception of the book: clearly a condition of critical alertness as if he were attending to a song-cycle by Bartok.
So Burke makes his hero a thoroughly unpleasant character, a
twisted creature, with whom the reader could not possibly
identify himself. The hero's skill in articulation would help
further to place his reader at a safe distance. Listening to John
Neal, a self-declared Outsider, the reader would feel no desire to
bring him in. So the character of John Neal was dictated by the
decencies of the stylistic occasion. Burke invents an alienated
hero by deciding that alienation, at least to begin with, is the
appropriate situation of the reader *vis-a-vis* the book.

The genesis of the fiction is therefore in the strictest sense verbal and stylistic. But, once the technique is under way, the possibilities of invention are limitless, since there is no end to the
resources of language. By trading on certain incongruities between style and action, Burke devises the most exquisitely comic
incidents. In the second chapter, for instance, he describes John
making an anguished telephone-call to his beloved Florence
from a public booth: '. . . and while Florence listened to words
as desolate as my talent and my predicament could make them,
I was grinning into the mouthpiece that the man beyond the
glass, waiting to speak here next, might not suspect my condition.'

Again, at a theatrical party of extremely low voltage, John
feels compelled to attack the lucky Anthony in a style of formal
Complaint: 'This idealism is facile and meaningless. . . . You
may advocate much, and thus ally yourself with goodness,
through being called upon to do nothing. You need face no

objective test. Under the guise of giving, you are receiving.'

So the plot is manipulated not according to the usual realistic laws but to allow for the necessary variety in the sentences. If a certain mood has been going on for some time, the time is ripe to change it, for that very reason. And the demands of the sentences, strictly obeyed, often produce scenes and actions wonderfully 'true'. When John meets Florence, after months of separation, he brings her on a walk to an old ruined house which he has often haunted: 'I have gone through the littered rooms, opened musty cupboards, and rummaged among rags with the rung of a broken chair. I have examined this decrepit house, waiting—and into its dismalness I now guided Florence, that her bright curiosity might give it different echoes.'

The motto for this is given about half-way through the book when John reflects, 'If one seeks new metaphors, will he not also find new women?' a conjunction, by the way, entirely consistent with the magical properties commonly attributed to metaphor by the coolest aestheticians. *Towards a Better Life* is written as a dance is created; where the choreographer designs the movements not, in the first instance, to tell a story, but to give the accomplished bodies an occasion to disclose their resources. Thus the love-scene with Florence has 'a minuet-like quality'. John abuses his friends, urged by the persuasions of his terminology, and by those alone; a gift for words being an imperative to use them in the ways most fitting to the gift. 'Yet I could as easily have loved these people,' John rightly says. In a fragment at the end of the book we read: 'speech being a mode of conduct, he converted his faulty living into eloquence. Then should any like his diction, they would indirectly have sanctioned his habits.'

The plot itself is guided by principles purely internal to the medium of language and the reader's desires. It begins in misery, worse still in John's twisted recollection. The misery is appeased; hence a change of scene, Genevieve, John's marriage, children, a move to the country. The appeasement is embodied in an unexpected and joyous meeting with Florence. But this proves, for the moment, a deception, in keeping with the fact that words often run before their deeds. Later the joy is made good. Then John dismisses Florence, as he will later dismiss Genevieve, not for any overt reason in nature but in keeping with the linguistic resource of the Negative; Thou Shalt Not. Finally he dribbles into total isolation, soliloquizing in Hell: hence, silence.

To give some impression of the dance-like quality of the book it is advisable to quote a long passage. John has been describing a group of people with whom he has been vaguely associated:

'Dare I go further among this uneven lot? No further than to mention briefly a beautiful, and even picturesque woman, a Madame Durant, loved by two men. Through letters, telegrams, sudden visits, and the intervention of relatives, she carried her drama tumultuously across many states. With her arms about Joseph, she would cry out that she loved Josephus and thereupon, misled by a desire for too literal a symmetry, would cross the room to embrace Josephus and protest her love for Joseph. For to be alone with one of them seemed far greater impoverishment than to be with neither, and whichever she lived with, she thought herself conscience-stricken for leaving the other, though in reality suffering most from a drop in the liveliness of her situation. She wept in contentment, insisting that she was degraded—and friends, stopping to rebuke her for her inconstancy, would become her suitors. On one occasion I drank a toast to her elopement, using for the purpose glasses given prematurely as a present for her prospective marriage to the groom now temporarily abandoned though on hand to bid her and his rival farewell—and I left in complex cordiality, loving her, her two men, her dog, and the darkening inhospitable sky which matched my lonesomeness.'

We read this prose as if it were verse, perhaps eighteenth-century poetic couplets in which the outside is simple so that the inside may be intricate. And it is not too fanciful to suggest that every detail in Madame Durant's complicated *ménage* is contained 'in principle' in the technical resources of language, not forgotting such choice items as rhyme, alliteration, assonance, and the remaining figures of speech and thought. If metaphor suggests a woman, would it not be possible to devise human relationships equivalent to simile, rhyme, oxymoron; as we already say that a certain relationship is paradoxical, and might go on to say that a full stop is a happy marriage, a comma an affaire, a semi-colon an engagement, a new paragraph a divorce? If speech is conduct, what is a dictionary?

Meanwhile we ask a prosaic question: what kind of book are
we reading? It is certainly not a novel, nor was it meant to be. In
ascriptions of this kind we are well advised to consult Northrop
Frye's account of the several forms of prose fiction. Then it
appears that Burke's book is not a freak, a sport of Nature, but an
example of a distinguished tradition, the anatomy. It answers in
every respect to Frye's description: it deals 'less with people as
such than with mental attitudes'; its characterization is 'stylized
rather than naturalistic', presenting people 'as mouthpieces of
the ideas they represent'. The anatomist sees evil and folly 'as
diseases of the intellect, as a kind of maddened pedantry'. The
narrative is 'loose-jointed'. The writing 'relies on the free play of
intellectual fancy and the kind of humorous observation that
produces caricature'. The anatomy presents 'a vision of the
world in terms of a single intellectual pattern'.[1] The masterpieces
of the genre include *A Tale of a Tub, Candide*, the *Anatomy of
Melancholy, Headlong Hall*, and *Brave New World*.

Let us say, then, that *Towards a Better Life* is an anatomy of
dissociation. John Neal is detached from Nature as from us: 'the
weather's metaphysical whisperings' do not sing to him. His
human relationships are never more than provisional, the most
tentative essays in a doomed genre. Throughout the book he is
so conscientious in husbanding grimness that, while buffeted beyond endurance, he is never surprised in principle. He is our
scapegoat. At the end of the book the quality of character has
drained away entirely from the people of his experience, col-
lecting itself now only in lamp-posts, street cars, and gutters
which takes on a frightful vitality. John sees these manifestations
of his curse as entirely in the nature of things, never a matter of
surprise; the last 'event' is a fixation upon a wooden policeman
outside a cigar-shop. This stage in his Gothic tale is conveyed by
unmailed letter to his dead mistress, the style a tissue of quotations from a favourite poet, William Blake. As he sits in his
room in New York ('this inexorable city') he says: 'Watch the
mind, as you would eye a mean dog. Wait. Die as a mangled
wasp dies.' Thereafter he delivers his testimony in fragments
broken from the aphoristic structure. There comes a time, he
says, when one must abandon his vocabulary, 'for the rigidness

[1] Northrop Frye, *Anatomy of Criticism* (Princeton. Princeton University Press,
1959), pp. 308 f.

of words, by discovering a little, prevents us from discovering more'. And this is the time for silence. The book ends: 'Not only not responding, but even refraining from soliloquy—for if we tell no one, the grave burden accumulates within us. Henceforth silence, that the torrent may be heard descending in all its fulness.'

It is not enough to say that *Towards a Better Life* is beautifully 'written', if by this praise we mean to consign the book to an anthology of Prose Style. However peculiar its origin, it is in fact one of the most moving books in modern literature, as well as one of the purest anatomies. Like John Neal, Burke is skilled in 'the hilarious aspects of distress'. I have already lodged a mild complaint against the fretful note in Musil, and would mention now that Burke's book is entirely free from this. The basis of Musil's fretfulness is the belief that Ulrich is right and the world is wrong; it is always the world that is in error, in sin. There is something of this also in Bellow. But in *Towards a Better Life* the absurdity is evenly divided between John and the world: neither has any reason to ascribe to the other a monopoly in ill will. This has the effect of keeping the book's air clear. John never denies the world, or complains of the arbitrary nature of its arrangements. Indeed, if his troubles were of this nature, this would have to be a different life, a different book. He says at one point: 'Throughout eternity there is hunger in the fact that the universe *needs to be*, and appeasement in the fact that the universe *is*.' This is his idiom. Another fragment reads: 'Had he found the matter ludicrous, he could have spared himself much indignation.' So he spares himself indignation by finding himself, in many respects, ludicrous. And if he is tempted to become a modern mind-man, he knows the answer: 'We would not deny the mind; but merely remember that as the corrective of wrong thinking is right thinking, the corrective of all thinking is the body.' Meanwhile he walks 'boldly through life, head erect and shoulders thrown back in shame'. We revert to Beckett and the saving spirit of Comedy.

But leaving aside the diverse excellences of Bellow, Musil, and Burke, we ask: how are we supposed to 'take' their images of man, dangling, dissociated, an alien in an alien world?

In the Preface to *Towards a Better Life* Burke pays tribute to Thomas Mann as an author of notable relevance; and we recall a celebrated essay, 'Thomas Mann and André Gide', in Burke's *Counter-Statement*. The essay is very much to the present point. Burke juxtaposes Mann's irony against Gide's experimentalism. Mann's concern, he notes, is with 'serious and lonely fellows, deviations from type, who are overburdened with a feeling of divergency from their neighbours'. These Outsiders 'watch, they compare themselves with others to their own detriment, they are earnest to the point of self-disgust, and they are weighted with vague responsibilities'. Mann has identified art as the problematical sphere of the human: implicit in the artist's work there is 'a deliberate entertaining of moral vacillation'. This attitude is summed up as irony, 'which merges the sympathetic and antipathetic aspects of any subject'. Gide, on the other hand, is an adept of curiosity, the question-mark. 'He views any set code of values with distrust, because it implies the exclusion of other codes.' He is on guard, Burke says, 'lest the possible be obscured by the real'.[1] Then the critic quotes a passage from Gide's autobiography which toys with the notion of writing the imaginary history of a nation to prove that the history of man might easily have been different. It is obvious, by the way, that Burke himself is close to Mann's irony, as Musil to Gide's experimentalism; and the author of *Herzog* seems to me blood-brother to Tonio Kröger, who wrote to Lisabeta Ivanovna of his longing for the bliss of the commonplace, his love for 'the average unendowed respectable human being'. (But this is by the way.)

At the end of the essay Burke proposes that we disown a too literal interpretation of Gide's 'corruption'. 'I should take the specific events in Gide,' he says, 'as hardly more than symbols: their parallel in life would not be the enacting of similar events, but the exercising of the complex state of mind which arises from the contemplation of such events with sympathy.' But this, however genially stated, is merely the old aesthetic based on therapy and the dramatic imagination; the idea that we are enlarged and improved by contemplating, in the frame of art, actions which we would disavow in practice. Such theorists would emphasize the intransitiveness of the artistic experience, and recommend it as a relief from our common preoccupations which are all-too-transitive. But Burke goes far beyond this

[1] Kenneth Burke, *Counter-Statement* (Los Altos, California. Hermes Publications, second edition, 1953), pp. 92 f.

position. He says: 'Irony, novelty, experimentalism, vacillation, the cult of conflict—are not these men trying to make us at home in indecision, are they not trying to humanize the state of doubt?' And later: 'Need people be in haste to rebel against the state of doubt, when doubt has not yet permeated the organs of our body, the processes of our metabolism, the desire for food and companionship, the gratification with sun and water?' Now I relish the certainties of the body quite as vigorously as Burke does, but I cannot separate them neatly from the uncertainties of mind. Burke goes on to say that society might well benefit from 'the corrective of a disintegrating art'; which 'converts each simplicity into a complexity'. An art may be valuable, he says, by 'preventing a society from becoming too assertively, too hopelessly, itself'. If action could be destroyed by such art as Gide's, this would be disastrous: 'but art can at best serve to make action more laboured'. And this is good.

The implication is clear. Art is Criticism. When society is a braggart, the most useful artist is Thersites. Society is now a braggart (1931), hence we need all the Gides we can find. But the case has altered, I think, in thirty-five years: even Society, crude as it is, has received the artist's message that we are all sick, alienated, and so forth. The deepest visions of alienation are now blurred for general consumption and sold at cut-price. This mode of criticism is no longer available. Lionel Trilling has recently complained that those to whom he teaches the masterpieces of modern literature take those great alienated works in their stride. They are not intimidated. The artist who would criticize our society at this moment would probably hold up before its eyes a heroic image, the implication being that we are incapable of rising to it. There is a literature of celebration as well as a literature of critique. Indeed, there is a case for such a literature now on strictly stylistic grounds, as the persistence of a certain mood in a poem over many stanzas calls for another mood, in relief. This is Burke's own principle, advanced in *Counter-Statement* with great rhetorical force. I find it embodied in *Herzog*, which points its dangling hero toward certain 'certainties', soul-certainties as well as body-certainties, in which he might rest. These are not 'answers'; but they imply that the gates may still be open.

Meanwhile, behind our several alienists, there is the image of

Paul Valéry. We think of his Monsieur Teste as one of the most insistent mind-men in modern literature. The mind seeing itself seeing has never had a more accomplished student. But there are other moments: as in *Le Cimetière Marin* we hear:

> Brisez, mon corps, cette forme pensive!
> Buvez, mon sein, la naissance du vent!
> Une fraîcheur, de la mer exhalée,
> Me rend mon âme . . . O puissance saleé!
> Courons à l'onde en rejaillir vivant.

And later:

> Le vent se lève! . . . il faut tenter de vivre!

These are not answers. But the moment in which the voices in Valéry's poems turn again toward the images of human life, to Yeats's 'fury and the mire of human veins', are among the most exhilarating in modern literature; the turning means so much, these voices being what they are. And just as Homer was Yeats's example, one looks ahead to Valéry in his last poetic years, to the 'final yes' of *Mon Faust*: 'Je vis, je respire, rien de plus!'

I have implied that in Burke's novel there is no turn. But this is not so. Indeed, in a recent discussion of the book with its author I was admonished to look more closely at the last few pages. Burke now reads his book as a ritual of rebirth, an example of a pattern which he finds in many modern novels and poems; which he calls the 'sprout-out-of-rot' literature. This description is to account for those works in which the *materia poetica* is unwholesome while the work itself gives an impression of hygiene and sanitation. He still thinks of *Towards a Better Life* as 'a terror-stricken novel', appropriately enough for the year of its inception, 1929, but he would now emphasize the intimations of renewal which sprout in its later pages. In this reading John Neal dangles between tragedy and comedy; the tragic grotesque is Burke's name for his hero's place. The squirming of the book is designed to force John from tragedy through the tragic grotesque into comedy. Towards a better life; that is, toward comedy. The principle reminds me of an aphorism in Lichtenberg: 'The healthiest, handsomest, and most regularly built people are the ones who will put up with anything. No sooner has a man an

affliction than he has his own view on things.'[1] John Neal has so
many afflictions that he is himself an affliction, but the aim of the
book is to get him to put up with things in the spirit of comedy.
This is why he is a fitting scapegoat. As he says near the end: 'all
I have pondered in malice, some one, coming after me, will
consider comfortably. What I have learned through being in
grave extremities, he will handle with case'.

So there are, Burke would insist, implications of a 'way out'
at the end. Or rather, the possibility of a 'new life' is both fore-
told and held in 'problematic abeyance'. John Neal does not
disown his affliction: 'let no man discredit your discoveries by
pointing to your troubles'. His affliction has given him whatever
he has, whatever he knows. All one can hope for is a slight but
crucial modification in one's circumstances; with a corresponding modification in one's stance. 'The sword of discovery goes
before the couch of laughter. One sneers by the modifying of a
snarl; one smiles by the modifying of a sneer. You should have
lived twice, and smiled the second time.' Burke gives the principle of this sequence in *Attitudes toward History*:

' "The progress of humane enlightenment can go no further
than in picturing people not as *vicious*, but as *mistaken*. When you
add that people are *necessarily* mistaken, that *all* people are exposed in situations in which they must act as fools, that *every* insight contains its own special kind of blindness, you complete
the comic circle, returning again to the lesson of humility that
underlies great tragedy." '[2]

And certainly, in looking for a way-out, one should note the
emergence, in the last section, of words like 'vision' and 'promise', which stand for allegiances hardly possible in contractual
terms. One such moment is: 'became bat-blind, that he might
have bat-vision'. Another recalls the scene in *Jane Eyre*, at the end
of Chapter 9, when Helen Burns has died and, fifteen years later,
a headstone in the graveyard at Brocklebridge is inscribed with

---

[1] Quoted in J. P. Stern, *Lichtenberg: A Doctrine of Scattered Occasions* (London.
Thames and Hudson, 1963), p. 215: 'Die gesundesten und schonsten, regelmas-
sigst gebauten Leute sind die, die sich Alles gefallen lassen. Sobald einer ein
Gebrechen hat, so hat er seine eigene Meinung.'

[2] Kenneth Burke, *Attitudes toward History* (Los Altos. Hermes, 1959), p. 41. I
should also cite Burke's Introduction to the second edition of *Towards a Better
Life* (Berkeley and Los Angeles. University of California Press, 1966); and his
essay, 'Art—and the First Draft of Living': *Modern Age*, Spring, 1964, pp. 155f.

her name and the word '*Resurgam*'. In *Towards a Better Life*, two pages from the end, we read, in one of John's last explosions: '*resurgam! resurgam!* I shall rise again! Hail, all hail! Here is a promise: *resurgam!*' The tone at least holds affliction in abeyance; as a storyteller, reciting an interminable tale of woe, might insist that the tale was, at any point, unfinished, and there was no telling how it might all turn out. The comedy of Beckett's *Molloy* is in this key, holding its readers sane while threatening to drive them mad.

In Burke the comic proof is style. While John Neal dangles, twists, and squirms, his author maintains his style as the last ditch of possibility. There is hope, the book implies, as long as the sentences stay true. Faith, hope, and charity are not dead as long as grammar, logic, and rhetoric continue to act. This is in keeping with a passage in *The Philosophy of Literary Form*, where Burke, posing the question, 'Style for its own sake?' answers: 'Decidedly, not at all. Style solely as the beneath-which-not, as the admonitory and hortatory act, as the example that would prod continually for its completion in all aspects of life, and so, in Eliot's phrase, "keep something alive", tiding us over a lean season.'[1]

It seems a good moment to let the matter rest.

[1] Kenneth Burke, *The Philosophy of Literary Form* (New York. Vintage Books. 1957), p. 140.

I I

Nuances of a Theme by Stevens

The theme, from 'Notes toward a Supreme Fiction':

A bench was his catalepsy, Theatre
Of Trope. He sat in the park. The water of
The lake was full of artificial things,

Like a page of music, like an upper air,
Like a momentary color, in which swans
Were seraphs, were saints, were changing essences.[1]

I

The occupant of the bench is the poet. Or rather the Poet: a
generic figure, hardly to be distinguished too carefully at any
moment. A flick of metaphor, even a second glance, will change
him into the pensive man of 'Connoisseur of Chaos', the pensive
giant of 'Notes toward a Supreme Fiction', the naked man of
'Montrachet-Le-Jardin'. Depending on the weather and the
make of the mind he will appear as the seeing man in 'The Blue
Buildings in the Summer Air', the 'figure of capable imagination' in 'Mrs. Alfred Uruguay', the dark-blue king in 'Extracts
from Addresses to the Academy of Fine Ideas'; in several poems
he is 'the hero', sometimes 'the fictive hero', sometimes 'a man
at the centre of men'. And at dusk he is liable to become 'major
man' by an obstinate metamorphosis; under great pressure the
very 'idea of man'. Stevens warns us, 'Give him no names'; if
we obey, we are then free to think of him in any one of a dozen
roles. In 'Of Modern Poetry' he is 'a metaphysician in the dark'

[1] *Collected Poems* (New York. Knopf, 1954), p. 397. Hereafter page-reference to
this book is given, italicized, in brackets.

and something of an actor, a mime, acute in improvisation. In
'Asides on the Oboe' he is

> The impossible possible philosophers' man,
> The man who has had the time to think enough,
> The central man, the human globe, responsive
> As a mirror with a voice, the man of glass,
> Who in a million diamonds sums us up. (250)

Call him, then, the man of thought. At all cost not the man of
action, since we are reading Stevens and not another poet. The
best chance is that he is Stevens himself raised to the nth degree,
sua voluntate; metaStevens. But this is still a long way off. Meanwhile the man on the bench aspires to a condition of philosophic
rigor: he will, perhaps, wear the philosopher's hat.

But he will not be a mere philosopher. Stevens agreed with
Whitehead that 'poetry and philosophy are akin',[1] and he
allowed for the existence of men like Jean Wahl and George
Santayana, poets and philosophers in high standing with both
communities.[2] If he said in his own behalf, 'I am not a philosopher',[3] he did so to acknowledge the fact; and having done so
he was free to collect philosophical ideas and to find in them
qualities to a high degree poetic. The ideas, shall we say, were
poetic in themselves as possibilities of the mind; but when they
were pressed to serve a palpable dogma, they quickly lost their
savour. In short, a lot of philosophical poetry is dull. And yet,
among the critics, Hegel tells us that this need not be so: in
Stevens's version, 'a poem in which the poet has chosen for his
subject a philosophic theme should result in the poem of poems'.[4]
Should, but never does. And yet Stevens would not agree with
T. S. Eliot, who maintained that it is quite possible for a great
poet to do no 'thinking' at all. To Stevens, 'the greater the mind
the greater the poet': hence 'the evil of thinking as poetry is not
the same thing as the good of thinking in poetry'.[5] So if you
propose to 'think' at all, you are well advised to think along
philosophic lines. Stevens would often condescend to the philosophers, as if they were second-class citizens making the noise of

[1] *The Necessary Angel* (New York. Knopf, 1951), p. 30.
[2] *Opus Posthumous* (New York. Knopf, 1957), pp. 183, 187.
[3] ibid., p. 195.   [4] ibid., p. 187.
[5] *The Necessary Angel*, p. 165.

'reason's click-clack' while poets played the sweet music of the imagination. Philosophers would give 'the official view of being',[1] but the unofficial view proffered by poets is more exciting, more daring. Since truth is unattainable in any form that would satisfy the strict philosopher, that man must end in despair: 'the philosopher comes to nothing because he fails'.[2] Meanwhile the poet lives dangerously in the life of the mind, a wild gambler in casual exfoliations. If the cards fall right, he owns 'the mundo of the imagination', a more vital possession than 'the gaunt world of the reason'.[3] And yet, despite this, the poets do well to familiarize themselves with the philosophic world, if only because many of the concepts in that world are poetic. Indeed, some philosophic ideas are the most beautiful materials the poet will ever find. If they have the look of despair—we can add this gloss —all the better: poets know this look, and know how to deal with it.

II

Hence the man on the bench will use philosophic ideas in his own way, as *materia poetica*, and he will entertain them not for their truth or even for their beautifully desperate failure, but for their 'poetic' nature, their suggestiveness. He will feel that some philosophic ideas are 'inherently poetic'; the concept of the infinity of the world, for instance. And the idea of God is 'the ultimate poetic idea'.[4] But if he offers any philosophic or ethical observations on his own behalf, he will ground them in an obstinate aesthetic. This will leave room for difference; even for contradiction. If he attends with adequate nobility and precision to the multitudinous seemings, he can let the One Being look after itself: 'let be be finale of seem', in 'The Emperor of Ice Cream'. After all, the most beautiful idea in the world says that at some level of abstraction all things are One; division sends us back to unity:

> It is the celestial ennui of apartments
> That sends us back to the first idea . . . (*381*)

A wave is a force 'and not the water of which it is composed,

[1] ibid., p. 40.   [2] ibid., p. 45.   [3] ibid., p. 58.
[4] *Opus Posthumous*, pp. 183, 193.

which is never the same'.[1] All things resemble one another. The
river of rivers in Connecticut is a force, 'not to be seen beneath
the appearances/That tell of it' (533). In 'This Solitude of Cataracts' the flecked river flows through many places 'as if it stood
still in one.' And, to crown all seemings, in 'A Primitive like an
Orb' the lover, the believer, and the poet conspire with earth
and sky to celebrate 'the central poem'. Meanwhile the poet does
what he can; writes poems: the central poem is the finale. He
does this for a hundred reasons, but chiefly because he is devoted
to the human imagination in its marvellous range, its plenitude,
its manifold powers. One thing at a time: let the fifteenth poem
wait until the fourteenth is written.

It is necessary to say this because the philosophic positions registered in Stevens's poems are severally in contradiction: we
have already implied this. The poet swings between Realism and
Idealism with a degree of facility which a mere philosopher
would envy. True, he had his favourite resting-places: there
were days on which he felt that nothing could withstand the
mind, and other days on which he felt with equal pleasure that
reality was its own master. In 'Sunday Morning' the woman
laments that even in Paradise we shall not find the objectivity,
the *alteracion* she desires; of the pear and the plum she says, 'Alas
that they should wear our colours there' (69). And there are
many poems in which Stevens insists that fruit will wear our
colours, the colours of the imagination: else he will deny its
'fruitfulness'. But before we convict him of intellectual confusion or indifference we have to understand why he would make
no philosophical commitments. He gives the reason clearly
enough in the first pages of 'The Noble Rider and the Sound of
Words' when he says: 'Adams in his work on Vico makes the
remark that the true history of the human race is a history of its
progressive mental states. It is a remark of interest in this relation.'[2]

It is a remark of crucial interest in considering Stevens; because
it means that any mental state is relevant to his 'true history'. As
soon as a mental state declares itself in Stevens, it immediately
becomes part of the whole story, and Stevens will value it as
such without cross-examining it too ruthlessly. If it is succeeded
by another mental state and a new 'allegiance', well and good,

[1] *The Necessary Angel*, p. 35.   [2] ibid., p. 6.

this is the natural progression of human things. Many of these mental states in Stevens were instigated by the contemplation of philosophic ideas; others were endorsed by them. A poem by Marianne Moore would join with an essay by the realist H. D. Lewis[1] and both with Stevens's mind. Or an intuition of a more idealist cast would look around for endorsement in Kant or, it might be, Joad. Stevens took his mental states where he found them without requiring them to swear a loyalty oath. So he would quote Joad: 'Philosophy has long dismissed the notion of substance and modern physics has endorsed the dismissal. . . How, then, does the world come to appear to us as a collection of solid, static objects extended in space? Because of the intellect, which presents us with a false view of it.'[2] And Kant, who says that the objects of perception are conditioned by the nature of the mind as to their form: the phrasing is Stevens's, in 'The Figure of the Youth as Virile Poet'.[3]

The happiest situation for Stevens, of course, is that reality and the imagination are equal and inseparable; a mutual tension, a fine acknowledgement of equals. And this credence is featured in many poems, such as 'In the Carolinas', 'Infanta Marina', 'Montrachet-Le-Jardin', and several others: for a motto, think of 'a nature to its natives all/Beneficence' (442) or, 'The partaker partakes of that which changes him' (392). And the theory of this happiness is 'The Noble Rider and the Sound of Words'.

But it is necessary to say that these philosophic commitments are severally contradictory; not merely to repeat, as an apologia, that Stevens was not a philosopher, a systematic thinker. Stevens did not play with philosophic ideas: he was too scrupulous to frivol with the gravity of other men. Moment by moment, poem by poem, he committed himself to the 'mental state' of the occasion, doing his best to make it lucid if nothing else. If it occurred to him that these local commitments were contradictory, he was not distressed, because he trusted that the work would conform to the nature of the worker, and no other conformity was required. Stevens's readers may yield him this

---

[1] *Opus Posthumous*, pp. 236–7. Cf. *The Necessary Angel*, p. 96. These sentences were taken by Stevens from an essay by H. D. Lewis. See Joseph Riddell in *Modern Language Notes*, LXXVI (1961), pp. 124–9.

[2] *The Necessary Angel*, p. 25.

[3] ibid., p. 56.

courtesy; or they may refuse. (As a lay epistemologist I have my own position, and I am a little sullen when Stevens subverts it, either in verse or prose.) The principle of complementarity which modern physicists espouse would have been useful to Stevens and may be essential to his readers; the simultaneous presence of incompatibilities on the field of action. Among the philosophers and anthropologists Joseph Campbell has recently used this principle to bring the consideration of symbolism to a high atmosphere. Starting at the easy level, he says. 'According to one mode or aspect of our experience, all things—ourselves included—are implicated in a context of space-time determinants and are therefore bound; and yet according to the other mode of our experience (which is impossible to reconcile with the first) all things—ourselves included—are freely creating themselves all the time.' But if we push the principle for what it is worth, contradictions wither: then, to cite one example, 'Prometheus defying Zeus is not the free individual and social and cosmological order. Rather, Prometheus and Zeus, I and the Father, are one.'[1] Stevens did not invoke this principle, so far as I recall: if we invoke it now, on our own behalf, it is to make our discussion civil, to fend off the brawling of yes and no, at least to ensure that we remain silent until the poems are heard. It was enough for Stevens, and it is enough for many of his readers, that the poems conform to the nature of the poet, to his 'progressive mental states', and that that nature be handsome. (Aristotle allowed that a man may persuade in this way.)

III

'Give him no names.' Agreed: but we must work toward a description, at the least. His professional purpose is easily given in his own words: 'It is very easy to imagine a poetry of ideas in which the particulars of reality would be shadows among the poem's disclosures.'[2] Since this note persists, we might call him an ideal poet; to bring in Plato, who cannot be left out of Stevens; and to remark an engaging link with the last plays of Shakespeare, which Northrop Frye calls 'ideal comedies', bearing

---

[1] 'The Symbol without Meaning': *Eranos*, Jahrbuch 1957, Band XXVI (Zurich, 1958).
[2] *Opus Posthumous*, p. 187.

down with all necessary pressure upon the meaning of the adjective. And if we want a motto in Stevens's own words, there is the last paragraph of 'Three Academic Pieces': 'In short, metaphor has its aspect of the ideal. This aspect of it cannot be dismissed merely because we think that we have long since outlived the ideal. The truth is that we are constantly outliving it and yet the ideal itself remains alive with an enormous life.'[1]

Or we might call him a metaphysical poet, for the sufficient reason that his themes are often metaphysical; Appearance and Reality; the One and the Many; Being (as, specifically, in 'Metaphor as Degeneration'); Knowledge; Image and Idea; Metamorphosis. But this would mean going against Stevens's wish. There is a remarkable passage in 'The Figure of the Youth as Virile Poet'—a page of dear, gorgeous nonsense to rival Plato's—in which Stevens says that when we find ourselves 'in agreement with reality' we 'cease to be metaphysicians'. In fact, we 'do not want to be metaphysicians'. In the radiant and productive atmosphere of poetry the virile poet sees metaphysicians in the crowd around him, but he has his own sufficient reasons for being himself; the poet, *ipse*.

Trying again: it would be possible and decent to think of Stevens as a mythological poet, on the particular authority of that passage in 'The Comedian as the Letter C' in which he says

> What counted was mythology of self,
> Blotched out beyond unblotching. . . . (*28*)

or that late poem in which he says that, 'A mythology reflects its region.'[2] And this, at the least, would be preferable to the poverty of calling Stevens a symbolist poet; especially after 'This Solitude of Cataracts'; in which the poet repudiates the language of wild ducks or mountains that are not mountains. But then we remark, with some embarrassment, that Stevens also wrote 'The Poem that Took the Place of a Mountain'; so we are advised to take another tack.

The last one: the man on the bench, 'Theatre/Of Trope'. Call him, then, a tropical poet. Since this implicates Santayana's *The Realm of Matter*—a crucial parallel text for Stevens—all the better. By trope Santayana means the 'essence of any event as

---

[1] *The Necessary Angel*, p. 82.
[2] *Opus Posthumous*, p. 118.

distinguished from that event itself'. Tropes 'belong to the region of Platonic ideas: they are unitary patterns, distinguishable
in the movement of things: they are no part of the moving substance, executing those patterns and overflowing them'.[1] This is
one way of putting it. Another way is Stevens's:

>   To get at the thing
>   Without gestures is to get at it as
>   Idea.   (295)

And then there is, beside this, his famous law of abstraction.
    We like this, or we do not. Stevens worked in this way be-
cause it was the nature of his mind to work in this way. One of
his favourite sentences was Focillon's: 'The chief characteristic
of the mind is to be constantly describing itself.'[2] And Stevens
dramatized this in 'The Man with the Blue Guitar':

>   Or, at the least, a phrase, that phrase,
>   A hawk of life, that latined phrase: (178)

When Renato Poggioli asked him what this meant, Stevens
answered: 'A hawk of life means one of those phrases that grips
in its talons some aspect of life that it took a hawk's eye to see.
To call a phrase a hawk of life is in itself an example.'[3] Or, alter-
natively, 'the image must be of the nature of its creator':[4] the act
—our own gloss—must be of the nature of its agent.
    My predicate runs somewhat on these lines. Stevens wrote his
poems for a hundred reasons, including this one: to pass the
time, to get through the evening. He wrote while waiting: for
what? For the maximum disclosure of his own poetic powers.
And because this is eight words he often reduced it to one, calling
it God: or sometimes to three, calling it the human imagination.
Hence and meanwhile there was something to be done. Good or
bad, it would be better than its alternative—nothing, the grand
zero. He had his own powers: and he had the language, in its
dazzling resource. Put the two together, and you have a Theatre
of Trope. Add the belief that the imagination is 'the will, as a

---

[1] *The Realm of Matter* (London. Constable, 1930), pp. 101–2, 113.
[2] *The Necessary Angel*, p. 46.
[3] *Mattino Domenicale, ed altre poesie* (Turin, 1954), p. 180,
[4] *Opus Posthumous*, p. 118.

principle of the mind's being, striving to realize itself in knowing itself'.[1] Then because this object is dauntingly far off, allow that the poet will push hard and live 'on the verge of consciousness'.[2]

He will push hard because 'the imagination is the power of the mind over the possibilities of things';[3] it is 'the will of things' (*84*); it must exert its mastery, reducing the monster (*175*). The pressure against it is often given as the moon, 'part of a supremacy always/Above him' (*314*); and sometimes it is the direct pressure of reality, society, bourgeois triumph, war. Hence the war between the mind and sky must continue because 'the mind is the end and must be satisfied':

> It cannot be half earth, half mind; half sun,
> Half thinking; until the mind has been satisfied,
> Until, for him, his mind is satisfied. (*257*)

Satisfied, assuaged, appeased; then 'the vivid transparence that you bring is peace' (*380*). In the Theatre of Trope the poet is Prospero, commanding Ariel to devise revels, masques, confections; poems all, at once 'makings of the sun' and 'makings of his self' (*532*). Tropical poets are always Prosperos; all they need is a little plot of ground, an ample language, and their own imagination. Then the water of a lake fills itself with imagined, artificial things; swans become seraphs, melting themselves in thin air, at the imaginations's caprice. 'The freshness of transformation is/The freshness of a world' (*397–8*). (But this is to anticipate.)

IV

'The image must be of the nature of its creator': a Kantian aphorism. Indeed, when we follow the man on the bench through his progressive mental states, the way calls for description in Kantian terms; somewhat as we trace a configuration and know that at some late stage it will make a way of its own, denying its paradigm; as Stevens does, at the end.

If we begin with Kant's term from the *Critique of Pure Reason*,

---

[1] *The Necessary Angel*, p. 10. Cf. *Opus Posthumous*, p. 242.
[2] *The Necessary Angel*, p. 115.
[3] ibid., p. 136.

'empirical intuitions of sensibility' :[1] ('The capacity for receiving representations through the mode in which we are affected by objects is entitled *sensibility*. Objects are given to us by means of sensibility, and it alone yields us *intuitions*. . . . The effect of an object upon the faculty of representation . . . is sensation. That intuition which is in relation to the object through sensation is entitled *empirical*.'). This is Stevens's first world, the world of *Harmonium* (except that *Harmonium* includes a few poems, like 'Sunday Morning', which point beyond that world). The first poems celebrate many things which seem to be 'rankest trivia' but are in fact the *sensibilia* upon which so much depends. They are the 'arrant spices of the sun' (*88*), the 'immense dew of Florida' (*95*), 'prickly and obdurate, dense, harmonious' (*35*), 'hallucinations in surfaces' (*472*). Stevens called them '*delectationes* of the senses':[2] Antonio Machado called them 'the *Olé! Olé!* of things'.[3] When we think of this world in Stevens we call it, quite simply, Florida; but this is to be a little too easy. More accurately, it is the world evoked by words and phrases, some Stevens's, some not, like these: 'gay is, gay was' (*385*), abundance, gallantry, elegance, epicure, euphrasy, regalia, panache, fastidious, swish, *vif*, dizzle-dazzle.

Most poets begin and end in this world. It is a dense, sufficient world as long as it remains so; or as long as the poet's mind is satisfied with it. But Stevens moved on. He said farewell to Florida and moved on and back to his 'North of cold'. Presumably he had his own sufficient reasons. But he would have had to move in any event, as a good Kantian. The quotidian, he says, saps philosophers (*42*); even the quotidian of Florida, presumably, has its attendant 'malady' (*96*). But in any event the Kantian's mind is never satisfied by *sensibilia*, however profuse: it always recognizes that there is a higher level of generalization, which must be possessed for the sufficient reason that it is there. In Kant this world operates through 'concepts of the Understanding'.

From the *Critique*: Objects 'are thought through the *under-*

---

[1] The following, and all subsequent, phrases from the *Critique* are taken from the translation by Norman Kemp Smith (London. Macmillan, 1929), pp. 65, 93, 106, 308, 310–11, 313, 550–1.

[2] *The Necessary Angel*, p. 166.

[3] *Juan de Mairena*: edited and translated by Ben Belitt (Berkeley. University of California Press, 1963), p. 44.

standing, and from the understanding arise *concepts*. . .
Understanding is the mind's power of producing representatio..
from itself, the spontaneity of knowledge. . . . Insofar as imagination is spontaneity, I sometimes also entitle it the productive
imagination. . . . Concepts of understanding contain nothing
more than the unity of reflection upon appearances, insofar as
these appearances must necessarily belong to a possible empirical
consciousness'.

This is the world of *Ideas of Order*; though its first and greatest
intimation is 'Sunday Morning'. Stevens speaks of it with un-
characteristic directness: 'Words add to the senses' *(234)*. And
again: 'The eye sees less than the tongue says.'[1] In 'A Collect of
Philosophy' he says that poets and philosophers are united in 'the
habit of forming concepts', probing for an integration.[2] In 'The
Relations between Poetry and Painting' he gives in his own
words Kant's theory of the productive imagination: the operative force is not the sensibility, it is a constructive force which
uses the offerings of sensibility for its own new purposes. And
its triumphs are *'deliciae* of the spirit'.[3] When we think of this
world in Stevens we think of words of a different order from
those of *Harmonium*: words like resemblance, liaison, relation,
integration, humility, sentence, anatomy. The anatomy of
Summer is not the same as Summer. 'A minimum of making in
the mind' *(473)* is a late phrase, but it will serve our purpose if
we take it to mean a necessary minimum, altogether necessary
and desirable; as Stevens in an even later poem gives us two
Romes, 'the two alike in the make of the mind' *(508)*. Readers
who love *Harmonium* so much that they want Stevens to make
his permanent poetic residence in Florida are never assuaged by
his concepts of the understanding: in *Ideas of Order* they miss the
poet's gibberish, the zay-zay and rou-cou-cou of the venereal
soil. If *Harmonium* is a holiday-poster, *Ideas of Order* is a lieder-
recital. There is room for both. And the later book has, as its
weather and consistency, a sustained rhetoric, a high style, a
sublime, which the *vif* of intuition hardly allows; except as an
occasional grace note in poems like 'Sunday Morning' and (in
part) 'The Comedian as the Letter C'. As in 'Evening without
Angels':

[1] *Opus Posthumous*, p. 170.   [2] ibid., p. 196.
[3] *The Necessary Angel*, pp. 165–6.

> . . . Evening, when the measure skips a beat
> And then another, one by one, and all
> To a seething minor swiftly modulate.
> Bare night is best. Bare earth is best. Bare, bare,
> Except for our own houses, huddled low
> Beneath the arches and their spangled air,
> Beneath the rhapsodies of fire and fire,
> Where the voice that is in us makes a true response,
> Where the voice that is great within us rises up,
> As we stand gazing at the rounded moon.   (137–8)

Most poets who achieve a grand rhetoric are satisfied: their minds are satisfied. But Stevens was a good enough Kantian to know that there was still one great resource of the mind lying unpossessed: the powers of the imagination would have to take one more country, or remain in part undisclosed. So he would push toward a higher level of generalization, the Kantian-Hegelian Universal. In Kant's terms; Ideas of Reason. In the *Critique of Pure Reason* he said that 'in the domain of theology we must view everything that can belong to the context of possible experience . . . as if the sum of all appearances (the sensible world itself) had a single, highest and all-sufficient ground beyond itself, namely, a self-subsistent, original, creative reason'. Stevens, of course, will deal with this by calling it God and equating it with the human imagination. Kant gives most of his thought by defending Plato: he speaks of Plato's 'flight from the ectypal mode of reflecting upon the physical world-order to the architectonic ordering of it according to ends, that is, according to ideas. . . .' And again: 'Plato knew that our reason naturally exalts itself to forms of knowledge which so far transcend the bounds of experience that no given empirical object can ever coincide with them, but which must none the less be recognized as having their own reality, and which are by no means mere fictions of the brain.' The idea, in short, is an heuristic concept.

Stevens's way of announcing this is to invoke a Supreme Fiction and say: *It Must be Abstract.* Indeed, *Notes toward a Supreme Fiction* is the culmination of Stevens's Ideas of Reason. For motto: 'This warmth in the blood-world for the pure idea' (256). Sometimes Stevens will insist on having the Idea in all its purity, as in the second part of 'The Owl in the Sarcophagus'.

At other times he will exert great pressure to reconcile Idea and Image: when he enters the place of metamen and parathings, they must still be men though metamen, things though parathings (*448-9*). In the second of the 'Contrary Theses' he will walk toward an abstract of which the sun, the dog, and the boy are 'contours': the abstract is the premise from which all things are conclusions (*270*). In 'The Noble Rider and the Sound of Words' the measure of a poet is deemed to be the measure of his power to abstract himself, 'and to withdraw with him into his abstraction the reality on which the lovers of truth insist'.[1] It is a hard saying, but Stevens will say it again; notably in 'Effects of Analogy', where he invokes 'a world that transcends the world and a life livable in that transcendence'.[2] And then there are moments in which the *sensibilia*, the contours, seem merely 'crude compoundings', and the poet on the verge of consciousness demands that the real come because his need is so great:

> To find the real,
> To be stripped of every fiction except one,
> The fiction of an absolute—   (*404*)

When the going is as hard as this, Stevens often plays solitaire under the oaks, escapes to 'principium',[3] reflecting—I assume—that major man is 'abler/In the abstract than in his singular' (*388*). And in such moments he always invokes Plato. Sometimes by loyal paraphrase: 'The aim of our lives should be to draw ourselves away as much as possible from the unsubstantial facts of the world about us and establish some communion with the objects which are apprehended by thought and not sense.'[4] This is from 'On Poetic Truth', and Stevens immediately protests that he, as a poet, is not prepared to dismiss 'the individual and particular facts of experience as of no importance in themselves'. But often, in the poetry, he escapes in precisely this way; sometimes by imagining a 'person' who has escaped in his behalf:

> If we propose
> A large-sculptured, platonic person, free from time,
> And imagine for him the speech he cannot speak,

---

[1] ibid., p. 23.
[3] *Opus Posthumous*, p. 111.
[2] ibid., p. 130.
[4] ibid., p. 236.

> A form, then, protected from the battering, may
> Mature: A capable being may replace
> Dark horse and walker walking rapidly.   (*330*)

The platonic person, the man on the bench is one of the extreme
reaches of his imagination, composes structures of his mind;
when a composition is complete, it has the composure and
finality that Rilke found in Valéry's language. The structures are
'stratagems of the spirit' (*376*), 'academies' (*386*), 'enclosures of
hypotheses' (*516*). When we think of them, or—the same thing
—when we think of their style, we say that the style is curial,
doctrinal, exquisite, lofty, vertiginous. Stevens, like Santayana,
is an inquisitor of structures, and he will test them as severely as
he can. He knows as well as any other modern poet that one can
be self-indulgent in words even more easily than in action or
evasion. And he knows and does not need Elizabeth Sewell to
tell him that words are a great defence of the mind against being
possessed by thought; a defence and an ease of mind. Words
alone are certain good, Yeats said, and only half-believed: the
other half of the belief was taken up by Stevens, for whom the
world had to issue in the word or declare itself redundant. As in
'Description without Place':

> Thus the theory of description matters most.
> It is the theory of the word for those
>
> For whom the word is the making of the world,
> The buzzing world and lisping firmament.
>
> It is a world of words to the end of it,
> In which nothing solid is its solid self.
>
> As, men make themselves their speech: the hard hidalgo
> Lives in the mountainous character of his speech; (*345*)

Everything is proved, justified, certified by the 'acutest speech'
which crowns it; and by that alone. Ideas of Reason have no
other ground than the nature of the imagination that constructs
them. When Stevens confronted this fact, he sometimes con-
strued it for his delight, and sometimes for his despair: the

ground was often enough, but often not. And sometimes he protests too much.

This accounts for a characteristic sequence in many of Stevens's later poems: he will begin by positing a situation, often a loss, sometimes an 'idea of reason' of some extremity; and then, whatever the situation, he will claim to rise above it because his imagination has encompassed it; and the claim sends him through the situation, through the poem. In 'Notes toward a Supreme Fiction', for instance, he begins a sequence: 'What am I to believe?' And then he posits an angel in a cloud, leaping down through evening's revelations and growing warm in flight. And then he asks: 'Am I that imagine this angel less satisfied?' He answers this in his own favour: the poet, imagining this ease, possesses it. 'I have not but I am and as I am, I am.' (As he says in the *Adagia*: 'Poetry is a purging of the world's poverty and change and evil and death. It is a present perfecting, a satisfaction in the irremediable poverty of life.')[1] Then from the consoling refuge of this 'structure of the mind'—this 'academy'—he turns back to survey the quotidian world:

> These external regions, what do we fill them with
> Except reflections, the escapades of death,
> Cinderella fulfilling herself beneath the roof?   (*405*)

Again, in 'The Plain Sense of Things': when the leaves have fallen it feels like the end of everything, even the end of imagination. 'The great structure has become a minor house.' No *vif*, no romance, the malady of the quotidian. And yet, and yet, and yet:

> Yet the absence of the imagination had
> Itself to be imagined.   (*503*)

Hence . . . and so on.

The trouble in the great structures of the mind, of course, is that they are miles beyond verification. By conforming to the nature of the mind which invents them, they come into being, achieve their identity. But by conforming to nothing else, they achieve nothing else. They have no status in the world, except that which accrues from the prestige of their creator. At best, they are 'supernatural preludes' (*414*) or 'putative canzones' (*420*). If men are made out of words, then life does indeed consist of

[1] ibid., p. 167.

propositions about life (355). This is either true or false: if it is false, then we must write a poetry or (better) live a life to refute it: if it is true, then indeed 'Reality is a vacuum'.[1] (And then we are reminded of Kant's great parable of the dove which, feeling the resistance of the wind, thought it would fly better in a vacuum.) In short, Ideas of Reason exist in a vacuum; they evade the resistance only too successfully. The man on the bench is poetically safe with his lakes and swans which change into seraphs; and he is still safe in the wilderness of essence and Trope if he brings his own resistance, his scruple. If not; not. The third phase of Stevens's poems invites description in these terms; the ease of mind, freedom of trope, resistances entirely adequate or not quite adequate, air or vacuum. But the story is not finished; there is still *The Rock*, and beside it there are several resistant poems in *The Auroras of Autumn*.

V

We posit for the man on the bench a certain scruple. He will quickly become dissatisfied if his ease of mind is too easy, and he will construe the cause with some severity. In the wilderness of essence one moves, presumably, with miraculous freedom; there are no obstacles of sensibility or understanding; the burdens of the past drop from us. And so on. But there is a passage in 'The Figure of the Youth as Virile Poet' which makes us ponder. Stevens has been thinking of the past, and the several images it throws before us. Now he imagines a young man emerging from one of these backgrounds; he represents 'the intelligence that endures'. He is the son, still bearing the burden of the father; Aeneas, carrying Anchises. 'It is the clear intelligence of the young man still bearing the burden of the obscurities of the intelligence of the old. It is the spirit out of its own self, not out of some surrounding myth, delineating with accurate speech the complications of which it is composed.'[2] This is the poet's programme for resistance. When the wilderness palls in its ease, Stevens—I speak now mostly of *The Rock*—brings resistance in the form of contingency, fact, appearance, even 'familiar things' (338).

This is not a return to *Harmonium*, a senior citizen's retirement

---

[1] ibid., p. 168   [2] *The Necessary Angel*, p. 53.

to Florida. It is not even a repudiation of Kant and Hegel and all the old immortals. Rather, in these great last poems Stevens is gathering all his resources, disowning nothing, and laying them all at the feet of humanity. He doesn't need a theory for this: besides, he has done his homework, he has been to school at the philosophers and aestheticians. If there is any theory behind these poems, it is Croce's Oxford lecture of 1933 in which the philosopher invoked an image of 'the whole man': 'the man who thinks and wills, and loves, and hates'.[1] Stevens quoted a few sentences in 'The Noble Rider and the Sound of Words' and returned to expand them in one of his last essays. The expansion has a certain interest, short of the highest interest, and it includes a sentence by Whitehead which Stevens quotes now (1955) and which he would not have quoted but for a radical change in his whole bearing. The sentence from Whitehead reads: 'Who shall say that to live kindly and graciously and meet one's problems bravely from day to day is not a great art, or that those who can do it are not great artists.' Then—for good measure—the next one reads: 'Aesthetics are understood in too restricted a sense.'[2] That these sentences were quoted and endorsed by Stevens is fantastic; Stevens, who asked, 'What is there in life except one's ideas?' and thought of 'the world as word'. But there it is. This is his final yes; to other people, other lives. His new text of the world is 'a scribble of fret and fear and fate' (494); and as if to deny to himself—the man on the bench—the pleasure of changing swans into seraphs, he says now:

> We seek
> The poem of pure reality, untouched
> By trope or deviation, straight to the word,
> Straight to the transfixing object, to the object
>
> At the exactest point at which it is itself,
> Transfixing by being purely what it is. . . .   (471)

Hence the rock itself. 'The rock cannot be broken. It is truth' (375). And again:

> The rock is the gray particular of man's life,
> The stone from which he rises, up—and—ho,
> The step to the bleaker depths of his descents. . . .   (528)

[1] ibid., p. 16.   [2] Opus Posthumous, p. 230.

The last word in the *Collected Poems* is 'reality'; its proof, its illustration is a bird's cry heard—heard, not posited or dreamed —in March.

Most of the evidence is in. If we try to trace the source of this new feeling in Stevens—the feeling for humanity that gets into the poems of the last nine or ten years of his writing life—the signs are thin on the ground. But there is, for one thing, his strange praise of 'the ignorant man'; praise common enough in Yeats, Synge, Williams, Eliot, but none the less strange when Stevens gives it:

> You must become an ignorant man again
> And see the sun again with an ignorant eye

he said in his first moments of *Notes toward a Supreme Fiction*. And there is his tone in 'In a Bad Time':

> But the beggar gazes on calamity
> And thereafter he belongs to it, to bread
> Hard found, and water tasting of misery.   (*426*)

This is one thing. And another is Stevens's response to particular lives. Santayana is only an extreme instance who prompts us to see that *The Rock* is more densely populated than any other book by Stevens; it is the only collection of Stevens's poems which one would invoke in a discussion of personalism, dialogue, *I and Thou*, Gabriel Marcel, Camus. For the first time Stevens has written a book which says *Thou*.

VI

So now we may think of the man on the bench coming out of his trance, his catalepsy, and asking himself, a little dazzled by the Theatre of Trope:

> I wonder, have I lived a skeleton's life,
> As a questioner about reality. . . .   (*42*)

And the wondering at once testifies to his scruple and enlarges it. This is 1947: for the remaining years of his life he will pay less devotion to the rhetorical handbook than to the 'handbook of heartbreak' (*507*): he will be touched by other lives, San-

[1] ibid., p. 89. Cf. ibid., p. 117.

tayana, an old man asleep, 'strong peasants in a peasant world' (*530*), even Ulysses and Penelope. He will listen to 'the cry of leaves that do not transcend themselves,/In the absence of fantasia'.[1] He will look at ponds that do not reflect him (*503*), and facts that proclaim his failure (*502–3*). There is still the imagination, and it still works by analogy, resemblance, metaphor, metamorphosis:

> A flick which added to what was real and its vocabulary,
> The way some first thing coming into Northern trees
> Adds to them the whole vocabulary of the South,
> The way the earliest single light in the evening sky,
>   in spring,
> Creates a fresh universe out of nothingness by adding
>   itself,
> The way a look or a touch reveals its unexpected
>   magnitudes.   (*517*)

But his acknowledgement of other people, of the quotidian in all its malady, imposes a resistance never felt in the wilderness of trope. Its symbol now is still the candle, the light of the imagination, but in 'To an Old Philosopher in Rome' it is

> A light on the candle tearing against the wick
> To join a hovering excellence, to escape
> From fire and be part only of that of which
> Fire is the symbol: the celestial possible.   (*509*)

But the saving grace is in the tearing, the wick, the sensible fire: so much so, that even at the end when every visible thing is enlarged it is 'no more than a bed, a chair and moving nuns': these, at the last, are the props and *personae* of 'the immensest theatre'; no longer a theatre of trope. It comes to this: the imagination lives even in a quiet normal life:

> There was no fury in transcendent forms.
> But his actual candle blazed with artifice.   (*523*)

Desdemona understood a fury in the words, but not the words. Yeats invoked an artifice of eternity. In Stevens, 'artifice' is a word for 'imagined'—nothing more—the humanist imagina-

[1] ibid., pp. 96–7.

tion, in time and place. This is the imagination of 'The World as Meditation', 'Long and Sluggish Lines', 'Final Soliloquy of the Interior Paramour', 'The Rock', 'St. Armorer's Church from the Outside', 'The River of Rivers in Connecticut', and 'The Course of a Particular'. It is a kind of total grandeur at the end.

12

A Reading of *Four Quartets*

Three modern poems seem to me particularly relevant to the questions we have discussed: *Four Quartets*, *Notes Toward a Supreme Fiction*, and the *Cantos*. They are all long poems; which means, among other difficulties, that we have to cope with what the poems 'say' and we cannot evade this chore by settling down to taste a phrase here, a rhyme there, or a particularly luscious piece of assonance ten pages back. The truth is that a long poem is necessarily a dogmatic poem, unless it elects the intrinsic justification of narrative—and perhaps it is necessarily dogmatic even then. So the first embarrassment in these three poems is that they are dogmatic in an undogmatic age. Stevens will try to provide 'the satisfaction of belief in an age of disbelief'. Eliot will write his poem precisely to render such satisfaction null, ashes in the mouth. But at least we can bring these poets together in one respect before sending them to their respective corners; for their poems assume that genuine 'ideas of order' must be, in the first instance, personal and individual and only at some later stage social. When each man has set his own house in order, 'society' will automatically flower in justice and security. In the *Cantos*, on the other hand, a genuine idea of order comes to the individual to the extent that he shares in a strongly ordered society. Pound wants 'society' to be so strong that it can tolerate a few Antonios and Sebastians, even if they do not step smartly into line. The question is: where do we look for Prospero?

But there is no point in drawing lines of connexion between our three poems. Each is very much the work of its own poet. Perhaps the only real connexion between them is a general sense of the problematic, a feeling that poetry is an uneasy lodger in the twentieth century, that long dogmatic poems must be particularly wary. In any event, these three poems will animate our questions, bringing our public topics to the quick of invention and critique. Our themes will persist and proliferate through the poems; the human image, the meaning of the past, the relation between human fact and human value, the possibility of commitment, the search for value in time and place, the Circe of transcendence, meaning imposed or discovered, Stevens's question in the *Notes*, 'What am I to believe?' Perhaps we can enclose all these in a fragment from Stevens's poem *Of Modern Poetry*:

> The poem of the mind in the act of finding
> What will suffice. It has not always had
> To find: the scene was set; it repeated what
> Was in the script.
> > Then the theatre was changed
> To something else. Its past was a souvenir.

—and start with *Four Quartets*.

INTRODUCTION

Four poems, each in five parts; clearly an elaborate structure, indicating that the meaning of the work is likely to be disclosed not in any culminating moment but in the organization of the whole, the relation between the parts, the correspondence of one part to its counterpart in the other poems. After *Burnt Norton* the later poems will exhibit not a development in the plot as beginning presses toward middle and middle toward end, but perhaps at every moment a new beginning, another raid on the inarticulate, as the poems indicate not positions reached but the reaching of positions, the struggle toward an object not promised, not in the contract. Hence while the poems have an unusually high proportion of abstract terms, suggesting that the experience has been brought to an unusually high degree of generalization, the poet will 'take the harm out of' these certitudes by going back over them and discarding those now deemed inadequate. The work will not be 'dramatic', it will not drive itself toward the fulfilment of a form at any moment unrealized. And yet while the leading analogies are musical (like those obtaining between air, earth, water, and fire) rather than logical (as in the parts of a syllogism or a detective story) the poems will be as dogmatic, in their way, as *The Dunciad* or *Night Thoughts*. The dogmas will be declared by making their substitutes illusory or incomplete. For this purpose the poet will use the camouflage of different voices; he will not, like the author of *Night Thoughts*, make everything depend upon the *fiat* of a single voice. The strategy of *Four Quartets* is to set up several voices, each charged with the evacuation of one area, until nothing is left but 'prayer, observance, discipline, thought and action'. And at that point, presumably, the reader is ready to 'know the place for the first time'.

I

THE STRUCTURE OF THE QUARTETS

The work begins with two fragments from Heraclitus; untranslated, but now to be translated conservatively as (i) 'Although the Word (Logos) is common to all, most people live as if each of them had a private intelligence of his own'; and (ii) 'The way up and the way down are one and the same.'[1] The second is a comforting thought, even in the flux, since if it is true the choice of direction will not matter. The first admonishes us to give up our private wisdoms, which are almost certainly mere egotistical delusions, the 'fancies' of *Burnt Norton III*, and to seek the Word which is true precisely because it is not our invention.[2] So a proper humility is launched.

Part I of each poem renders a mode of being in which we impose upon our experience our own meaning and think that it is total; but it is sometimes illusory and, at best, incomplete. In *Burnt Norton* it is the deception of the thrush, the rose-garden of experience. In *East Coker* it is the 'daunsinge'-scene, handsome, archaic; Sir Thomas Elyot's couples are led off with half-gentle irony, blessings on their heads. In *The Dry Salvages* the anxious women try to reckon the sea in their own terms, 'calculating the future', forgetting that 'the sea is all about us', a reality encom-

---

[1] Translation by Philip Wheelwright. See his *Heraclitus* (Princeton University Press, 1959), pp. 19, 90: fragments 2 and 108.

[2] Dryden says in the Preface to *Religio Laici*: 'Let us be content at least to know God by his own methods; at least so much of him as he is pleased to reveal to us in the sacred Scriptures; to apprehend them to be the word of God is all our Reason has to do; for all beyond it is the work of Faith, which is the Seal of Heaven impressed upon our humane understanding.'

passing us for which we are not responsible, incorrigibly real because—like the Word—it is not our invention. And in *Little
Gidding* the pilgrimage is only 'a shell, a husk of meaning' because we, the pilgrims, have chosen our object and (worse still)
the choice is in accordance with our own mere 'sense and
notion'.

To take one of these Parts in some detail: *Burnt Norton* begins
with four statements about Time, each spoken perhaps by a
different voice. First, Time as a continuous chain of events:

> Time present and time past
> Are both perhaps present in time future,
> And time future contained in time past.

Second, Time as eternally present and therefore unredeemable
because it excludes history, process, and the flux. Third, Time as
a continuum of events which might have been different. And
lastly, these possibilities are pointed toward a divine purpose not
ours and therefore 'the ground of our beseeching':

> What might have been and what has been
> Point to one end, which is always present.

Burnt Norton was written as a separate poem, several years before
its companions, but it almost seems as if these opening statements
embodied a cadence which the poet was to deploy as the musical
figure of the entire work; that each of the four statements becomes the ground of meditation for its corresponding poem in
the sequence. This would go some distance to meet one of the
persistent problems of the *Quartets*, the tone of *The Dry Salvages*,
the idea being that the poem has to work out the implications of

> What might have been is an abstraction
> Remaining a perpetual possibility
> Only in a world of speculation

—hence, in the verse, the note of speculation, the feeling of
words issuing from a merely speculative universe of discourse.
(But this problem can wait.)

The next lines in *Burnt Norton* translate 'what might have
been' into footfalls which echo in the memory

> Down the passage which we did not take
> Towards the door we never opened
> Into the rose-garden

—a purely linguistic event featuring all the unfulfilled possibilities strewn across our past lives, offering themselves only as a fantasy sound-box in which 'my words echo'. To disturb the fictive past is futile, but it will be disturbed, because we have filled the garden with our own echoes, and nothing is sweeter than our own deception. The rose-garden is each man's fantasy-refuge, the realms of experience which he declares his private property. In the garden what we hear is not sound, Keats's 'heard melodies', but the 'unheard music' which is Absolute Sound, since we will settle for nothing less: when we impose our own meaning we are never satisfied by finite gratifications, we lust for the Absolute. So we arrange the scene to disclose ourselves; the roses are our guests, the dry pool is filled with water out of sunlight for our benefit because a vital harmony between ourselves and Nature is our great romantic illusion. But we exaggerate our control over Reality:

> Then a cloud passed, and the pool was empty.
> Go, said the bird, for the leaves were full of children,
> Hidden excitedly, containing laughter.
> Go, go, go, said the bird: human kind
> Cannot bear very much reality

—even the reality of laughing children. In *East Coker III* 'the laughter in the garden' is invoked again as part of our fantasy, but there it is defined immediately as 'echoed ecstasy', not something that must be abandoned or evacuated but 'requiring, pointing to the agony/Of death and birth'. Here in *Burnt Norton* when we have connived with the deception of the thrush, we get as much as we deserve if the thrush chases us sadly from the garden; if the illusion is broken we have only ourselves to blame. Part I ends with the several variants of Time gathered together now and 'pointing' toward one end, 'which is always present'. In Part V when the hidden laughter of children in the foliage is pointed in this way, the time is redeemed.

Part 2 of each poem is a statement of the true condition, set off against the preoccupations which prevent its recognition. In

Burnt Norton it is given as the dance of consciousness, concentration, the still point, *Erhebung*; against the diverse impediments of garlic, sapphires, the practical desire, 'the enchainment of past and future'. In *East Coker* it is the true wisdom of humility, set off against the vortex, 'the autumnal serenity/And the wisdom of age', the goodwill of mere Tradition, 'the knowledge derived from experience', and the fear of old men. In *The Dry Salvages* it is, quite simply, 'the meaning', the Annunciation; menaced by the 'currents of action' which cover our past lives. And in *Little Gidding* it is the refining fire of the dancer; obscured by the vanities of spiritless culture, last year's words, 'the gifts reserved for age'.

In *East Coker* this second Part is particularly vivid. The true condition is given, as in *Little Gidding*, only at the end of this Part, when the ground has been cleared and the necessary discriminations imposed. The motto for this process is given in the opening lines of the third Part of *Little Gidding*:

> There are three conditions which often look alike
> Yet differ completely, flourish in the same hedgerow

—the discrimination of conditions or modes of being whose signs are often identical. In a secular or neutral context no discrimination is possible; only the vision of spirit can reveal the differences, the difference—to take one example—between the darkness inhabited by 'distinguished civil servants, chairmen of many committees', in *East Coker III* and that other darkness which is the 'darkness of God'. So the second Part of *East Coker* begins with an experimental jeremiad, an answer to the 'reconciliation' passage in the corresponding Part of *Burnt Norton*. Instead of the still point there is the vortex, which extends to the whole world the fate of three victims in *Gerontion*:

> De Bailhache, Fresca, Mrs. Cammel, whirled
> Beyond the circuit of the shuddering Bear
> In fractured atoms.

That was a way of putting it; but the poet now begins again, rejecting the jeremiad, or rather translating it into more urbane terms. Not that the poetry matters: if it must be evacuated along with the rest, well and good; a fresh start is more important. The first obstacle is the dead weight of an unemployed past; this must be cleared away, especially if it comes with the self-righteous panoply of words like 'calm' and 'serenity'. If Tradition is merely an antique drum, we must get rid of it: the past is dead, by definition, unless it is alive. Eliot holds the vaunted terms close to the light of a genuinely live tradition; under this scrutiny the serenity is only 'a deliberate hebetude', the wisdom 'only the knowledge of dead secrets'. The editorial plural of 'it seems to us' is the voice of antiseptic discrimination; its object is 'the knowledge derived from experience', a platitude from whose warmth we must be ejected. The ejecting force is the concept of Tradition as 'a new and shocking/Valuation', every moment, of all we have been. The tone becomes more astringent as the editorial 'we' focuses in a single rebuking voice:

> Do not let me hear
> Of the wisdom of old men

and the wisdom is given as a self-congratulating fiction, a mere mockery. In *Ash Wednesday* the speaker prays to be delivered from this hall of distorting mirrors: 'Suffer us not to mock ourselves with falsehood', meaning our private intelligences. And in the second Part of *Little Gidding* Eliot will make yet another attempt, using Yeats's *Purgatory* and the Ghost of Hamlet, now merging the wisdom of old men with the gifts reserved for the senile humanist. For *East Coker* the answer is: 'Humility is end less.'

Part 3 of each poem is a statement of our time-ridden condition, and a proper admonition to 'wait' without choosing our object. In *Burnt Norton* it is the tube-station 'flicker' of apathy and distraction, followed by the warning, 'Descend lower.' The descent, if we agree to it, is guided by Heraclitus and St. John of the Cross, and it features the voiding of all claims to property, sense, fancy, and even—the last surrender—spirit. This is the 'awful daring of a moment's surrender/Which an age of prudence can never retract', in the fifth section of *The Waste Land*. The key-word is Evacuation. But the lines which will form the starting-point for the corresponding Part of *East Coker* are

> This is the one way, and the other
> Is the same, not in movement

> But abstention from movement; while the
>   world moves
> In appetency, on its metalled ways
> Of time past and time future.

In Part 3 of *East Coker* this 'scene' is extended. Some of the travellers are named, notably those who travel by limousine:

> Industrial lords and petty contractors, all go into the dark,
> And dark the Sun and Moon, and the Almanach de Gotha
> And the Stock Exchange Gazette, the Directory of Directors.

But if we gloat upon the discomfiture of the rich, 'we all go with them, into the silent funeral'. Silent because anonymous; since we have obliterated our own identities, 'there is no one to bury'. The proper admonition is: 'Be still'; wait, without choosing even the objects of our faith, hope, or charity. Then this admonition, in turn, is intensified in the last lines of this Part, and will eventually become Celia's story in *The Cocktail Party*: 'You must go by a way wherein there is no ecstasy.' The last line should probably be read: 'And where you *are* is where *you* are not.' In *Little Gidding*—to defer the special problems of *The Dry Salvages*—Part III gives our time-ridden condition as indifference, desire, the enchainment of past and future; and the admonition, under Lady Juliana's auspices, is to purify the motive:

> And all shall be well and
> All manner of thing shall be well
> By the purification of the motive
> In the ground of our beseeching.

Lady Juliana's *Shewings* are the Logos common to all, now partially revealed through her but independently of her will: their truth does not depend upon her. She does not suggest that the visions were important because they attended her. There is a reality not ourselves, not our property, not our 'supreme fiction'. This is the transition between Parts 2 and 3 of *The Dry Salvages*. When a discursive voice says, 'I sometimes wonder if that is what Krishna meant,' the fresh start, the new version of our time-ridden condition, is the facile notion of Time itself as a spatial category in which the self occupies a gratifyingly secure present tense, looks 'back' to a fixed past and 'forward' to a future rich in anticipated pleasures. The anxious worried women of Part 2 were at least in a more dignified position,

> Between midnight and dawn, when the past
> is all deception,
> The future futureless. . . .

F. H. Bradley had already undermined the cosy assumptions of the travellers in Chapter 4 of *Appearance and Reality*: Eliot's admonition is given in two voices, the nocturnal voice which snubs the travellers, 'you who think that you are voyaging', and the voice of Krishna, persuading Arjuna to go with purified motive into battle. The first voice comes from a reader of Bradley:

> You are not those who saw the harbour
> Receding, or those who will disembark

and virtually challenges the travellers to declare their 'personal identity' and prove it. But the travellers can still be saved, if they heed Krishna. The quoted lines are taken from Canto VIII of the *Bhagavad-Gita*, with a glance at Canto II. The relevant sentences are these:

'He who at his last hour, when he casts off the body, goes hence remembering Me, goes assuredly into My being. Whatsoever being a man at his end in leaving the body remembers, to that same he always goes, O son of Kunti, inspired to being therein. Therefore at all times remember Me, and fight; if thy mind and understanding are devoted to Me, thou wilt assuredly come to Me. . . . In Works be thine office; in their fruits must it never be.'[1]

Eliot's version is:

> At the moment which is not of action or inaction
> You can receive this: 'on whatever sphere of being
> The mind of a man may be intent
> At the time of death'—that is the one action
> Which shall fructify in the lives of others:
> And do not think of the fruit of action.
> Fare forward.

[1] Translation by Lionel D. Barnett: *Bhagavad-Gita* (London. Dent, 1905), p. 123. Cf. Canto II, verses 38 and 47.

This is as close as we are likely to come to the dogmatic centre of this dogmatic poem. The moment which is not of action or inaction is presumably the moment of incarnate thought, concentration without elimination, in our own lives hardly more frequent than Wordsworthian 'spots of time', since human kind cannot bear very much reality. Krishna's message concerns the moment of death as his pupil goes into battle, but Eliot's Heraclitean parenthesis gives it a strangely Christian latitude; if we die every moment and if at every moment we are intent upon the highest sphere of being, then—the Dantean promise runs—this 'intention' will fructify in the lives of others. This is another version of the promise made in Part 2, after the equation of 'the meaning' with 'the one Annunciation'; that the past experience revived in the meaning 'is not the experience of one life only/ But of many generations. . . .' And of course it is also, looking back to *East Coker*, the 'lifetime burning in every moment'. If we add, from *Ash Wednesday*, 'Redeem the time', and, from *Burnt Norton*, 'only through time time is conquered', we have a node of Christian emphasis, depending upon the Incarnation, which is as close as the *Quartets* at any one moment will come to 'the meaning'.

Part 4 of each poem is a lyric of purgation; not a persuasion toward that act but the act itself. In *Burnt Norton* when we have renounced the pretentions of action and the black cloud has carried away the sun, we are at the 'ABC of being'—Wallace Stevens's phrase—and in a fit state to ask the appropriately modest questions. 'Will the clematis/Stray down, bend to us' is one of four questions, each a preparation for prayer. Clematis, the Virgin's Bower of blue, Mary's colour, and the fingers of yew point the questions toward death and the Christian hope of immortality. But the last lines are provisional: the harmony between the kingfisher's wing and nature's light is less than a final comfort; these are merely 'notes toward' prayer. In *East Coker* the lyric of purgation hovers over Adam's curse, Original Sin. The tone is strangely crude; indeed, this is one of the weaker parts of the poem. The analogies of health and disease, surgeons, patients, but hospitals are marginally appropriate, but far too dependent upon our reading 'the wounded surgeon' as Christ, 'the dying nurse' as the Church, the hospital as the earth, 'the ruined millionaire' as God the Father, the briars as the thorns of

Christ. When we have effected these translations little remains but the satisfaction of having done so. The corresponding Part of *The Dry Salvages* is much finer, a direct prayer continuous with that of Part 5 of *Ash Wednesday*. Then the last version, in *Little Gidding*, is the Pentecostal Fire, the Descent of the Holy Ghost. The German bomber which was the 'dark dove' of Part 3 is now transformed:

> The dove descending breaks the air
> With flame of incandescent terror

and if the old dove was deadly the new one is far from being domesticated. Heraclitus's account of the Death of the Elements is relevant, but the entire lyric is an extended version of the lines in the corresponding Part of *East Coker*:

> If to be warmed, then I must freeze
> And quake in frigid purgatorial fires
> Of which the flame is roses, and the smoke is briars.

—with a glance at Adam's curse and 'the one discharge from sin and error'. The first lyric, in *Burnt Norton*, was all question; the second, in *East Coker*, a sermon of rude reminders; the third, the prayer of *The Dry Salvages*; and now the question can be answered:

> Who then devised the torment? Love.
> Love is the unfamiliar Name
> Behind the hands that wove
> The intolerable shirt of flame
> Which human power cannot remove.
> We only live, only suspire
> Consumed by either fire or fire.

In the third Part of *Ash Wednesday* the devil of the stairs wore 'the deceitful face of hope and despair'. In *East Coker* the faith and the hope and the love were all 'in the waiting'. And now the tenable hope is specified in 'the choice of pyre or pyre', taking up where Part I left off, 'pentecostal fire/In the dark time of the year'. The collocation of Fire and Love, as the poet remarked of the ascetic conjunction of the Fire Sermon's 'Burning burning burning burning' and St. Augustine's 'O Lord Thou pluckest me out', in *The Waste Land*, 'is not an accident'.

Part 5 of each poem is a meditation on the redemption of Time. In *Night Thoughts* Young asks, innocently enough, 'Redeem we time?' In *Ash Wednesday* the voice intones:

>   Redeem
> The time. Redeem
> The unread vision in the higher dream
> While jewelled unicorns draw by the gilded hearse.

Part 5 of *Burnt Norton* is the first attempt, a tentative and frustrated figuring of time redeemed in Love. It begins with a Chinese jar which 'still/Moves perpetually in its stillness', but this is merely a slight specification of the 'daylight' of Part 3,

> Investing form with lucid stillness
> Turning shadow into transient beauty
> With slow rotation suggesting permanence.

But clearly the Chinese jar won't do; nor will the stillness of the violin. Then the syntax lurches in dazed considerations of beginning and end. The words strain and crack because they are not the Word, they are one man's fancies, his 'private intelligence', his disconsolate chimeras, the 'merely' human voices which, in *Prufrock*, 'wake us, and we drown'. Or perhaps the 'daemonic, chthonic powers' of *The Dry Salvages*. The last lines give up the attempt to offer comparisons from a familiar medium and confront the problem head-on, beginning with Aristotle's God as the Unmoved Mover, Dryden's Universal He, 'Unmade, unmov'd; yet making, moving All.' Eliot's version is

> Love is itself unmoving,
> Only the cause and end of movement,
> Timeless, and undesiring
> Except in the aspect of time
> Caught in the form of limitation
> Between un-being and being

—which I interpret as the Incarnation, a later version of a choric passage in *The Rock VII*:

> A moment not out of time, but in time, in what we call
> history: transecting, bisecting the world of time, a
> moment in time but not like a moment of time,

A moment in time but time was made through that moment:
for without the meaning there is not time, and that
moment of time gave the meaning.

'Un-being' is what *The Rock* calls 'negative being': 'being' is the
still point. *Burnt Norton* ends:

Sudden in a shaft of sunlight
Even while the dust moves
There rises the hidden laughter
Of children in the foliage
Quick now, here, now, always—
Ridiculous the waste sad time
Stretching before and after.

This sounds definitive, the great moment, especially when it is
set off against the waste sad time. But each of its terms has already been circumscribed. God as the Timeless is immanent in
the temporal, yes, here as in the *Paradiso*. He descended into history and thereby 'made time'. But we have already seen that the
rose-garden is each man's fantasy-refuge, not absurd or trivial
but incomplete, like the children's laughter. And the proof is in
the shaft of sunlight which will flash again across the corresponding Part of *The Dry Salvages*, focusing upon an experience declared incomplete. Two conditions are described in this Part, and
they are distinguished as firmly as in *The Cocktail Party*. In that
play the conditions are that of the saint, Celia, and that of the
rest of us, Edward and Lavinia at the end of the play, 'a good
life' but not sanctity or the refining fire. Critics who were
scandalized by this separation in the play did not remark that the
same plot is inaugurated in Part 5 of *The Dry Salvages*. This Part
begins with an account of 'men's curiosity' which 'searches past
and future/And clings to that dimension'. But then there is
sanctity:

But to apprehend
The point of intersection of the timeless
With time, is an occupation for the saint—
No occupation either, but something given
And taken, in a lifetime's death in love,
Ardour and selflessness and self-surrender.

Celia, clearly. But most of us are Edwards or Lavinias, and for us

> there is only the unattended
> Moment, the moment in and out of time,
> The distraction fit, lost in a shaft of sunlight,
> The wild thyme unseen, or the winter lightning
> Or the waterfall, or music heard so deeply
> That it is not heard at all, but you are the music
> While the music lasts

—the unheard music in the shrubbery of *Burnt Norton*. In that poem the words crack and strain before the birth of Celia. When she goes on the 'way of illumination' in Part 5 of *The Dry Salvages* the rest of us do what we can in the middle style:

> And right action is freedom
> From past and future also.
> For most of us, this is the aim
> Never here to be realised;
> We are only undefeated
> Because we have gone on trying;

—a counsel from which we extract whatever juice we can, perhaps more and perhaps less than Edward when he remarked:

> But Sir Henry has been saying,
> I think, that every moment is a fresh beginning;
> And Julia, that life is only keeping on;
> And somehow, the two ideas seem to fit together.

In Part 5 of *East Coker* the meditation on Time is carried a little further than in *Burnt Norton*, beginning with a rather damp consideration of life 'in the middle way', where, 'For us, there is only the trying.' Eliot seems now to repudiate the rose-garden,

> Not the intense moment
> Isolated, with no before or after

in his rush to define the great mode as

> a lifetime burning in every moment
> And not the lifetime of one man only
> But of old stones that cannot be deciphered

—which is an interim version of 'a lifetime's death in love', prefigured now in *East Coker* as

> Love is most nearly itself
> When here and now cease to matter.

The last lines seem to imply, even yet, that we can all still make ourselves Celias:

> We must be still and still moving
> Into another intensity
> For a further union, a deeper communion
> Through the dark cold and the empty desolation,
> The wave cry, the wind cry, the vast waters
> Of the petrel and the porpoise

—an impressive account of Kinkanja, and a reminder that even the 'way of illumination' leads through the temporal; as Reilly declared that the Saint in the desert, with spiritual evil always at his shoulder, also suffered from 'hunger, damp, exposure/ Bowel trouble, and the fear of lions'.

The distinction between the saint and the rest of us occupied the last moments of *The Dry Salvages* because it bore down hard upon the redemption of time, and the same distinction was to be worked out even more problematically in the plays; but in Part 5 of *Little Gidding* the distinction is set aside in a vision of time redeemed. The hint is picked up from *East Coker*: 'Old men ought to be explorers.' Our words are not the Logos, but if we resist our self-engrossing fancies and try to apprehend 'the meaning'—and this is what the exploration amounts to—instead of imposing our own, then 'every phrase and every sentence is an end and a beginning'. The temporal is the locus of value, because it is the only locus we have and value must exist; in the temporal we may still try to apprehend the meaning of the Incarnation; it is our condition; at its best, a condition of complete simplicity, costing 'not less than everything'. Hence the poet gathers up, still in time, all the broken images, the hints and guesses, Dante's scattered leaves ('Nel suo profondo vidi che s'interna,/legato con amore in un volume,/cio che per l'universo si squaderna') and folds them into 'one simple flame', the light of Eternal Love.[1]

---

[1] The most relevant passages of the *Paradiso* are Canto XXXI, lines 10–24 and Canto XXXIII, lines 85–145.

II
A SPECIAL PROBLEM: *The Dry Salvages*

In recent years the critical reception of *Four Quartets* has taken a curious turn. I shall describe it briefly, especially where it bears upon *The Dry Salvages*.

The new reading began with Hugh Kenner's essay 'Eliot's Moral Dialectic' (1949) and was pushed to a formidable extreme some years later by Donald Davie.[1] Mr. Kenner argued that the structural principle of *Four Quartets* is to be found in the pattern of *Burnt Norton*; two terms, opposed, falsely reconciled, then truly reconciled. Light and Darkness, opposed, are falsely reconciled in the tube-station 'flicker', then truly and paradoxically reconciled in the Dark Night of the Soul. In *Little Gidding* Attachment and Detachment, opposed, falsely reconciled in Indifference, are truly reconciled in Love. In his recent book *The Invisible Poet* Mr. Kenner does not urge us to acknowledge this pattern in each of the four poems. Instead, he suggests that the structural principle of *Burnt Norton* applies also to the organization of the *Quartets* as a whole. The 'recurrent illumination' of *Burnt Norton* and the 'pervasive sombreness' of *East Coker* are to be taken as opposing terms, 'alternative ways in which the mind responsible for their existence deceives itself'; they are then falsely reconciled in the 'conciliating formulae' of *The Dry Salvages*, and truly reconciled in the taut revelations, the 'refining fire' of *Little Gidding*. This implies, of course, that everything leading up to the last Part of *Little Gidding*, from the first words of *Burnt Norton*, is, more or less, parody; the disclosure of moral positions which Eliot—the suggestion runs—has never inhabited or from which he has detached himself. As if the poem were a long *Gerontion*. This is hard to take. I cannot believe that when the voice of *East Coker II* says

> The only wisdom we can hope to acquire
> Is the wisdom of humility: humility is endless

[1] 'Eliot's Moral Dialectic': *Hudson Review*, Vol. II (1949). See also Hugh Kenner, *The Invisible Poet* (New York. McDowell, Obolensky, 1959). Donald Davie's essay, first published in *The Twentieth Century*, April 1956, is conveniently reprinted in Hugh Kenner (editor), *Twentieth Century Views on T. S. Eliot* (New York. Prentice-Hall, 1962).

we are to interpret this as yet another moment in which the mind responsible for its existence is deceiving itself.

A more modest version of Mr. Kenner's case argues that *The Dry Salvages* becomes the 'flicker' stage in the plot of *Four Quartets*; this follows Mr. Davie's suggestion that *The Dry Salvages*—he does not include the other three poems—is deliberate parody.

And yet, even this modest version; is it credible? Who is parodying what?

> And on the deck of the drumming liner
> Watching the furrow that widens behind you,
> You shall not think 'the past is finished'
> Or 'the future is before us'.

This does not sound like *The Hollow Men*, but it is clearly not parody; it is [a] praeceptorial voice making our clichés uninhabitable; just as, later, a similar voice performs a similar function in

> Men's curiosity searches past and future
> And clings to that dimension.

There is more in *The Dry Salvages* than conciliating formulae.

And yet perhaps this is the hint we need. Mr. Kenner, if he cared, might have made his structural pattern cover *The Dry Salvages* by taking Action and Passion as the opposing terms, falsely reconciled in the mere Motion of Part 2, the 'currents', and truly reconciled in the 'Right Action' of Part 5 which is 'freedom/From past and future also'. This would have acknowledged that the poem is all transit, comings and goings, with the attendant temptation of choosing our direction and the attendant danger of getting lost. But let that be. There is a great deal in *The Dry Salvages* which requires explanation or apology. My own impression is that after the dark admonitions of *East Coker* the poet, for a fresh start, sought a new tone, something much more conversational. The new voice should be much more discursive, to begin with; becoming sharper as the decorum changes and the consideration of 'what might have been' becomes more arduous. I think Eliot wanted the voice to begin like Lord Claverton and end like Harry Monchonsey. Indeed, the passage beginning

> You cannot face it steadily, but this thing is sure,
> That time is no healer: the patient is no longer here.
> When the train starts, and the passengers are settled
> To fruit, periodicals and business letters

is taken up again after many years for *The Elder Statesman*:

> It's just like sitting in an empty waiting room
> In a railway station on a branch line,
> After the last train. . . .

And the voice which speaks of human questioning as mere curiosity is like Harry Monchonsey's, engaged in the demolition of family inquests:

> What you call the normal
> Is merely the unreal and the unimportant.

So there can hardly be any possibility of parody. If *The Dry Salvages* is bad it is bad because it fails to be good, not because Eliot meant it to sound 'bad' in a sophisticated way.

The Lord Claverton voice begins, 'I do not know much about gods,' and speculates about the river as a 'strong brown god'. The river, as I read the passage, is everything in ourselves which we elect to ignore, all the intractable forces within the self which we disregard because they do not lend themselves to our cliché-purposes—conveying commerce, building bridges, dwelling in cities and worshipping machines. Dazzled by the cliché-fancies of our own invention, we ignore the river, but it proceeds, however deviously, to a place alien to our purposes. And yet it was always with us:

> His rhythm was present in the nursery bedroom,
> In the rank ailanthus of the April dooryard.

The syntax is as flabby as Mr. Davie says it is. If Eliot wished to suggest a spectral presence in the April dooryard, he would have done better with something like *The Waste Land's*

> Who is the third who walks always beside you?
> When I count, there are only you and I together
> But when I look ahead up the white road
> There is always another one walking beside you
> Gliding wrapt in a brown mantle, hooded

or the later version of this which he uses in *The Cocktail Party*. 'The river is within us, the sea is all about us'; the sea being, I assume, an omnivorous impersonal reality alien to man and therefore suicidally attractive as a refuge from his consciousness. It has many voices and it measures 'time not our time', but we deceive ourselves like the anxious women and try to take the sea's measure, using our own counters.

But the real embarrassments begin in Part 2. My guess is that Eliot wanted now to make his anxious women of Part 1 into a choric voice, like the Women of Canterbury in *Murder in the Cathedral*, expressing the usual loud laments in their own terms; and then to bring in a Monchonsey voice to evacuate the whole area of plangent cliché and point to one Meaning. The hint is clear enough in

> The backward look behind the assurance
> Of recorded history, the backward half-look
> Over the shoulder, towards the primitive terror

and in the fact that the notorious rhymes of Part 2 are inaugurated in the last lines of Part I with the phrase, 'The future futureless.' The first stanza of Part 2 is very beautiful. But the decision to add five stanzas and to make each line-end rhyme with its counterpart in the other stanzas was disastrous. There is nothing as difficult in the choruses of *The Rock* or *Murder in the Cathedral*. The poet may have been impressed by the air of world-wide plangency which Coleridge evoked from 'measureless' in *Kubla Khan*, or perhaps by Hopkins's efforts with 'motionable' in *The Wreck of the Deutschland*, but for an artist whose vocational concern was speech there is no excusing the coinage of 'oceanless', 'erosionless', and 'devotionless'. The N.E.D. gives a certain pale authority for 'emotionless', but when Eliot writes

>   the trailing
> consequence of further days and hours,
> While emotion takes to itself the emotionless
> Years of living among the breakage
> Of what was believed in as the most reliable—

I do not know what he means. Does he mean that our undisciplined squads of emotion, instead of leaving the symbolic sea of Part I well alone ('emotionless' meaning, if anything, emotionally null) are constantly trying to take possession of it; and the more successful the emotions in these exploits, the more impoverished our lives, the more—if we are to 'live'—we shall have to renounce? The next stanza is an early version of the 'gifts reserved for age' in *Little Gidding*. 'The unattached devotion which might pass for devotionless' can hardly mean much more than 'the capacity for devotion which continues even when it lacks an object'; but I do not know why it should try to 'pass for' devotionless, playing possum. After the apocalyptic chorus Eliot returns to the Claverton voice, 'It seems, as one becomes older . . .' to modulate into the Monchonsey voice which will clear the way for the Meaning. The anxious worried chorus feared that the whole human scramble was ridiculous; rather like the fears of the Aunts and Uncles in their trance-moments in *The Family Reunion*. But the stern voice now says that 'the meaning' redeems time and because it is the Rock, is itself:

> in the sombre season
> Or the sudden fury, is what it always was.

We need not go through the poem: most of its sore thumbs have been at least noted. I think the defects of *The Dry Salvages* are real and serious; where they occur, they are the result of Eliot's failure to conduct a piece which he scored for an unmanageable number of voices. It would be easier in the plays, where he could take whatever time he required to establish his voices. In the other poems and especially in *Little Gidding* the voices are fewer, clearly distinguishable, and under impeccable control.

III

Eliot's problem in *Four Quartets* is a strategic one; how to evacuate practically all the areas in which his readers live. A proposal of this kind is tolerated only in wartime, and indeed Eliot wrote most of the poem during a World War and perhaps he wanted to use the idiom of war in order to enforce a deeper discrimination of peace-time commitments. The critique is religious, dogmatic, and Christian. Eliot's hope is to clear a space, or if necessary to take over a bombed-out area, and there to build a new life of the spirit; to realize 'the idea of Christian society'. He will approach the Meaning from several experi-

mental directions, making several fresh starts, because he can
hardly hope—the conditions being unpropitious—that one will
suffice. For there is a sense in which he himself is the object of
his own persuasion. The redemption of time will be his theme,
his case, but he will have to resist a Manichean force within himself which is notoriously subversive; it doesn't really believe that
time can be redeemed, it fears that the human scale of action is
puny beyond or beneath redemption. This is to give the Manichean force an extreme form, and it will not always be so intransigent; but that it is a complication in Eliot's Christian poetry
I have no doubt. Indeed, it is probably inevitable—or an occasional hazard, at the least—in all those 'varieties of religious experience' which are ascetic before they are anything else; taking
their bearings from the idiom of cleansing, surgery, and 'voiding'. It is difficult to propose the voiding of all human allegiances
without implying that they are in any event meretricious. The
idiom of renunciation is more hopeful, since the value of renunciation is all the greater if what is renounced is indisputably fine.
And therefore an 'ideal' strategy for a secular age would consist
in persuading one's reader to void his allegiances by showing up
his daily preoccupations as mere 'fancies'; and then to translate
this voiding into renunciation, a positive sacrifice which he is
encouraged to make to a God now certified by the quality of the
sacrifice itself. This is largely what Eliot tries to do in the
Quartets.

There is a passage in *The Trembling of the Veil* which throws
light upon Eliot's object. Yeats has been discussing 'Unity of
Being' in his habitual idiom of Image, Mask, and Anti-Self. But
he goes on to say that there are people to whom all this is irrelevant:

'I now know that there are men who cannot possess "Unity of
Being", who must not seek it or express it—and who, so far from
seeking an anti-self, a Mask that delineates a being in all things
the opposite to their natural state, can but seek the suppression of
the anti-self, till the natural state alone remains. These are those
who must seek no image of desire, but await that which lies beyond their mind—unities not of the mind, but unities of Nature,
unities of God—the man of science, the moralist, the humanitarian, the politician, Saint Simeon Stylites upon his pillar, Saint
Anthony in his cavern, all whose preoccupation is to seem no-

thing . . . their imaginations grow more vivid in the expression of something which they have not created.'[1]

The great example is George Herbert, a hero, incidentally, in Eliot's mythology. Eliot would probably say, 'all whose pre-occupation is to *be* nothing', since seeming is not enough—he is not Wallace Stevens. The authority—if he needs one—comes from St. John of the Cross, 'To be all things, be willing to be nothing.' These men are the great exemplars, but they are only the most extreme forms of Eliot's ideal reader, his ideal man. In this sense the poetry does not matter: it merely 'points' the reader—and perhaps the writer, too—toward one end.

Our argument, then, is that the course of Eliot's persuasion in *Four Quartets* is to translate voiding into renunciation, negative into its corresponding positive. For some of the rhetoric whistles in the dark, warding off the ghosts. There are certain moments in the *Quartets* when Eliot couldn't quite convince himself of human value, and even the pretty, inoffensive things are voided and cleared away before they can be redeemed. Like the poor dancers of *East Coker*:

>   Keeping time,
> Keeping the rhythm in their dancing
> As in their living in the living seasons
> The time of the seasons and the constellations
> The time of milking and the time of harvest
> The time of the coupling of man and woman
> And that of beasts. Feet rising and falling.
> Eating and drinking. Dung and death.

It is a gruff dismissal, when all is said. And it points to the deepest embarrassment—or so I think—in Eliot's poetry; the feeling, in part, that all the declared values of human life are somehow illusory and, in part, that nevertheless God so loved the world that He gave up for its redemption His beloved Son. In *Four Quartets* when the first part of this feeling is predominant, the persuasion is all voiding; when the second part asserts itself, the persuasion is all renunciation. The poems are dogmatic, yes, but there is often 'the backward half-look/Over the shoulder, towards the primitive terror'. For many readers, I should guess,

---

[1] W. B. Yeats, *Autobiographies* (London. Macmillan, 1955), pp. 247–8.

it is this half-look which redeems a poetry otherwise too imperiously above redemption.

This is to say that the poem is animated, however precariously, by a profound sense of the process, the struggle, the writhing of ignorance and purpose. The motto is given in the second part of *The Dry Salvages*:

> And approach to the meaning restores the experience
> In a different form. . . .

The meaning is given as the Incarnation, Love, figured in the Dance. The reader takes these terms as he finds them and makes of them what he can. But the poem does not depend upon his goodwill, his belief, or his disbelief. It depends, rather, upon his response to 'the approach', the degree to which his own sense of the process is animated by Eliot's words. The approach is featured in several versions. There is the struggle to make a pilgrimage of what, unmade, is mere wandering, errancy, footloose. There is the struggle to make valid sentences, the wrestling with last year's words. There is, to stand for everything, 'the trying'. 'The rest is not our business.' Eliot's greatest poetry is written in the tension between these polar terms, between the ineffable Meaning and the temporal Approach; between the Logos and the mere words, the dialect of the tribe. It is relevant also to note the Augustinian distinction between the meaning of a sentence and the syllables of which it is composed; which Kenneth Burke has recently linked to the distinction between Spirit and Matter.[1] If men are syllables, God is the meaning. So the higher term includes all the lower terms and transcends them; the tone of the transcendence can be urgent or reluctant. There is clearly a relation between the transcendence, the abstraction of Eliot's later poems and his sense of the burden of objects, the despotism of finite things. The object, often cancelled as an object, is entertained as form or shadow. But Eliot is not Mondrian or Kandinsky: he does not cancel the object in a fine flourish, his mind made up from the start. In the early poems the objects are seen from a distance and thus controlled: the distance is often the measure of the poet's distaste, the low vision, as in the 'young man carbuncular' of *The Waste Land*. The later mode is disciplinary and ascetic; and incidentally a way of buy-

[1] Kenneth Burke, *A Rhetoric of Religion* (Boston, Beacon Press, 1961), p. 81.

ing the highest and dearest property, the salvation of one's soul. But there is misgiving, either way. It is the poignancy of misgiving that keeps the poetry human.

Here is a passage from *Little Gidding*:

> If you came this way,
> Taking the route you would be likely to take
> From the place you would be likely to come from,
> If you came this way in May time, you would find the hedges
> White again, in May, with voluptuary sweetness.
> It would be the same at the end of the journey,
> If you came at night like a broken king,
> If you came by day not knowing what you came for,
> It would be the same, when you leave the rough road
> And turn behind the pig-sty to the dull façade
> And the tombstone.

This is not dramatic poetry. It does not find glory in the plenitude of the event, the thing, the object. In *Anna Karenina*, when the train is coming into the station at Petersburg, in the luggage-van, Tolstoy mentions, a dog is whining. This is not a symbol; it is an imaginative fact, part of Tolstoy's vision of the event, the scene. Eliot's later poems do not go in this way: they are meditative poems, dealing with their objects at the remove of contemplation and generalization. In this kind of poetry we do not get the particular object, or even the feeling of that object: we get the feeling of all such objects, attracted into a single cadence. In an easy comparison one thinks of Herbert:

> I know the wayes of Pleasure, the sweet strains,
> The lullings and the relishes of it;

where the lullings and the relishes bring together, as flesh to flesh, all those experiences which, in a decorous generalization, are called Pleasure; but not any particular instance of Pleasure. In the lines from *Little Gidding* the white hedges are provisional, moments in the approach to the Meaning, and Eliot is prepared, at need, to set them aside. But meanwhile the poetry acknowledges that kind of whiteness, that kind of sweetness, the merging of subject and object in those sensory terms; even if the cadence prepares us to disengage ourselves from all such occasions, at need. Hence the short name for Eliot's later cadences is nostalgia. He writes of objects and experiences as if he had already left them—with whatever degree of reluctance—behind. In these lines the elaborate complicity with the 'you' ('If you came this way in May time . . .') is partly to register the delicacy of the occasion, partly to make up for the poet's rejection of the objects; because he has contracted to reject them, however reluctantly. The short way to say this is perhaps too short, that Eliot's Christianity was not Franciscan; but his poetry was enlivened by a Franciscan scruple. Perhaps this explains why the technical resources of the passage are lavished upon the voluptuary sweetness; the single line, in the first part, which is released from the elaborate grammatical chain.[1]

For me, the poetry is saved by the scruple. The way in which it is saved may be indicated, perhaps, in a passage from *Varieties of Religious Experience*, where James discusses the character of sanctity, particularly its ascetic quality. He remarks that while it is normal and, apparently, instinctive for us to seek 'the easy and the pleasant', at the same time it is also normal 'in moderate degree' to seek the arduous: 'Some men and women, indeed, there are who can live on smiles and the word "yes" forever. But for others (indeed for most) this is too tepid and relaxed a moral climate. Passive happiness is slack and insipid, and soon grows mawkish and intolerable. Some austerity and wintry negativity,

---

[1] A few points to note in a technical analysis. (*a*) The coincidence of clause and metre. (*b*) The semantic stresses, normally four to a line, also serve the purposes of metrical stresses, keeping the lines going, in this case, at the speed of refined conversation. (*c*) More important: in these unrhymed lines grammar takes the place of rhyme. The italicized phrases, below, are grammatical cousins, running in the sequence, ABBA; two sets:

A   *If you came this way,*
B   Taking *the route you would be likely to take*
B   From *the place you would be likely to come from,*
A   *If you came this way* in May time, you would find the hedges
     White again, in May, with voluptuary sweetness.
A   *It would be the same* at the end of the journey,
B   *If you came at night* like a broken king,
B   *If you came by day* not knowing what you came for,
A   *It would be the same,* when you leave the rough road
     And turn behind the pig-sty to the dull façade
     And the tombstone.

This has the effect, one among many, of pointing up the odd-lines-out precisely because they are thus released from the grammatical 'rhymes'. (Donald Davie shows a similar procedure at work in *Ash-Wednesday*, the opening lines. See his *Articulate Energy* (London. Routledge and Kegan Paul, 1955), pp. 90 fol.)

some roughness, danger, stringency, and effort, some "no! no!"
must be mixed in, to produce the sense of an existence with
character and texture and power.'[1]

Perhaps this is how *Four Quartets* lives, and how it communi-
cates with those readers who do not share its Christian belief; by
giving us the sense of an existence with character and texture and
power. This is the tone of its 'approach'. Eliot has always implied,
incidentally, that the satisfactions of poetry are in this tone. The
great poem helps to purify the dialect of the tribe by making our
stupidity unendurable. Discussing *London* and *The Vanity of
Human Wishes*, Eliot remarked:

'Those who demand of poetry a day-dream, or a metamorphosis of their own feeble desires and lusts, or what they believe
to be "intensity" of passion, will not find much in Johnson. He
is like Pope and Dryden, Crabbe and Landor, a poet for those
who want poetry and not something else, some stay for their
own vanity.'[2]

Four Quartets is offered to the same readers for the same ascetic
purpose. Indeed, if the intimate procedures of Eliot's early verse
invite attention to those of Tennyson and Swinburne as well as
Baudelaire and Laforgue, the later poems should be read with
Dante, Dryden, Pope, and Johnson in mind; read as a stay
against our own vanity. Hence 'humility is endless'.

---

[1] William James, *Varieties of Religious Experience* (London. Collins, 1960 reprint), p. 295.
[2] T. S. Eliot, *Selected Prose* (London. Penguin Books, 1953), pp. 168-9.

13

On *Notes Toward a Supreme Fiction*

I

The basic motive of *Notes Toward a Supreme Fiction* is to offer man a substitute for God; to show him how he may transfer to himself the attributes and reverberations of the divine. This involves the replacement of certain fundamental terms in accordance with the idea that 'God and the imagination are one'. If they are one, the former may be replaced by the latter. So the idea of God is replaced by the idea of the imagination. Theology becomes Poetry, Metaphysics becomes Aesthetics. Faith is now addressed to the relation between the imagination and the structures of its own invention. The priest is replaced by the poet. Hence the Supreme Fiction is the Theme, of which only a few variations are known; the theme itself is not known, since it is beyond all the variations. The purpose of the *Notes* is to find the most persuasive variations; hence to imply the Theme by urging the imagination to reach it. The relation between theme and variations is like the relation between the body's beauty, which never dies, and the body, which always dies; or the relation between perfection and 'the imperfect', which is meanwhile 'our paradise'; or the relation, in 'The Comedian as the Letter C', between the text and its glosses; or the relation, in 'The Emperor of Ice Cream', between the 'be' which is the finale and the 'seemings' which lead up to it.

Meanwhile Stevens offers to translate the old terms. If God is the human imagination, Life is what the human mind has come to know: time is the continuum in which the mind acts: the self is the locus of the imagination. Fact is the instrumental matter through which the mind declares itself; as Focillon says in a sentence already quoted, 'The chief characteristic of the mind is to be constantly describing itself.' Value is the glow surrounding the acts of the mind. Notes toward a Supreme Fiction: supreme, meaning 'fully answerable to man's needs and desires', leaving no ache behind; fiction, meaning a structure of man's invention, corresponding not to an impersonal, objective reality but to the nature of the inventor; great because he is great. 'The image must be of the nature of its creator.' So the nearest work, in philosophy, to the *Notes*, in poetry, is Vaihinger's *The Philosophy of 'As If'*, an exhilarating account of man's working fictions which, false in themselves, have enabled man to do and say true things. The fiction is in man's image as the theologians say that man is created in God's image.

II

Notes Toward a Supreme Fiction seems to have been written between February and May 1942. The title is strange, not typical of Stevens, and if the chronologies would blink, the reader would recall T. S. Eliot's *Notes Towards the Definition of Culture*. Indeed bearing in mind that *Burnt Norton, East Coker*, and *The Dry Salvages* were completed by 1941, we are tempted to read Stevens's *Notes* as a humanist answer to the *Four Quartets*. Think of the poems together, the unwilling light they cast upon each other. Both are didactic, large statements, couched in grand terms with the support of many earlier experiments in the resource of language. The structure of Eliot's poem is theological and admonitory; persuasive because it makes the alternatives to religion seem uninhabitable. In *The Dry Salvages* the hints and guesses come into the open:

> The hint half guessed, the gift half understood, is
> Incarnation.

Imagine an untheological poet reading *The Dry Salvages*. He is a sophisticated man, wry, amused, and as a rhetorician he is interested in all kinds of things. He regards Christianity as a seducing hymn, redundant after a lustre of the moon; at best, a solacing majesty, until he feels that 'I can do all that angels can'. This poet may wish to chant his own Quartets, dissolving Eliot's terms or finding for them a strictly untheological and subversive meaning. He respects Christianity because it has engendered a set of notable 'hallucinations'—as in Joan of Arc[1]—but the word 'Incarnation' will lose its capital and will mean, as in 'Credences of Summer', any manifestations, a rock, April's green, a tree. When Eliot says

> Love is most nearly itself
> When here and now cease to matter

Stevens counters that here and now never cease to matter, are always the ABC of Being. When Eliot points to the Negative Way, the way of purgation, Stevens translates the admonition into humanist terms; each of us must become 'an ignorant man' again, until we can see the sun clearly 'in the idea of it', the dazzle of perception.

Perhaps, then, ignoring chronologies, we might read the *Notes* with the *Four Quartets* in the back of our minds. Stevens's object is to see how much of human life is in the power of the imagination. If the answer is: All; then man is indeed God.

III

In the first lines Stevens, addressing the Supreme Fiction, gives a phrase which we may use as a motto for the poem: 'the uncertain light of single, certain truth'. The single truth is certain, presumably, because man has conceived it, but care is required to deal with the uncertain light. The best gloss on this is the poem 'Man Carrying Thing', where 'a brune figure in winter' illustrates the aphorism that 'the poem must resist the intelligence almost successfully'.[2] The brune figure and the thing he carries are equally resistant: we are to accept them as 'parts not quite perceived of the obvious whole, uncertain particles of the certain solid'. Stevens says:

> We must endure our thoughts all night, until
> The bright obvious stands motionless in cold.

The bright obvious is the supreme fiction, to be approached only through the 'parts not quite perceived', the thoughts to be endured. In the same way the certainty of Poetry is to be approached through the opalescence of uncertain poems—includ-

[1] Wallace Stevens, *Opus Posthumous* (New York. Knopf, 1957), p. 240.
[2] ibid., p. 171.

ing this one, the *Notes*—since all poems are deemed 'secondary' to 'the primary free from doubt'. And, finally, 'major man' is 'more fecund as principle than particle'.

So the poem begins (*It Must Be Abstract*) by directing the reader beyond the particles toward the principle of which the particles are 'contours';[1] beyond the fixed name, Phoebus, toward the solar principle which must not be named; the sun must be seen 'in the idea of it'. The cleanliness of 'the first idea' must be perceived through the opaque particulars of reality, the 'ravishments of truth so fatal to the truth itself', the ancient cycle of desire in which we are beguiled. It must be abstract. In a letter to Hi Simons in January 1943 Stevens said 'the fictive abstract is as immanent in the mind of the poet as the idea of God is immanent in the mind of the theologian'.[2] Hence the function of the poem, as distinct from the nature of Poetry, is to mediate between the reader and 'the first idea'; as Keats's 'heard melodies' direct the willing reader toward the 'essential' sweetness of those unheard, that is to say, Absolute Sound. In *Abstraction and Empathy* Worringer says that the impulse to abstraction arises from 'a great inner unrest inspired in man by the phenomena of the outside world': in this unrest 'life as such is felt to be a disturbance of the aesthetic enjoyment'.[3] True, this is more relevant to the principle of Stevens's poetry than to the particles of his poems; but it is relevant. Now in the *Notes* he invokes the primitive 'hoobla-hoobla-hoobla-how' of the Arabian moon, a kind of Action Music like the labials of the ocean which are the delightful resemblances among *differentia*; 'Life's nonsense'. In the next poem the situation is given in much grander terms: since the first idea was not our own and the clouds preceded us,

we live in a place

That is not our own and, much more, not ourselves
And hard it is in spite of blazoned days.

Worringer says that 'where the abstract line is the exponent of the will-to-form, art is Transcendental, is conditioned by the need for deliverance'. Stevens's *Notes* is, in one aspect, a cry for

---

[1] Wallace Stevens, *Collected Poems* (London. Faber and Faber, 1955), p. 270.
[2] *Letters of Wallace Stevens*, edited by Holly Stevens (New York. Knopf, 1966), p. 434.
[3] Wilhelm Worringer, *Abstraction and Empathy*, translated by Michael Bullock (London. Routledge and Kegan Paul, 1953), pp. 15, 24.

deliverance from the arbitrariness of the phenomenal world. The difference between that arbitrariness and the arbitrariness of a fiction is that the fiction is grounded in the nature of the human imagination. Stevens has sponsored 'ecstatic identities between one's self and the weather', several times, and notably in 'Extracts from Addresses', but just now there is no identity: we mime the clouds, adding to them our own meanings; and the addition makes all the difference. The poem is an addition, and a deliverance.

In another aspect this becomes Stevens's declared theme, the interdependence of reality and the imagination. Later in the poem he will sing its praise, but now he teases the ephebe for the adolescent languor of his imagination; by contrast with the lion, the elephant, and the bear, who have the strength to impose themselves upon reality. He has not forgotten his own warning, that to impose is not to discover. The interdependence of reality and the imagination points toward the first idea; but the first idea cannot be realized or even approached through daily apprehensions and desires. Stevens can only describe it, experimentally, in terms of what it is not, in terms of illusory advances ('Not to/ Be spoken to . . .'), but after several improvisations he gives up, reverting to an earlier idiom. At last he comes back to reality and imagination, 'the weather and the giant of the weather'.

Perhaps the solution is to waive the question of 'a thinker of the first idea' and to enjoy the credences of consciousness, the Swiss perfections, when they occur. This demands an act of faith, that there is a principle behind these particles, a theme behind the variations. Stevens has already made this act of faith, notably in 'A Thought Revolved', where the poet striding among the cigar stores is still aware of commanding the relevant abstraction:

> One man, the idea of man, that is the space,
> The true abstract in which he promenades.

In the *Notes* the credences lead to the sharpest consciousness, and we 'behold/The academies like structures in a mist'. If the academies are 'ideas of order', they take the place of the brune figure in winter, in a mist because they are 'parts not quite perceived of the obvious whole'. In any event they are as native to the mind as rain to rainy men.

That the first idea is not to be equated with the divine, or the Gods, is the argument of the next poem. The relation between 'the MacCullough' and 'MacCullough' is obscure. The general subject is the futility of trying to restore the Gods; a topic brightly considered in one of Stevens's essays, 'Two or Three Ideas', virtually a prose translation of the verse. Stevens has been describing the dispersal of the gods, an annihilation in which, he says, we share. The gods in dispersal left nothing behind, 'no thrones, no mystic rings, no texts either of the soil or of the soul'. It was as if, he says, 'they had never inhabited the earth. There was no crying out for their return. They were not forgotten because they had been a part of the glory of the earth. At the same time, no man ever muttered a petition in his heart for the restoration of those unreal shapes. There was always in every man the increasingly human self, which instead of remaining the observer, the non-participant, the delinquent, became constantly more and more all there was or so it seemed; and whether it was so or merely seemed so still left it for him to resolve life and the world in his own terms.'[1] 'But the MacCullough is MacCullough.' In the same letter to Hi Simons Stevens glosses this: 'MacCullough is any name, any man. The trouble with humanism is that man as God remains man, but there is an extension of man, the "leaner being", in fiction, a possibly more than human human, a composite human. The act of recognizing him is the act of this leaner being moving in on us.' This seems to say that Man is any man, a god if he wants to be a god, and certainly a god in relation to his own generic life. So, instead of the pensive giant prone in violet space, we have MacCullough lounging by the sea; finally achieving that interdependence of the imagination and reality which releases the Word. The 'increasingly human self' is then the 'beau linguist', speaking 'the poem of the act of the mind'. This is an elaborate way of saying, 'You too can be a god; if only you will work your imagination hard enough, committing yourself to your fictive possibilities. You will then go far beyond the timidity of humanism.' It is also a devious way of saying that God is made, or gods are made, in the image of man; say, the *n*th degree of man. Stevens is unwilling to lose the feelings which attached themselves to the divine idea: his stratagem is to attach them to man, but to urge man 'beyond' himself

[1] *Opus Posthumous, supra*, pp. 206–7.

in the reach of his imagination. The poem of the act of the mind is the persuasive means.

But the poem must be described, since it is to be the origin of 'the major man'. It cannot be 'romantic intoning' or 'reason's click-clack'. The major man comes from the meditative imagination, as in Milton's lonely tower. The previous poem insisted that major man is not to be identified with 'man', that is, with the idea of man. Nor is he to be fixed or named:

> Yet look not at his colored eyes. Give him
> No names. Dismiss him from your images.
> The hot of him is purest in the heart.

In the heart of each of us, I presume, when our contemplation is freed from the fixity of names.

Stevens brings all this together in the next and last poem of 'It Must be Abstract':

> The major abstraction is the idea of man
> And major man is his exponent. . . .

The human imagination, that is to say, at its furthest reach encompasses the idea of man; beyond which, since the human will is satisfied, there is nothing. The idea of man is therefore the 'single, certain truth', fully in accord with the nature of its inventor. The 'uncertain light' discloses 'major man', an heroic part of the 'commonal' but not itself the commonal. 'The major abstraction Is the commonal,/ The inanimate, difficult visage'; difficult because each of us must imagine it for himself and the enterprise is a lonely act:

> What rabbi, grown furious with human wish,
> What chieftain, walking by himself, crying
> Most miserable, most victorious,
>
> Does not see these separate figures one by one,
> And yet see only one, in his old coat,
>
> His slouching pantaloons, beyond the town,
> Looking for what was, where it used to be?

In 'Le Monocle de mon Oncle' the inquiring figure is now a dark rabbi observing the nature of mankind, and a little later a rose rabbi pursuing 'the origin and course of love'; clearly a dignified role in each case, appropriate companion to the chieftain walking, however, by himself. Presumably Stevens is saying that the distinction between the idea of man and its exponents, between the major abstraction and major man, is valid but difficult; we are only human if we blur the distinction and let our imaginations rest and fix upon a single, generic, abstract image somehow compounding both parts of the distinction. The image must be generalized, and above all must not be named; hence the Chaplin-figure is as far as Stevens is prepared to go. The figure is probably drawn from that of Leonidas, invoked in Stevens's essay 'Effects of Analogy', or from all those intimations which crowded into Stevens's aphorism, 'The poet is a god, or, the young poet is a god. The old poet is a tramp.'[1] This does not matter. Drawn from whatever source, the figure is purely human, fallible, pathetic, 'looking for what was, where it used to be'. And yet,

> It is of him, ephebe, to make, to confect
> The final elegance, not to console
> Nor sanctify, but plainly to propound.

From the figure in pantaloons, the 'purely human', the ephebe will construct the final elegance, the supreme fiction; and this act will be the 'type' of all human acts, acts of the imagination. 'Not to console,' since we do not acknowledge a loss; nor to sanctify, since we have declined apotheosis and watched the Gods disperse in mid-air; but plainly to propound, since in these matters the plain style is 'acutest speech', a style strangely proper to man, composed in his own image.

The second part of Stevens's creed; the Supreme Fiction, which must be abstract, must also change.

This is Stevens's answer to many questions, many prayers; to the Romantic 'quest for permanence', with all its beauty an interminable whine; to Aristotle's God as Unmoved Mover; to theological talk of eternal verities; to the fixity of religious ritual. Things change, Stevens will imply, because we want them to change; this is the 'motive for metaphor', that we desire 'the exhilarations of changes', shrinking from 'the weight of

[1] ibid., p. 173.

primary noon'.[1] And in 'Mr. Burnshaw and the Statue' Stevens rebukes the high-toned old 'mesdames' for not understanding this, for whining farewells, for dragging companions from the past, for a protective indifference; 'It is only enough/To live incessantly in change.'[2] This does not encourage us to console ourselves with the cyclic movement of things—the 'myth' celebrated by Mircea Eliade and others—or to put on the elegance of nostalgia. Stevens knows that we cling to a 'repertory of poetic ideas'—such as the idea of an earlier life or a later life or a different life[3] and he does not hold us severely to account for these weaknesses; but he recites them with some impatience. He is particularly severe on the attempt to arrest the course of things by ritual; as in the Churches:

> The old seraph, parcel-gilded, among violets
> Inhaled the appointed odor, while the doves
> Rose up like phantoms from chronologies.

In any event, 'the seraph/Is satyr in Saturn, according to his thoughts', that is, according to the quality of his imagination and the different modes of freedom it claims. Again we are dealing with an equation typical of Stevens: if change is the law of life—and by implication an excellent law—then the more change, the better. In the present poem he says, 'the distaste we feel for this withered scene/Is that it has not changed enough'; although the scene in itself is pretty, perhaps poetic. Eliot says in *East Coker* that 'to apprehend/The point of intersection of the timeless/With time, is an occupation for the saint.' Stevens has no interest in saintly occupations. Hence the parable of the President and the Bee.

In 'The Noble Rider and the Sound of Words' Stevens argued that the imagination can be urged, persuaded, but not commanded. The President 'ordains the bee to be/Immortal', but the bee refuses. The bee is partly the human imagination, partly that scruple in life itself which refuses the lure of immortality. Life rejoices in its own death and a new beginning in another bee, 'the new-come bee'. To the extent that we share this scruple, Stevens implies, we are human; if we fend it off, we re-

[1] *Collected Poems, supra*, p. 288.
[2] *Opus Posthumous, supra*, p. 50.
[3] ibid., p. 203.

lapse into the vestigial state of mind which he deplores in the next poem, on the statue of a mythical General Du Puy. As he wrote to Hi Simons, in a gloss: 'We cannot ignore or obliterate death, yet we do not live in memory. Life is always new; it is always beginning. The fiction is part of this beginning.'

Up to this point Stevens has been speaking of fixities, things torn away from the imagination and therefore congealed; their permanence is deadly. The motive which engenders them is destructive. Stevens's law is: one thing, then another, then another. The congealed things are offensive because they evade the dignity of a natural death; but they have lost all genuine vitality because the life of the imagination no longer flows in them. In the next poem (II. iv)—perhaps the most beautiful passage in Stevens's entire work—the tone changes from the asperity of an impatient aesthetician to the wonder of a humanist marvelling at the flow of the imagination where he finds it, in relationships, harmonies beyond prediction:

> Two things of opposite natures seem to depend
> On one another, as a man depends
> On a woman, day on night, the imagined
> On the real. . . .

It sounds like 'the Romantic reconciliation of opposites',[1] and yet it is hardly that, because the Romantic critics (and notably Coleridge) had in view the imaginative force required to subdue the opposition and command the reconciliation; but here no force is required, this is a beautiful fact of the world, these relationships are 'dialogues', their members call to one another and rush to embrace. Stevens gives the exact tone further down in the same poem: 'The partaker partakes of that which changes him'; and, to leave no room for error, 'The child that touches takes character from the thing,/The body, it touches.' These accords are unpredictable liaisons, marvellously in keeping with the interdependence of reality and the imagination, and they say 'yes' to time and change: the wonder of it touches Stevens and excites him to his greatest poetry. But at the end of this poem he will slide away from 'dialogue' into a realm more characteristic of his own nature:

[1] See Frank Kermode, '*Notes Toward a Supreme Fiction:* A Commentary': *Annali dell'Istituto Universitario Orientali* (Naples, 1961), p. 186.

> The captain and his men
> Are one and the sailor and the sea are one.

Yes, in the sense of a shared quality, a shared passion. But the next lines dissolve the identity of each 'member'; or, more accurately, dissolve the Other in the 'I':

> Follow after, O my companion, my fellow, my self,
> Sister and solace, brother and delight.

Dialogue, which depends upon the mutual acknowledgement of identity, goes as far as 'companion', perhaps even struggles through 'fellow', but breaks down in 'self'; in Stevens, characteristically if not always, the imagination is Narcissus. Indeed, the best gloss on these lines is the discussion of Narcissus in the first of 'Three Academic Pieces': Narcissus sought his image everywhere, Stevens says, 'because it was the principle of his nature, as it is of ours, to expect to find pleasure in what he found'. This principle is, presumably, beyond discussion: we are not reading *I and Thou*. In Buber—this is the real difficulty—a sense of reality increases our sense of the Otherness, the integrity, of each of its members; in Stevens, it sets up another reality, in rivalry, because this new reality is 'made' in the image of its maker; how else? Stevens remarks that 'the intensification of reality by resemblance increases realization', but he continues: 'It is as if a man who lived indoors should go outdoors on a day of sympathetic weather. His realization of the weather would exceed that of a man who lives outdoors. It might, in fact, be intense enough to convert the real world about him into an imagined world. In short, a sense of reality keen enough to be in excess of the normal sense of reality creates a reality of its own.'[1]

Hence the next poem, the difficult fable of the Planter and the Island, develops several related issues: the search for self-resemblance (Narcissus), a sense of reality creating a reality of its own, and the ambiguities secreted in the relation between reality and the imagination.

The poem falls into four parts; three scenes, and a comment. The first scene is the blue island, after the planter's death; the fallen house, a few scraggy trees. But these fruit-trees were the planter's meaning:

[1] Wallace Stevens, *The Necessary Angel* (New York. Knopf, 1951), p. 79.

> These were his beaches, his sea-myrtles in
> White sand, his patter of the long sea-slushes.

The planter was the imagination imposing itself upon reality·
But—the second scene—'there was an island beyond him', an
island of pineapples and bananas. This I take to be a reality 'independent of the planter's constituting consciousness': because
it is beyond him, he does not seek there—as he had sought on his
own island—images of himself; he is not on this second island at
all. There is a reality, Stevens is positing for the moment, not
ourselves. And—now in the third scene—

> He thought often of the land from which he came,
> How that whole country was a melon, pink
> If seen rightly and yet a possible red.

In the third part of 'Someone Puts a Pineapple Together'
Stevens speaks of

> The slight incipiencies, of which the form,
> At last, is the pineapple on the table or else
> An object the sum of its complications, seen
> And unseen. This is everybody's world.
> Here the total artifice reveals itself
> As the total reality.

So, too, the land from which the planter came is a condition in
which reality glows in the light of the imagination. Here the
imagination does not impose itself upon reality: the melon is not
seen as the observer wishes. Reality is seen in the light of the
imagination and only then seen rightly, as the melon is pink if
seen rightly. And yet it is also 'a possible red', to allow for those
indoor-men who suddenly go out and convert reality to their
own dazzling faith. Stevens ends this poem by defending the
planter's purity of motive:

> An unaffected man in a negative light
> Could not have borne his labor nor have died
> Sighing that he should leave the banjo's twang.

It is not immediately clear what this has to do with 'It Must
Change'; except that when the planter thought of the land from
which he came he thought also of the former self which he

brought along. Of course he acknowledged the change in himself as in the land. The later self seeks its own resemblances with its own persistence. The question of the relation between the several selves is not raised. It does not need to be. The good Law of Change is enough. If we need anything further to save the poem from a certain moral jauntiness, we think of those old men in 'Of Ideal Time and Choice' 'who have chosen, and are cold/ Because what they have chosen is their choice no more'. Stevens's gloss on the planter is a help: he is 'the laborious human who lives in illusions and who, after all the great illusions have left him, still clings to one that pierces him'. This last illusion is likely to be 'some little thing like a banjo's twang'. In this sense the planter may be considered, tentatively, 'a symbol of change'.

The next poem presents the desire for change as a revulsion from 'granite monotony'. All the different sounds of nature are drowned in one, the Presidential Ke-Ke. In this monotony, Stevens says, 'the sound ceases to be minstrelsy'. All the different faces become one:

> One sole face, like a photograph of fate,
> Glass-blower's destiny, bloodless episcopus,
> Eye without lid, mind without any dream—

meaning, 'as all fates become a common fate, as all the bottles blown by a glass blower become one, and as all bishops grow to look alike'. One of the problems, in reading Stevens, is that to approach the meaning at all we have to translate the given particulars into corresponding 'universals', retaining the sense that they are at once universal and particular. This is the way he wants the reader's imagination to proceed, apparently. In the present poem he relies upon the reader to jump to the right universal by giving him several particulars of the same kind, the same shape: they remain particulars largely because of the vitality with which the parody of Shelley is enforced: 'Bethou me, said sparrow, to the crackled blade' making fun of Shelley's 'Be thou me, impetuous one'. The fact that Stevens himself often makes the same demand is, for the moment, forgotten.

The next poem recalls the dialogue of 'Sunday Morning', and especially the man's voice. The woman felt 'the need of some imperishable bliss', perhaps an enduring Sabbath. In the *Note* this voice is not heard; perhaps the man has won, and the need is dissolved. Now 'the lover sighs as for accessible bliss', not the romantic kind, not the *frisson* of impossibility. The best and only tense is the present; the best and only place is here: this is the persuasion of the poem. The good life, the embodied value, consists in

> the heat of the scholar, who writes
> The book, hot for another accessible bliss:
> The fluctuations of certainty, the change
> Of degrees of perception in the scholar's dark.

So change is good even when it involves fluctuations of perception; as Bergson observed that the vision I now have of a motionless object differs from the vision I have just had, 'if only because the one is an instant later than the other'.[1] Here they are fluctuations; elsewhere 'propagations', like 'precious scholia jotted down in the dark'; the scholar-major-man in his Miltonic tower. Hence the search for an inflexible order—conducted in the next poem by Nanzia Nunzio in bridal metaphors—is misconceived, since 'the bride is never naked', never at the ABC of Being, because

> A fictive covering
> Weaves always glistening from the heart and mind.

It comes back, yet again, to the relation between reality and the imagination; or rather the infinite number of relations, since each term is in constant fluctuation. And this in poetry itself:

> The poem goes from the poet's gibberish to
> The gibberish of the vulgate and back again.
> Does it move to and fro or is it of both
> At once?

Valéry would say that it is of both at once, alas, and would urge the poet to wrench from the gibberish of the vulgate his own gibberish and cleave to that. Or in Stevens's terms, to set up his own imagination as the God-term, and leave 'reality' to the care of the mob. But Stevens is not quite prepared for this: he still wants to write the poem of Earth, using the gibberish of the vulgate animated by his own imagination; reality and the imagina-

[1] ibid., p. 25.

tion, each wearing its fictive covering, new moment by moment, in dynamic mutuality:

> It is the gibberish of the vulgate that he seeks.
> He tries by a peculiar speech to speak
> The peculiar potency of the general,
> To compound the imagination's Latin with
> The lingua franca et jocundissima.

This lingua, which evades 'our bluntest barriers', is the acutest speech of a reality constantly in change, wearing a fictive covering always glistening from the heart and mind of each observer, each participant. In this sense—in the next and last poem—'the water of/The lake was full of artificial things', imagined coverings, sharing a general 'will to change'. The eye of reality is 'the eye of a vagabond in metaphor/That catches our own'. Not the casual: 'the casual is not enough', as the imagists and surrealists should have known. Only 'the freshness of transformation' will satisfy, acknowledging the benign law of change:

> The freshness of a world. It is our own,
> It is ourselves, the freshness of ourselves,
> And that necessity and that presentation
> Are rubbings of a glass in which we peer.
> Of these beginnings, gay and green, propose
> The suitable amours. Time will write them down.

This is addressed to the ephebe in one of the most ravishing parts of the entire work. The rubbings are scholia—beautiful if not notably erudite—jotted down in the poet's dark. The ephebe, the good pupil, will accept them as beginnings; the suitable amours are to be imagined in equal gaiety, as given day you could perhaps imagine night, given morning you could imagine afternoon, given a woman imagine a man, 'two things of opposite natures' which seem to depend on one another as reality and the imagination depend upon one another 'and forth the particulars of rapture come'. It is as if we were given, as an image, a storm at sea; and the ephebe, proposing for this an arpeggio of suitable amours, were to write *The Tempest*.

The third and last part of Stevens's creed; the Supreme Fiction, which must be abstract and must change, must also give pleasure. One of the most compelling patterns in Stevens takes this line: why do we do such-and-such?; because we like doing it. And why do we like doing it? Because doing it satisfies something in our nature. But why does it satisfy? We do not know—to proceed beyond this is to 'say more than human things with human voice,' and, 'That cannot be.'

The poem begins with a list of common enthusiasms to be rejected; the first disposes of institutional religion, the next of the kind of racial unity invoked by Yeats in such poems as 'At the Galway Races' and 'At the Abbey Theatre'. 'This is a facile exercise', reality too blunt to receive the imagination:

> But the difficultest rigor is forthwith,
> On the image of what we see, to catch from that
> Irrational moment its unreasoning,
> As when the sun comes rising, when the sea
> Clears deeply, when the moon hangs on the wall
> Of heaven-haven. These are not things transformed
> Yet we are shaken by them as if they were.
> We reason about them with a later reason.

This is one of the credences of Summer, and the poem of that title gives us a setting for its reception. Stevens was fascinated by the irrational element in life as in poetry; by life's gibberish. To catch from an irrational moment its unreasoning is one of life's deepest satisfactions, not to be achieved by the rational anatomy of summer but by the 'later reason' which is the imagination. So we look at the image 'in its essential barrenness', without apotheosis, without souvenir, and 'we accept what is as good'. Above all, 'let's see the very thing and nothing else'. This is the programme of the next poem, the apprehensions featured in the blue woman. A sentimentalist, Stevens implies, wants things to be transformed, as a Christian wants wine to become blood, but the blue woman is happy that 'the frothy clouds are nothing but frothy clouds'. If the clouds change, well and good: granite texts are useless. Stevens's proof of this is the Old Testament figure in the next poem:

> A lasting visage in a lasting bush,
> A face of stone in an unending red . . .

and so on, one of the most opulent passages in his entire work, where one phrase added to another shows the arrogant effulgence faded and then we desire its death. If, as Stevens says in 'Two or Three Ideas', all gods are created in the images of their creators, then the Old Testament god has sinned by claiming to survive. Stevens's gloss is almost as vivid as the text it annotates: 'The first thing one sees of any deity is the face, so that the elementary idea of God is a face: a lasting visage in a lasting bush. Adoration is a form of face to face. When the compulsion to adoration grows less, or merely changes, unless the change is complete, the face changes and, in the case of a face at which one has looked for a long time, changes that are slight may appear to the observer to be melodramatic. We struggle with the face, see it everywhere & try to express the changes. In the depths of concentration, the whole thing disappears: A dead shepherd brought tremendous chords from hell/ And bade the sheep carouse, etc. This dead shepherd was an improvisation. What preceded it in the poem made it necessary, like music that evolves for internal reasons and not with reference to an external program. What the spirit wants, it creates, even if it has to do so in a fiction.'[1] Stevens will always listen to the voice of internal requirement, because it implies change and change is good. One of the values of the Christian Revelation, in his eyes, is that it thundered into time and cracked the imposing granite, speaking a new *lingua franca et jocundissima*:

> Children in love with them brought early flowers
> And scattered them about, no two alike.

This plenitude is good, in the next poem, because it satisfies a principle of nature in those who dispense it; like the 'mystic marriage' of the great captain and his maiden Bawda. The marriage takes place on earth because, as Robert Frost says, 'Earth's the right place for love.' This marriage will give pleasure, not only because bride and groom are very much 'of their place and time', but because they are conscious of being so. Stevens will not allow his pupils to evade the obligations of consciousness even in the shiver of their bodies. It is surprising, in this marriage at Catawba, to find the elements and the whirlwind given as obstacles; we are used to Catawba as the place of Summer credences. But even if the signs are 'love's characters', the poet is still aware of the mind at war with the sky. Reality and the

---

[1] Letter of 28th January 1943: *Letters*, p. 438.

imagination are, ideally, in harmony, but there are times when we feel 'the pressure of an external event or events on the consciousness to the exclusion of any power of contemplation'. The only answer, at these times, is enormous resistance, possible perhaps only to 'individuals of extraordinary imagination'.[1] This explains why the marriage in Catawba is 'mystic'.

It may also explain why Stevens introduced at this point the fable of Canon Aspirin and his widowed sister. This is difficult: so it may be useful to paraphrase the story, citing Stevens's own gloss where it is available. The Canon is a man who has 'explored all the projections of the mind, his own particularly', but he has not yet acquired 'a sufficing fiction'. He comes back to visit his sister and her children. His sister lives her daily life: she 'has never explored anything at all and shrinks from doing so'. She does not dream. The Canon approves. But he does not sleep as soundly: he dreams. At night he has a sense 'of nothingness, of nakedness, of the finality and limitation of fact'. So he returns to 'night's pale illuminations'. He must evade 'human pathos, and fact', he must 'go straight to the utmost crown of night'. Stevens says: 'He might escape from fact but he would only arrive at another nothingness, another nakedness, the limitation of thought. It is not, then, a matter of eluding human pathos, human dependence: thought is part of these, the imagination is part of these, and they are part of thought and of imagination. In short, a man with a taste for Meursault, and lobster Bombay, who has a sensible sister and who, for himself, thinks to the very material of his mind, doesn't have much choice about yielding to "the complicate, amassing harmony".'[2] Stevens gives this, in the poem, as an epic act; hence the Miltonic blank verse in which the Canon tries to save his Paradise.

In the next poem Stevens tries, I think, to cheer himself up; insisting that the disclosure of 'the real' is 'possible, possible, possible':

> It must be that in time
> The real will from its crude compoundings come,
> Seeming, at first, a beast disgorged, unlike,
> Warmed by a desperate milk. . . .

[1] *The Necessary Angel, supra*, p. 23.
[2] Letter of 29th March 1943: *Letters*, p. 445.

In 'The Figure of the Youth as Virile Poet' Stevens says that the poet who has elected to exercise his power to the full begins 'by studying it in exercise' and then proceeds 'little by little, as he becomes his own master, to those violences which are the maturity of his desires'.[1] Those violences are the beast disgorged; answering a desire in the poet and in him only as an extreme instance of man. In the next poem, still in Miltonic idiom, Stevens imagines an angel 'leaping down through evening's revelations', taking possession of the fiction that Stevens has conceived. Earlier, the lover sighed as for accessible bliss and now the poet is satisfied 'without solacing majesty'. If man has invented the gods, his 'irremediable poverty' includes their riches: hence, 'I can do all that angels can.'

'I have not but I am and as I am I am,' Stevens says. Perhaps: but at once the poet lists his possessions, just to make sure that 'being' is not ashamed in the eyes of 'having'. The result of the tally is impressive. Speaking of the angel, he asks: 'Are the wings his, the lapis-haunted air?/Is it he or is it I that experience this?' The easy answer is that it is certainly 'I'. The poet is clearly richer than the angels whom he has invented; richer, too, in his 'poverty' than the 'too weedy wren', the 'forced bugler', the 'red robin' tied to instinct and its repetitions. The birds repeat; and in that sense repeat themselves. But the 'man-hero' is 'he that of repetition is most master'. Man, that is, may 'be' the sum of his experiences; and these extend through all worlds—birds, beasts, and angels—to the limit of his imagination; stopping only there.

For of all his pleasures, the greatest—since we are reading Stevens and not another poet—is consciousness. In the last poem of the present sequence Stevens locates the source of human pleasure in the 'fat girl, terrestrial, my summer, my night':

> How is it I find you in difference, see you there
> In a moving contour, a change not quite completed?
> You are familiar yet an aberration.

He finds her in difference as in the children's flowers of III. iii, 'no two alike'. In 'Contrary Theses II' he spoke of walking toward an abstract 'of which the sun, the dog, the boy were contours', here again a version of 'the uncertain light of single,

[1] *The Necessary Angel, supra,* p. 64.

certain truth'. She is familiar yet an aberration because the devotee who sees her—Stevens himself, let us say—has achieved
now the difficultest rigor,

> On the image of what we see, to catch from that
> Irrational moment its unreasoning

—its irrational element, 'the fiction that results from feeling'.
Yes, that:

> They will get it straight one day at the Sorbonne.
> We shall return at twilight from the lecture
> Pleased that the irrational is rational,
>
> Until flicked by feeling, in a gildered street,
> I call you by name, my green, my fluent mundo.
> You will have stopped revolving except in crystal.

To call her by name in this way is not to subdue her to fixity; it
is to find her reality in the acutest speech of the poet. As Stevens
said in 'The Noble Rider and the Sound of Words', 'A poet's
words are of things that do not exist without the words.' Hence,
'Poetry is the supreme fiction, madame.'

The *Notes* should have finished at this point. But Stevens
added an Epilogue, an address to the Soldier-Hero, reminding
him that the war between the mind and sky never ends. The
addition is redundant. Even though we have a lovely poem,
'The Death of a Soldier', for proof, we may think that Stevens
resigned himself too glibly to the suffering of others. The
Soldier-Hero invoked in 'Examination of the Hero in a Time of
War' carries (in certain rejected stanzas) the burden of 'the
common man against evil',[1] and this is warmer, more human,
than the grappling of imagination and reality featured in the
Epilogue. If we want to clear away the impression of glibness,
we might bear the 'Examination of the Hero' in mind: meanwhile the Epilogue adds a few stanzas to a poem already complete.

IV

But the last phrase of the Epilogue stays in mind; 'the bread of
faithful speech'. If we are ironists we reflect that man may in

[1] *Opus Posthumous, supra*, p. 84.

some sense live on this bread, but only after his requirements in the more prosaic kind of bread are satisfied. This is one of the dissatisfactions which persist; the feeling that to Stevens bread is something to which we listen rather than something we eat. Things become metaphorical and figurative before they have long established themselves as things. Yeats said that *Marius the Epicurean* taught him and his fellow-poets 'to walk upon a rope tightly stretched through serene air', and they were left to keep their feet upon 'a swaying rope in a storm'.[1] Stevens is a virtuoso in this manœuvre. What Pater called 'the gypsy phrase' is an essential part of his poetry: finding little nourishment in the gibberish of the vulgate, he had to rely upon his own. He cared little for the dialect of the tribe: he did not feel called upon to purify it.

There are other sources of dissatisfaction. Stevens never quite persuades us that consciousness is the centre of all human circles. While reading him we are persuaded that the only relevant human act is consciousness, but when we put down the book and read something else or nothing at all, we cease to believe him. Other things assert their importance; spontaneous, daily things, hardly conscious at all. Sometimes in Stevens the imaginative act seems too easy, the resistance not great enough. Reality seems to be merely an instrument for the disclosure of the human mind: the world is merely adjectival to the noun, the imagination. Thinking of this, we recall a passage in *Man's Freedom*, where Weiss, speaking of 'independent objects which are other than the knowledge we have of them', says: 'A world exhausted by my experience would be a world in which there was nothing still to know, in which there was no action or causation, no past to be remembered, no future to anticipate, no present to be known.'[2] But the real difficulty in Stevens is that the individual John Smith tends to be dissolved in the idea of John Smith and finally in the idea of Man. The reason is clear. If John Smith lives and moves without my *fiat*, his life and motion are an affront to my imagination. Stevens does not always think so, as we have seen, but the thought came easily when it came at all. He would sometimes allow that 'the plum survives its poems', but this allowance came hard. This is why he would have asked

[1] W. B. Yeats, *Autobiographies* (London. Macmillan, 1956), p. 302.
[2] Paul Weiss, *Man's Freedom* (New Haven. Yale University Press, 1950), p. 21.

to live in essence rather than in substance or existence. He found it a little too easy to abstract himself.

The ready answer is: a poet writes the poems he writes, does what he does. This is compelling, up to a point: especially as the satisfactions in reading Stevens are so great that to qualify our pleasure seems the work of a churl. But vagabond doubts persist. I think it a limitation in the *Notes* that they seek a Supreme Fiction rather than a viable Truth. In the *Adagia* Stevens says, 'In the long run the truth does not matter,' and we respect his meaning. But if you opt out of a search for truth your traversing acquires the gaiety of freedom at the cost of being arbitrary. You can assert that there is a relation between the proffered image and the nature of its creator, but you can merely assert it; there is no proof. This is why the reader remembers, in Stevens, the labials of certain exquisite moments, moments of a consciousness almost Decadent, making us revel in Decadence against our sharper judgement; and then we put down the book and move back into the world of gutturals, half in relief. Fiction is such a relief from fact, until fact becomes a relief from fiction. Paul Weiss says that 'the truth of the fiction is one with its consistency, with the way it follows out the implications of its own determinations. The great virtue of idealism is that its coherence theory of truth allows it to do full justice to the logic of fictions. Its great limitation is that for it all assertions are treated as referring only to fictions.'[1] The reader of *Four Quartets* is impelled to say, 'Yes, the poetry does not matter': the reader of *Notes Toward a Supreme Fiction* comes close to saying, 'Only the poetry matters.'

But this is to be extreme, and somewhat glum. In Stevens's greatest poetry the purity of the fiction is wonderfully thwarted by his sense of the palpable world, the sundry of things, and especially in his later poems he gave the world its due. I have argued elsewhere that in *The Rock* the poetry is sustained by a vigorous tension between principle and particle; between 'intelligence' and 'soil', to use the terms of 'The Comedian as the Letter C'.[2] Where the tension fails, the poetry is slack; and slackness is Stevens's characteristic fault. He is not a dramatic poet:

[1] Paul Weiss, *Nature and Man* (New York. Henry Holt, 1947), p. 123.
[2] Denis Donoghue, *Connoisseurs of Chaos* (New York. Macmillan, 1965. London. Faber and Faber, 1966).

his bearings are aesthetic at some cost to all the other considerations, moral, social, and political. He tends to place his qualified spectator at a suitable vantage-point, looking at the world with his own imaginative eyes: hence the poetry of meditation and survey. But the tension between thesis and instinct on these occasions often results in Stevens's greatest poetry; as in this passage from the *Notes*, where the blue woman is standing at her window, looking:

> It was enough
>
> For her that she remembered: the argentines
> Of spring come to their places in the grape leaves
> To cool their ruddy pulses; the frothy clouds
>
> Are nothing but frothy clouds; the frothy blooms
> Waste without puberty; and afterward,
> When the harmonious heat of August pines
>
> Enters the room, it drowses and is the night.
> It was enough for her that she remembered.
> The blue woman looked and from her window named
>
> The corals of the dogwood, cold and clear,
> Cold, coldly delineating, being real,
> Clear and, except for the eye, without intrusion.

It is easy to feed these lines back into the general bod y o Stevens's poetry, glossing the blue woman and finding a special meaning in the coldness and clarity of the dogwood. It is always a temptation, because always a pleasure, to do this; to find the images cohering in Stevens's poetic world. But it is unnecessary. Sternly looking at the lines, safely outside, we see that the progression of indicatives is noble; never glib or chic. Stevens's command of the rhetoric is complete, but the rhetoric is not applied, from outside; it moves with the momentum of the scene, the perception. The felicities of the verse are many, but they are not readily detachable from the precision of tone, the adjustment of feeling. When the heat enters the room, 'it drowses and is the night'; a felicity, yes, but the felicity is inseparable from the precision, itself remarkable. The blue woman is not described, apart from the objects of her perception and her memory, but these are so vivid and so deeply companionable that they flood back, not to drown the woman but to sustain her. This is Stevens's happiest element, 'veracious page on page, exact', where the poet, a stern theorist, lays by his trouble and relents.

14

Ezra Pound's School Book

There are many factors in the work of Ezra Pound which we can take for granted. The following is a brief list:

(i) that he has a marvellous command of language;

(ii) that he is a good linguist but not as good as Erich Auerbach, E. R. Curtius, or Leo Spitzer, notable scholars but not poets;

(iii) that he has—or has had—certain economic theories which are patently absurd, quaint or archaic;

(iv) that his orientations in other respects are, to the chagrin of many of his readers, vaguely Catholic/Fascist/Anti-Semitic/Medieval;

(v) that this conglomeration of notions and allegiances has frustrated the clear flow of his poetry;

(vi) that he is, when he understands his powers, a splendid lyric poet;

(vii) that he is not a thinker, and should never have aspired to systematic thought;

(viii) that in the early days he was a force for Good, and that even now the moral value of his work is, in some strange way, impressive;

(ix) that he is a good priest who went wrong.

I list these items, not to shame them or to declare their banality, but to invoke a certain general opinion of Pound's work with which, on the whole, I agree. What follows may be read either as a footnote to item viii, above, or as a general introduction to the *Cantos*.

The central concern of the *Cantos* is figured in a passage in
Canto 54: 'History is a school book for princes.' This sends the
reader to the *speculum principis*, the 'mirror for magistrates',
a tradition which has fallen on such evil days that it requires some
effort even to invoke it. The effort is, however, worthwhile.

At the base of this tradition there is an image of the ideal
prince. Isocrates sketched many of its elements and Cicero endorsed them. The ideal prince is a man of wide learning—
Pound says in Canto 79, 'and if the court be not the centre of
learning'—his learning issues, as Cicero says in *De Oratore*, 'ex
intimis sapientiae fontibus'. The prince is a man of civil prudence, a wise man. When St. Augustine translated Cicero's
doctus orator into Christian terms, the way was clear for the political images of John of Salisbury, St. Thomas Aquinas, and Eras-
mus. John of Salisbury—Huizinga's 'man with the serious smile'
—is a crucial figure in this tradition, because the ideas embodied
in his *Policraticus*, supplemented by the rediscovery of Aristotle's
Politics in the thirteenth century, virtually determined the image
of the good prince until the middle of the sixteenth century. The
ideal prince is a man of learning, eloquence, and wisdom, dedicated to civil order and justice. Behind the *Policraticus* there is
the organic conception of the state: John went further than
Aristotle and quite as far as modern jurists in exploiting the
metaphor. Under the sign of Plutarch he went beyond St. Paul
in naming the classes analogous to each part of the body; the
senate as the heart, the officials and soldiers as the hands, and so
on.[1]

A full account of the *speculum principis* would include many
texts which we do not mention, and several which we mention
and pass over, like Gilbert of Tournai's *Eruditio Regum et Princi-*

---

[1] *Policraticus*, ed. Webb, I, 283, Sec. 540c. 'Cordis locus senatus optinet, a
quo bonorum operum et malorum procedunt initia. Oculorum aurium et lin-
guae officia vendicant sibi judices, et praesides provinciarum. . . .' Cf. Isaac de
Stella, XXXIV (Migne, *Patrologia Latina*, CXCIV, 1801c) in which the organic
metaphor is applied to the *corpus mysticum* 'the head of which was Christ and
whose limbs were the archbishops, bishops, and other functionaries of the
Church'. (Ernest H. Kantorowicz, *The King's Two Bodies: A Study in Medieval
Political Theology*, Princeton, 1957, p. 200.) Hannah Arendt notes in *The Human
Condition*, Anchor Books, 1959, p. 315, that while the early Christian writers,
'stressed the equality of the members, which are all equally necessary for the
well-being of the body as a whole, the emphasis later shifted to the difference between the head and the members, to the duty of the head to rule and of the
members to obey'. But the metaphor retained its familial connotation,

pum, Occleve's *The Governaunce of Princes*, the fourth Book of *Il Cortegiano*, and Elyot's *The Governour*. But perhaps we can imply these works in thinking of the *Basilikon Doron*, that gift which James prepared for the young Prince Henry in 1598. The primary emphasis in this particular mirror for magistrates is on the relation between right thinking and right speaking; style, shall we say, as a moral achievement. James advises his son: 'In your language be plaine, honest, naturall, comelie, cleane, short, and sentencious: eschewing both the extremities, as well in not using any rusticall corrupt leide, as booke-language, and pen and inke-horne tearmes: and least of all mignarde & effoeminate tearmes. But let the greatest parte of your eloquence consist in a naturall, cleare, and sensible forme of the deliverie of your minde, builded ever upon certaine and good groundes; tempering it with gra-vitie, quicknesse, or merrinesse, according to the subject, & occasion of the time.'[1]

I would propose, then, as a way-in to the *Cantos*, that the unity of the poem is that of its dominant figure, Pound himself, the controlling intelligence, teaching the moral significance of history as a mirror for magistrates. His role is that of the great counsellor, close to the strong Prince, governing his state in terms of a coherent political intelligence. This will explain, to start with, why the form of the poem is not a real problem: as long as the words issue from the single controlling intelligence, and as long as the speaker's role remains unchanged, the unity of the poem is built-in, thus guaranteed. The speaker is deemed to be a fixed point, centre of an ever expanding circle of reference; himself immutable. This marks the main difference between Pound and his nearest relative Walt Whitman. Whitman assumes that the self 'is' through the collusion of its world, the objects it makes its own. Hence these objects, because they contribute to the opulence of the self, should be as vivid and manifold as possible. The equation in his case is $X = A$ plus B plus C plus D, and so on. Each object apprehended enriches the observer. But Pound conceives the self as a being, immutably set off against a world upon which it imposes—or in which it sometimes finds—an idea of order congenial to its nature. In the *Cantos*, in Pound, there is no sense of a self 'endlessly become'—to

[1] *Basilikon Doron*, ed. Craigie (Blackwood, 1950), pp. 179–81. The text is the Waldegrave edition of 1603.

use Helen Mary Lynd's phrase;[1] the self of a mature man is formed; not determined, congealed, or fixed, but operative in the degree of its formation. This will have its own dangers; in poetic practice, it is very easy for the single intelligence choosing and 'mastering' its material to see the whole range of human history in similar terms, thus endorsing its political equivalent, which is dictatorship. Indeed, it is not too fanciful to suggest that Pound was drawn to admire a man like Mussolini largely on 'literary' grounds, that is, because the poet deals with his material as a dictator or at least a benevolent despot. (Whitman's politics was 'literary', too.)

I have said that in Pound the self is operative in the degree of its formation, and it must be added that Pound regarded this degree as largely a matter of choice. It was foolish to expose yourself to a multitude of casual or trivial experiences; this was the error of democracy. You should choose and seek out the experiences likely to be of use to you. And the likeliest source of these was in great literature and the record of great event; say, poetry and history. Hence the acquisition of superior languages. This would have another advantage. If the linguistic anthropologists are right in arguing that each language has its own special insight into reality, its own special vision of life, then to acquire that language would to some extent provide us with that special insight. Several such visions, held and adjudicated by a fine critical intelligence, would redeem the critic from some of the limitations of the fixed 'point of view'; he would now 'choose' to remain an immutable self, strongly set off against a world which he would view and assess; but his survey would be conducted from the notable height effected by his linguistic powers.[2] From this height, in effect, he could give—quite simply —better advice to his Prince.

Provided he has a Prince. If you make a great mirror for magistrates and find that there are no magistrates, or that they have no intention of looking into it, what then? This is, I should argue, precisely Pound's situation; he is an adviser without a prince. He has, he believes, certain marvellous things to say, and

[1] *On Shame and the Search for Identity* (New York. Harcourt, Brace, 1958), p. 203.
[2] On the limitations of the fixed 'point of view' see Marshall McLuhan, *The Gutenberg Galaxy* (London. Routledge and Kegan Paul, 1962).

he wants to say them to a man of power, a Prince, but the men of power are not listening, have never listened, and have never intended listening. I believe that this predicament accounts for the humiliating factors in the *Cantos*; the stridency, the scream, the hysteria, the venom, the extremity. It will also account for the anti-Semitism; if you choose for yourself the role of 'adviser to Prince' and you make your mirror and the prince looks the other way, you will find out who is obscuring your light, and if you think the princely court is cluttered up with a host of Jews closer to the prince's ears than you are; then hatred and venom are almost inevitable. I think this, or something like it, has occurred in the *Cantos*; though in this case to understand is not to condone.

But it is a commonplace in modern literature that many of the poets who have extended hospitality to political ideas have been extraordinarily wilful in their choice of guests. Lionel Trilling has pointed out that the broadly based politics of liberal democracy, which has seemed to satisfy many thousands of ordinary people, has won the allegiance of very few artists of any stature. The reason may well be found in the nature of the imagination itself, which subjects its images to a critical stress far greater than may be sustained by the 'ideas' in common use. Hence in a democratic age the last refuge of the imagination may indeed be sought in an aristocracy of image; the common name for this being 'obscurity'. But perhaps we can bring the matter nearer home. Yeats and Pound were, as everyone knows, deeply attracted to aristocratic images and times. Each poet dallied with the luxury of a sixteenth-century Italian birthright. Yeats spent many poetic hours enjoying racial memories of patrician splendour; and so on. But there was a difference. When Yeats thought of such scenes as the great conversation in Castiglione's *Courtier*, with those great sensibilities gazing at the dawn through the casement, he was entranced by the beauty of it all, but only by that. Even when he flirted with crypto-Fascist gestures, in his late bitterness and disgust, this was merely his way of being 'different' from the noisy men who ignored his voice in the Irish Senate; he was not committed to these gestures. This is one of the notable aspects of Yeats, his grain of common sense even in the throes of his nonsense. Above all, his dream of the Italian Renaissance was largely a 'dream of fair women', of beautiful architecture, great sculpture; he was never engrossed by the reality of power and force behind the dream. Pound was: in Pound the dream of aristocratic beauty was sustained only as a grace—what Stevens would call a flick—on the faces of power-ful men; and when he dreamed most deeply, it was the power he saw and touched.

Much of this is clear in the images through which Pound directs his role in the *Cantos*. In Canto 76, after the passage on the fall of Brendan Bracken and the mendacity of the B.B.C. Pound says:

> As a lone ant from a broken ant-hill
> from the wreckage of Europe, ego scriptor

and in Canto 81, from the famous 'What thou lovest well re-mains'—one of the few passages, incidentally, ever actually quoted to prove anything—'The ant's a centaur in his dragon world.' The redemptive ant moves with remarkable persistence through the later Cantos, perhaps because of the hope declared in Canto 83:

> When the mind swings by a grass-blade
> an ant's forefoot shall save you
> the clover leaf smells and tastes as its flower.

The lone ant from Europe's broken ant-hill, moving against dreadful odds to start a new, strong civilization: Pound's chosen role. Or, in another version, a martin sending urgent messages, Cantos 76 and 77. The messages are many, but their centre is the moral significance of history. In Canto 62 we read, 'IF moral analysis/be not the purpose of historical writing . . .'; in Canto 83, a more florid version, 'If deeds be not ensheaved and gar-nered in the heart/there is inanition'; and perhaps all this is con-tained, in gist and summary, when Pound speaks of memory—as in Canto 80:

> Quand vous serez bien vieille
> remember that I have remembered,
> mia pargoletta,
> and pass on the tradition
> there can be honesty of mind
> without overwhelming talent
> I have perhaps seen a waning of that tradition

—one of the most moving passages in the entire poem. What Pound has remembered has nothing to do with Jung or Yeats or the *anima mundi* or the collective unconscious; he has remembered what he has seen and heard and felt and suffered—and read in good books. He has, literally, no time for the densities of subterranean experience; too much is already available on top of the soil. He has gone through the world in search of facts that he can use; facts which chime with his own nature and his own vision. Many of the *Cantos* are simply 'books I have loved', turned into impeccable verse, but this is not at all a damaging observation; because Pound loves books not when they provide him with a place to lie down, but when they make something 'new', say something of enduring significance. Hence these books become his meaning, or another version of it. Like a good adviser, he tries to keep a clear space surrounding his Prince; into that space he admits only those presences—in documents, facts, the record of history—which the Prince needs for his enlightenment. The *Cantos* are as much an essay in exclusion as anything else; they engross the mind so that that mind will not, at this time, be engrossed by inferior matter. It may be argued that Pound is a peculiarly insistent and overbearing adviser, constantly browbeating his Prince: the point is well taken. But it merely sends us back to the distressing ambiguities of Pound's role; and these were always clear to an outsider.

The message of Pound's school book is that there is a difference between good government and bad government, and that it is possible to opt for the former. Bad government is murk and fog:

> whenever
> we leave principles and clear propositions
> and wander into construction we wander into a wilderness
> a darkness wherein arbitrary power
> set on throne of brass with a sceptre or iron . . .

from Canto 54; or, in Canto 80,

> and when bad government prevailed, like an arrow,
> fog rose from the marshland
> bringing claustrophobia of the mist
> beyond the stockade there is chaos and nothingness.

And good government is clear law. In Canto 99,

> VIII. Let the laws be made clear,
>   Illumine the words of procedure,
>   Peace comes of good manners,

which recalls, in Canto 64, 'actus/legis nulli facit injuriam'.

Hence the Confucian centre, the axis, the pivot, is the fulcrum, not the still point in the turning world and certaintly not the centre of a cyclone; the fulcrum of intelligence, imposing balance. Pound came upon it in Chinese texts, presumably because the wind bloweth where it listeth, and he acknowledged what he found. He could and would say, like the Kung of the beautiful Canto 13,

> The blossoms of the apricot
>   blow from the east to the west,
> And I have tried to keep them from falling.

And he would say, like the same counsellor in the same Canto,

> Anyone can run to excesses,
> It is easy to shoot past the mark,
> It is hard to stand firm in the middle.

Indeed, Canto 52 is a sustained account of the Good Life, again an Oriental vision of order and harmony; set off against such intimations of malice domestic as this—

> I think wrote Miss Bell to her mama
>   that when not against the interests of Empire
> we shd/keep our pledges to Arabs.

—and we should not delude ourselves that whenever Pound talks of these matters or uses a phrase like 'the true base of credit' the poetry immediately dies. This is the 'violence without' pressing against the 'violence within'—Stevens's terms—and it kills the poetry only when the first violence is too great and the second not great enough and the result is frenzy or hysteria. But when the violence within is engendered and propelled by the 'memory' of great men and of high civilizations—such as the civilization embodied in the Siena frescoes—the two violences meet and the battle is constantly drawn.

This is the vision which Pound would declare to his Prince; the violence without, 'answered' by an equal and opposite vio-

lence within. The second violence is that of intelligence, but intelligence of a certain cast and form: Pound implies this in Canto
59,

>De libro CHI-KING sic censeo
>   wrote the young MANCHU, CHUN TCHI,
>less a work of the mind than of affects
>brought forth from the inner nature. . . .

and, further:

>Ut animum nostrum purget, Confucius ait, dirigatque
>ad lumen rationis
>   perpetuale effecto.

And this intelligence—Pound insists—will never harden into a
crust; the great litany in Canto 90 is dedicated to the preserva-
tion of intelligence as a live, responsive idiom,

>   not arrogant from habit,
>   but furious from perception.

It must be a force, a spring of light and energy, within the self;
the Prince will be a good Prince because his 'inner nature', to
start with, is richer and nobler than that of others; and because
he has been stimulated, notably by his Poundian adviser, to love
certain images of order:

>And Kung said, and wrote on the bo leaves:
>   'If a man have not order within him
>He can not spread order about him;
>And if a man have not order within him
>His family will not act with due order;
>   And if the prince have not order within him
>He can not put order in his dominions.'   (Canto 13)

A later version of this, from Canto 59, is 'Urbanity in externals,
virtu in internals', elsewhere (Canto 53) translated loosely as

>Swine think of extending borders
>Decent rulers of internal order

—the latter embodied in a few great men such as Apollonius of
Tyre (Canto 94) and, in many Cantos, John Adams.

Intelligence has normally been presented, in Western Literature, as Light; sometimes a direct beam of light, often the entire

ambience in which things and facts are seen. In any event, it is a visual recognition, featured in such words as 'clarity' and 'definition', which thereupon becomes value-terms beneath or beyond justification. Pound will speak this language, using these clusters of feeling as shortcuts when he is in a hurry, or as 'places' of remembrance:

> Honour to CHIN-TSONG the modest
> Lux enim per se omnem in partem
> Reason from heaven, said Tcheou Tun-y
>   enlighteneth all things
> seipsum seipsum diffundit, risplende
>   Is the beginning of all things. . . . (Canto 55)

And he will often use commonplaces in this way, to stir up tired remembrances, so that the reader, the Prince, may proceed better equipped to understand. In Canto 94,

> pity, yes, for the infected,
>   but maintain antisepsis,
> let the light pour—

the light is at once the intelligence which prompts good medicine and our general feeling that this is 'good'. An earlier, discursive version is simply, from Canto 85, 'We flop if we cannot maintain the awareness,' tightened in the next page to read, 'Awareness restful & fake is fatiguing,' further down in the same page, 'The 5 laws have roots in an awareness,' and so on. And even when Love, the term of terms, is invoked, it becomes the place of intelligence, residence of vision:

> Trees die & the dream remains
>   Not love but that love flows from it
>   ex animo
>   & cannot ergo delight in itself
>   but only in the love flowing from it.
> UBI AMOR IBI OCULUS EST.   (Canto 90)

In Canto 104 the poet will suddenly inject an attendant aphorism, 'No science without clear definitions,' from the general bank of his meaning to remind us that even Venetian bloodstreams need common sustenance. This is one of Pound's characteristic gestures; to make a great commonplace suddenly rise from an otherwise free-flowing narrative; reminding us that a lesson from an Oriental text, if true, survives transplanting. But the moving centre is always the intelligence, light, vision, clarity, definition, as in

> that the body of light come forth
> from the body of fire
> And that your eyes come to the surface
> from the deep wherein they were sunken. . .
> (Canto 91)

Hence the characteristic 'moment' in Pound's poetry is one in which an identifiable form emerges from the clouds of possibility. He is a connoisseur of emergence, waiting for the light to break through behind a form now visible for the first time. These are the perfect moments, when a limited, clear something emerges from dusk; as the light of intelligence presses facts, things, events to disclose themselves as real. This disclosure is figured in the beautiful line which reverberates through the early Cantos, 'In the gloom, the gold gathers the light against it,' which is sung first in Canto 11 and put to a new melody in Canto 17:

> In the gloom the gold
> Gathers the light about it. . . .

—where it becomes virtually a motto, a tone, for the entire poem. And when that particular melody is silent, its voice is heard in several other invocations, notably in the harmony of light and crystal; as in Canto 91:

> Light & the flowing crystal
> never gin in cut glass had such clarity
> That Drake saw the splendour and wreckage
> in that clarity
> Gods moving in crystal. . . .

And in the emergence of form from the stone, as in sculpture. To Pound, it would seem from the *Cantos*, sculpture is the art of arts, a perfect emblem of human possibility. It has all the attributes we need for our consolation; its matter is brute, inert —unless by chance the stone has within it an implicit form which the sculptor can then discern, rejoicing—it responds to the artist's will; it is warmly substantial, earthy; it exhibits, in its final state, the marvellous unity of form and content, substance and accident, Chance and Choice; it receives the artist's personality and holds it, as the light in crystal.[1] We need not extend the list; except to note that no other art discloses as majestically the form emerging from its willing matrix. Musical form is nothing till complete, completely realized; verbal forms, incompletely realized, are nonsense; even the pictorial forms are inconsequential till their consequences are clear. But every moment in the development of a sculptural form is charged with moral life, incorrigibly 'there', and the last form is but the pressure, the emergence of a vision 'made new' in the light. 'That the body of light come forth from the body of fire' is the prayer of the *Cantos*; and the coming forth is its centre. Sculpture, light, and crystal are the analogues which 'fix' the discursive passages of the poem; passages like the Jefferson letter in Canto 21 or Malatesta's letter in Canto 8. Without the analogues, these passages would be totally dependent upon the tone of the speaker's voice; the analogues once in place, the letters and documents spread their meaning over a larger course. Jefferson's effort to find a gardener who could at the same time play the flute is the light of intelligence and civility pouring itself on ground far more ample than the lawns at Monticello. And so on. 'In the gloom the gold gathers the light against it.' And, from the same cluster of values, in Canto 97, 'the temple is holy,/because it is not for sale'.

Emergence of forms, of distinct ideas, of relations hitherto obscure; these are the great moments, the 'crede̅ ̃es of summer' in Pound's poetry. Very often the point of a narrative, in the *Cantos*, will be to show that intelligence is not a modern invention, that there have been intelligent people long before now, that we have not invented the light. In Canto 105, for instance; on the first page we read, 'Anselm "Monologion" scripsit, 1063.' This is a thought to conjure with. But twenty lines further down, we find, 'Guido C. had read "Monologion".' This is the emergence, a relation seen and held as light in crystal. And lest there be any mistake or inertia, the next lines read

[1] See Donald Davie, *Ezra Pound, Poet as Sculptor* (London. Routledge and Kegan Paul, 1965).

vera imago
>   and via mind is the nearest you'll get to it. . . .

This is Pound holding up the mirror, directing his Prince to see himself and his role in its light. Cavalcanti reading the *Monologion* is an utterly un'democratic' fact; it is the result of an intelligence, a vision entirely 'aristocratic'. Hence this—and not sheep running through a gap—must be our example.

This brings us to one of the crucial problems of the poem. If you opt for an aristocracy of intelligence and you set up your images of value in that light, it will be very difficult to find a human and dignified 'place' for the millions of ordinary people who are not outstandingly intelligent. A similar difficulty arises in *Four Quartets*, where 'ordinary people' acquire unwholesome lungs and unhealthy souls simply, it appears, because they can't afford to travel by taxi. (One wonders what Martin Buber thought of *East Coker*.) Admittedly, a democratic poetics has its own dangers, notably the sentimentality which presents an anonymous figure absurdly endowed: a man is not ten feet tall, in fact. But what is Studs Lonigan to do? And who is to be blamed if Augie March does not read the *Monologion* of Anselm and therefore does not see what Cavalcanti saw? Pound's speculum is designed for magistrates, an imaginary Prince, an exceptional man; its meaning for 'us' is derived, handed down from that height. Hence the early Cantos are occupied largely by 'exceptional men', personages rather than persons. These poems are a land fit for heroes to inhabit; but only for heroes. *Hugh Selwyn Mauberley* was more hospitable; like Yeats's *The Wild Swans at Coole*, a home in which a man might live, without souvenir, without transcendence. With the Pisan Cantos there is a change. When we speak of these as more humane than the early and middle Cantos, we mean that the speculum now for the first time willingly includes a man named Whiteside, otherwise unknown, because at a certain place on a certain day he said,

>   ah certainly dew lak dawgs,
>   ah goin' tuh wash you. . . .   (Canto 79)

and his saying this is morally significant. People can now enter the Cantos even if they are not fixed points in a political spectrum. This is also part of the achievement of *Paterson*, a much more democratic poem than the *Cantos*, but a poem in which a letter from Josie takes its proper place beside an invocation to Sappho without any suggestion that the differences are negligible. Williams always wanted to write an 'impure' poetry, because he valued the multiplicity of life and knew that only a very small fraction of life is inherently poetic. The way to 'make it new' was to say it without fog or halo; and if over a long course the poem seemed to reach for an inhuman purity, then you would take on a lot of ballast, letters, documents, flotsam—if necessary—to keep it on earth. Pound reached this commitment more slowly, as *Lustra* shows; but he reached it. His motive was probably different from Williams's: Williams simply wanted to be true to life; Pound wanted—or so it seems in the later Cantos —to expose his poem to a more ample set of co-ordinates. There is no evidence that he would ever renounce his trust in the mind: 'via mind is the nearest you'll get to it' continues to be his motto. But he seems to have felt, especially in the later poems, that to equate Sanctity with Consciousness was not the whole story. Irving Howe has observed that modern literature—Conrad was his occasion—exhibits a notable excess of Consciousness over Being; modern writers find it profoundly difficult to develop a vision of life and thence a 'style' answerable to a fully organic and dynamic sense of the flow of Being. Yeats is a relevant text. So is Eliot. And Pound. Indeed, in Eliot's case most of the dissatisfactions which persist even after a devoted and admiring engagement with the poems arise precisely from the equation of Sanctity with Consciousness and, even more, from the poet's reluctance to challenge his own position. Pound has accepted the challenge. This is why he can say, in the lovely Canto 99,

> There is worship in plowing
> and equity in the weeding hoe. . . .

and we do not think this mere talk.

But it is wrong to quote from the long turbulence of the *Cantos* in single lines or short pieces. Sometimes phrases and lines will leap from the page—especially now that recitation is defeated, as the poem becomes once again a visual construct— and these fragments will seem particularly and to an extraordinary degree the cries of their occasions. This poet's gibberish is peculiarly his own, like a birthmark—which it is; and he has

had the misfortune, as well as the loneliness, of using a sensibility
entirely his own. The exposure of being an adviser without a
prince is one thing, one predicament; but it discloses another and
sinks into it, the exposure of having only one's own mind and
never even the holiday of another mind to sing to or to rest on.
This may explain why even the great modern writers who figure
in the *Cantos* become the Possum, or Willy, or Jimmie, or James
(H. J.) and get full names only when they don't count. The
Eliots and Joyces are not invoked 'familiarly'; nor are they deci-
mated; they are simply fended off, fixed in an element not
Pound's and therefore, by definition, half-frozen; as you freeze
Yeats's poetry if you call it minstrelsy. Using a sensibility almost
entirely his own, Pound makes it hard for us to get the beauty of
the *Cantos*, as it were, hot; so we cling to dazzling phrases and
hope that these will bring us further into their poem. And they
will. But never as deeply as we want. For if we fasten upon the
images—the moments of great emergence—we miss what R. P.
Blackmur writing of Eliot calls the trouble between the images;
and that is to miss nearly everything.

So we need a passage short enough to disclose its transitions,
long enough to show its directions. From Canto 83:

> in the drenched tent there is quiet
>   sered eyes are at rest
>
>
>   the rain beat as with colour of feldspar
>   blue as the flying fish off Zoagli
> pax, ὕδωρ   ΥΔωΡ
>
>   the sage
> delighteth in water
>   the humane man has amity with the hills
>
>
> as the grass grows by the weirs
>   thought Uncle William   *consiros*
> as the grass on the roof of St What's his name
>   near 'Cane e Gatto'
>   soll deine Liebe sein
> it would be about a-level the windows
>   we grass would, or I dare say above that
>   thhen they bless the wax for the Palio

Olim de Malatestis
    with Maria's face there in the fresco
    painted two centuries sooner,
    at least that
before she wore it
      As Montino's
in that family group of about 1820
    not wholly Hardy's material
    or παυτα ʽρει

as he was standing below the altars
    of the spirits of rain
'When every hollow is full
    it moves forward'
to the phantom mountain above the cloud
But in the caged panther's eyes:

          'Nothing. Nothing that you can do . . .'

green pool, under green of the jungle,
caged: 'Nothing, nothing that you can do.'

To touch the images and feel the trouble between them we have to listen to the voice and follow it. The association of Water and Peace begins with the first line of the Canto, a page back, and is picked up again. The sered eyes are the panther's, part apocalyptic but all desolate, and if the analogy of water and peace begins almost as a prayer, the end is not the release of elevation. But, for the moment, the rain is peace. For the movement of feeling begins; going first to the beautifully felt relation between a man and his world—what Stevens would call a liaison. And then Pound recalls an early poem by Yeats in which the girl tells her lover to take life and love easy, as the grass grows on the weirs; a Yeatsian liaison. 'But I was young and foolish, and now am full of tears'; *consiros*, with grief. Now one grass reminds Pound of another, dearly remembered, 'soll deine Liebe sein', at Siena. And then from Siena to Rimini, the Tempio, and Maletesta. 'Olim de Maletestis' is a hint to Pound as much as to ourselves; it sends us back to Canto 76 and Canto 80, where it was used before, and it sends Pound back to Malatestine intimations already given, intimations of *caritas* and 'care in contriving'. Maria is a beloved face in the fresco, a pictorial memory set astir by Yeats's wise girl. And thence to another face, Montino's —a name unfamiliar to me, unless Pound meant Vincenzo Monto, who translated the *Iliad* and the *Odyssey*. 'Not wholly Hardy's material' may mean little more than 'a face too Mediterranean to pose for *Under the Greenwood Tree*'; in which case the Heraclitus-tag, 'All things flow', should be read as 'or else there are no boundaries at all'. But the flowing river of Heraclitus and the pouring rain bring Pound the panther back to his cage. The 'he' is, I think, a generalized figure, in the first instance, but merging easily into the caged panther. 'When every hollow is full/ it moves forward'; with one exception, here in Pisa, caged. 'Nothing. Nothing that you can do.'

It seems, then, that the voice moves from one point to another by an inner music rather than an outer law; one thing leads to another according to a music of feeling, an intuitive syntax, which can no more be challenged than predicted. But if this is so, does it not contradict everything we have been saying about consciousness, intelligence, the light of the mind, and the *speculum principis*? A princely adviser should not work by random association. And so on. But we must take this slowly. Indeed—to give the argument against my case its full weight— there is a remarkable passage in Yeats's essay of 1931 on Berkeley which cites the early Cantos to prove a large discrimination. Here is the gist of it: 'The romantic movement with its turbulent heroism, its self-assertion, is over, superseded by a new naturalism that leaves man helpless before the contents of his own mind. One thinks of Joyce's *Anna Livia Plurabelle*, Pound's *Cantos*, works of an heroic sincerity, the man, his active faculties in suspense, one finger beating time to a bell sounding and echoing in the depths of his own mind. . . .'[1]

This is marvellously eloquent but, I believe, wrong. In the long section quoted from Canto 83 Pound is not helpless before the contents of his own mind. The transitions are wonderfully delicate, often elusive, but they are not—as my analysis implied —the result of random association. Controlled association, yes. Pound is not the slave of Memory; he will seek her guidance, he will even entrust his fortunes to her—though with a wary eye—

[1] *Essays and Introduction* (London. Macmillan, 1961), p. 405.

but he does not bind himself. He remains his own man. For in any event Memory—in Pound—is what he chooses to remember; 'remember that I have remembered'. The contents of his mind are there by specific and sustained invitation, by his choice; this is the basis of his criticism and the saving light of his poetry. Joyce—since Yeats links him to Pound—took far greater risks, was much more 'wilful' than Pound. Indeed, I have argued strongly against the procedure which, given a word such as 'drift', jumps to 'swift' and thence to Stella and Vanessa. Joyce is not helpless before the content of his own mind; he is not in trouble, he is in sin, the sin of Pride. Pound is in so much trouble that there is nothing else to which he can give himself; unless it be the record of a carefully stocked memory. His memory contains all the images of order and chaos which he has found and taken from history, from books, ledgers, poems; this plus his own personal stock, which is largely his own trouble. Hence when he opens the doors of memory—especially now in the cage of Canto 83—we get images and the trouble between the images. If he goes from the grass by the sally garden to another grass on the roof of St. What's his name, his motive is a quality disclosed by both, a shared devotion, a shared grief, a hazard of relation. Hence also the impression, in this verse, of stored up energy now in release; the memory of years, packed tight, and then the doors are opened. Most poets give the impression of building up or working up to large effects: Pound's verse is a release, getting the thing down and done. This is what the transparent style comes to; the verse, going about its business, has no time for spectacular climaxes or effects. William Carlos Williams said that a poem by Marianne Moore is an anthology of transit; in a caged panther transit is release. Even when Pound makes what in another poet would be a large showing, the words are released from his mind; there is no explosion. As in Canto 76 he will say,

> nothing matters but the quality
> of the affection—
> in the end—that has carved the trace in the mind
> dove sta memoria

—which is his way of saying, with T. S. Eliot, 'the poetry does not matter'.

Conclusion

There is none. 'The humane man has amity with the hills'; but not now. One of the few generalizations we make of contemporary literature is that the private and the public worlds are now deemed to have nothing whatever to do with each other. Literature does not criticize society: it has already disowned society. There is nothing left but the 'universe within', the little world made cunningly of our own fantasies. The cult of apocalypse is one manifestation; significant because it involves a denial of the finite, a rejection of history and politics, the transfer of value to self. Psychedelic experiments, whatever else we choose to think of them, are clearly designed to break the ennui of self; to give the inner world the interest, the variety, the liveliness traditionally found in the world at large. This is not new. A full account would go back beyond Symbolism to the Transcendentalists. In *Character and Opinion in the United States* Santayana observes:

'To discredit the intellect, to throw off the incubus of an external reality or truth, was one of the boons which transcendentalism in its beginnings brought to the romantic soul. But although at first the sense of relief (to Fichte, for instance) was most exhilarating, the freedom achieved soon proved illusory: the terrible Absolute had been simply transplanted into the self. You were your own master, and omnipotent; but you were no less dark, hostile, and inexorable to yourself than the gods of Calvin or of Spinoza had been before. Since every detail of this mock world was your secret work, you were not only wiser but also more criminal than you knew.'

In 'Sunday Morning' Stevens's dreaming woman laments that the things of Paradise are smeared with our mystery, are images of ourselves, exist only in our terms:

> Alas, that they should wear our colors there,
> The silken weavings of our afternoons,
> And pick the strings of our insipid lutes!

The man, Stevens's pagan, has already accepted this; that the earth shall seem 'all of paradise that we shall know'. The poem of earth is the greatest poem, the ultimate poem.

The paganism is touching, almost pious, devout. Even if the speakers cannot distinguish between the hills and their sense of the hills, the dialogue has a Sabbath propriety. It is good to speak of paradise. Indeed, there is an exemplary moment in modern poetry when talk of paradise brings together many of the themes which have concerned us in this book.

In the winter of 1913–14 Ezra Pound provided secretarial and advisory services for Yeats at Stone Cottage, Coleman's Hatch, 'in Sussex by the waste moor'. Pound's version is given in Canto 83 which we have already quoted, in part. The issue between them, it soon becomes clear, is the status of the object, the given world. At the end of *A Vision* Yeats speaks of finding everything in the symbol. In 'Sailing to Byzantium' he asks to be gathered into 'the artifice of eternity'. In Canto 83 the secretary answers, 'Le Paradis n'est pas artificiel.' This is, to begin, an answer to Baudelaire: one of Baudelaire's books is called *Les Paradis artificiels*, an elaborate chorale to hieroglyphic dreams and symbols.

Canto 83 rebukes Baudelaire and the entire Symbolist tradition as well as Yeats; tactfully, because the critical point has already been made in Cantos 74, 76, and 77. Paradise, Pound implies, is not *artificiel*, an assertion of Symbolist will: it exists, finite and historical, if 'only in fragments', like excellent sausage, the smell of mint, and Ladro the night cat. So he makes fun of Yeats:

> And Uncle William dawdling around Notre Dame
> in search of whatever
>
>   paused to admire the symbol
> with Notre Dame standing inside it.

I read this as a reflection not upon the church but upon Yeats's sense of it, his tendency to replace the given world by a figment of the Symbolist imagination. Pound is warning Yeats that the given world, such as it is, is more durable than all the bronzes of

Symbolism: it stands forth, bodied against the hieroglyphic dream and the golden bird. This criticism of Yeats has often been repeated, but it is wide of the mark. Yeats is not Baudelaire. Indeed, in the context of modern literature his commitment to the finite world as a structure in its own right is remarkable. To relate him to Berkeley and Blake and Nietzsche, without admitting this qualification, is wrong. Sturge Moore saw that in 'Sailing to Byzantium' the goldsmith's bird is 'as much nature as a man's body', and that it sings of natural things. True, Yeats wrote 'Byzantium' partly to answer Moore, but even there the spirit, as we have seen, cannot finally disdain the gong-tormented sea.

This is to say that Yeats was not a Symbolist. We have already argued for this reading. It is also to say that the Gnostic contempt for the given world and the Symbolist resentment of its claims tend to coalesce; and, coalescing, to sponsor that severance of the private and the public worlds which we have mentioned. We come back to the inescapable question: wise and criminal as we are, how to live in this 'old chaos of the sun'.

Index